Barefoot Through The Bindies

Growing up in North Queensland in the Early 1900s

Marion Houldsworth was born in Mount Morgan, Queensland, and educated at Rockhampton Girls Grammar School and the University of Queensland. She taught for many years in New Guinea and the Northern Territory where she and her family survived Cyclone Tracy. She has published three books on childhood. Her special interest is the history of Queensland. With grandchildren in Townsville and West Sussex she commutes regularly between both places but regards North Queensland as home.

Also

Hearts Bright With Hope: A Grammar School Diary, 1948–51

The Morning Side of the Hill: A Townsville Childhood, 1939–45

The Immigrant Boy: A Townsville Boyhood, 1912–1918

Barefoot Through The Bindies

Growing up in North Queensland in the Early 1900s

•

Marion Houldsworth

First published in 2002 by Central Queensland University Press

Second published in 2012 by Boolarong Press, Salisbury, Brisbane, Australia.

National Library of Australia Cataloguing-in-Publication entry

Author:	Houldsworth, Marion.
Title:	Barefoot through the bindies / Marion Houldsworth.
ISBN:	9781921920615 (pbk.)
Subjects:	Children--Queensland, Northern--Biography.
	Queensland, Northern--Biography.
	Queensland, Northern--Social conditions--20th century.
Dewey Number:	305.23099436

Typeset in 12 on 13½ pt Monotype Garamond by Frank Povah, at the Busy Broody, Dunalley

Cover design: Jane Dorrington

Cover Photograph: JCU Archives

Many of the newspaper items reproduced throughout this book first appeared in the pages of the NORTH QUEENSLAND REGISTER. This publication, so closely interwoven with Northern Queensland's history, is a rich source of material for the researcher.

Printed and bound by Watson Ferguson and Company, Salisbury, Brisbane, Australia.

Foreword

STUDENTS OF Professor Brian Dalton, for over twenty-five years Head of the School of History and Politics at James Cook University's School of History and Politics, North Queensland, were encouraged by him to follow the philosophy that the oral tradition has a significant and legitimate role not only in teaching about us our past but helping to equip us to face the future. Brian Dalton was instrumental in setting up of the North Queensland Oral History Archive, for which hundreds of audio-taped interviews were conducted with representatives from many walks of life, each of whom had contributed to the formation of North Queensland's distinctive character.

By 1980 a full-time Research Officer had begun a programme of interviewing identities then in their seventies and eighties. These interviews formed the pool from which Marion Houldsworth has selected the set of reminiscences that go to make up *Barefoot Through the Bindies: Growing Up in North Queensland in the Early 1900s.*

Having read Marion's typescript it was gratifying to observe (*The Australian,* 8 April 1998) the remarks of Professor Greg Dening, former Chair of History at Melbourne University, on the significance of 'Living History' in reviewing Professor Henry Reynold's latest book, *The Other Side of the Frontier:* which 'came out of a remarkable Department of History at James Cook University, Townsville, where the students didn't learn history so much as make it. They made it out of the living histories and cultural memories of the regional north… Living histories are more likely to well up in tears than in words, or come out in shouts or solemn silences. Living history does not belong to the artificial world of learning and schools but to human realities. It is about truth, not accuracy.'

With the publication of *Barefoot Through the Bindies: Growing Up in North Queensland in the Early 1900s,* Marion Houldsworth provides us with an invaluable insight into what it was like to be a child growing up in the North in the Federation years, so many decades ago. All the voices are now silenced by time, yet the Narrators live on through Marion's prose and her dedication to her task.

This volume complements Marion's previous contribution to 'living history' in North Queensland, *The Morning Side of the Hill* which so vividly conveyed her own childhood and the experiences of the Townsville community during World War II, in the foreword to which Brian Dalton wrote: 'This account of wartime Townsville is remarkable for its clarity and for its rich, concrete and exact detail…' That same clarity, rich, concrete and exact detail, complemented by annotations and illustrations, characterises *Barefoot Through the Bindies: Growing Up in North Queensland in the Early 1900s.*

Marion Houldsworth's empathic use of the North Queensland Oral History Collection provides an inspiration for a new generation of students and a vindication of Brian Dalton's initiative in setting up the Archive a quarter of a century ago. There are still hundreds of 'voices' within the collection, each with a story to relate, each able to contribute to the mosaic of living histories of the North and its people.

Barefoot Through the Bindies: Growing Up in North Queensland in the Early 1900s is an achievement to be recommended. It is poignant and captivating, a sheer delight to read.

Professor Kett Kennedy
James Cook University
Townsville

Acknowledgements

KEN HALL, of Sydney, has generously loaned the many beautiful photographs from the Frederic Charles Hall Collection. The Reverend Frederic Charles Hall was a Church of England Minister in the early years of the twentieth century whose vast parish in the Gulf country of northern Queensland included small townships, cattle properties and mining settlements. With his keen interest in photography he captured on the unwieldy glass plates of the period not only the grandeur of the landscape, but the beauty, strength and character of the people. He must have been a very welcome visitor wherever he went, as the faces of his subjects – at bush weddings, Sunday School outings and homesteads reflect the joy at his having come among them. I am grateful to the family for the privilege of being allowed use of the unique collection.

The most pleasurable part of writing this book has been the many trips out bush in search of old wagon tracks, deserted mining towns and homesteads. For these I am grateful to my son Michael and his wife. Mr and Mrs R. Fryer of Hervey's Range station helped us to locate the grave of Mary Langton, overgrown by lantana in dense bush at the foot of Thornton's Gap. Clearing the headstone it was a shock to learn that she had been only twenty-eight, although described by one of the Narrators in this book as his grandmother. Ron and Beryl Quelch took me to historic Ravenswood and to the site of the original Macrossan bridge on the Burdekin, and located 'the big flat rock' on Castle Hill, of which Connie Hill speaks.

My daughters Elizabeth and Airlie have been unfailingly supportive, my son-in-law Kristian Kebby, and nearly son-in-law Nick Wood have provided the technical back-up (as in, 'Help! Where did those seven thousand words go!') and my lifelong friend Pearl Mahony, with her shared love of Queensland history, has been a never-failing source of exhortation and advice.

This book would not have been written had it not been for the encouragement of the late Professor Emeritus Brian Dalton, of the School of History and Politics, James Cook University, whose sudden death in September 1996 deprived the North of one of its most esteemed personalities. A New Zealander by birth he had come to look upon North Queensland as home and was instrumental in the setting up of the North Queensland Oral History Archive. He wanted the part played by ordinary people, especially its women and children, in the development of the North, to be more widely known and appreciated.

I would like to thank the James Cook University Oral History Archive for access to the Collection and for their copyright release.

For
the Children of the North,
especially
Robert, Edward, William and Genevieve.
and also
Julius, Alexander, Kristian and Sebastian

'Take now the fruit of our labour,
Nourish and guard it with care,
For our youth is spent, and our backs are bent,
And the snow is on our hair.'

from 'The Pioneers' by Frank Hudson
in the old *Queensland School Reader.*

Introduction

Of all the nostalgias that haunt the human heart the greatest is an everlasting longing to bring what is youngest home to what is oldest, in us all.[1]

I LOVE CHILDREN and I love old people. Most of all I love to hear the stories old people tell of their childhood.

The topic of childhood has an endless fascination because we are all children at heart.'We are but older children, dear, who fret to find their bedtime near,' says Lewis Carrol in *Through the Looking Glass.* John Dryden adds, 'Men are but children of a larger growth', and Jung stresses the profound significance of the symbol of the child, representing a link to the past as well as a link to the future. In mythologies around the world the child represents renewal, zest for life, spontaneity, even immortality. We all carry within us an eternal child, a being of innocence and wonder.

My special interest is in the childhood of the Federation era, so it was a 'Yes!' moment to be offered, by Professor Emeritus Brian Dalton of James Cook University, the chance to explore the North Queensland Oral History Collection for childhood experiences of the early 1900s.

The North Queensland Oral History Project was funded by the Australian Research Council in 1980 with the aim of recording the life histories of North Queenslanders from all walks of life and especially those who were then in their late eighties or nineties.

When I selected the first tape, at random, and switched it on, I was thrilled to hear the sweet, feathery voice of Constance Grace Hill, born in 1897, describing her family's experiences in Cyclone Leonta. In rising wind, with 'the pennants up on Pilot Hill',[2] their mother had gathered the children and hurried them across the road to shelter with a neighbour. They had watched and waited to see their own 'little old place with verandahs' disintegrate, but 'only a paw-paw tree got blown down and a kerosene tin went spinning around the yard'. The chuckle which Constance Grace gave at this almost-century-old memory gave me a sense of privilege, as of being taken by the hand and invited to step back through time. A pinafored child seemed to be beckoning; 'Come with me, and I'll show you what it was like.' Suddenly it was March, 1903. I could see the flattened paw-paw tree and the ridiculous kerosene tin bowling over and over. I understood that in remembering that moment this very old lady had stepped forth from the worn garment of age and become a child again, filled with wonder at the power of the storm yet secure in the assurance of her mother's love. Who would not feel enriched to share such a moment?

Soon I had a gallery of friends from the period. There was Oscar Crowther, who remembered the horse-teamsters' camp at Belgian Gardens, and Edward Cummings, whose family would have perished in the sinking of the *Yongala* had not their mother been so well organised that they caught an earlier ship instead. There was Henry Brown who described how he and his friends would float down the flooded Ross River on logs, something I have done myself in the flooded Herbert. There was Florrie Toombs, who endeared herself to me utterly with her story of having to sweep out the schoolroom at the convent before being allowed to go home in the afternoon. Seventy years later her voice was still burdened at the memory. These were all people who might have seemed ordinary, but who weren't ordinary at all, who had each cherished quiet hopes and aspirations of being something better, who had delighted in the goodness of others.

I wanted to present their stories because I could identify with them in many of the circumstances of their childhoods. My parents were settlers from 'the Old Country' who emigrated after the Great War. Filled with hopes for the future they bought land in the Dawson River Valley and cleared it by axe to grow cotton. Their home was a tent with a bark hut attached for sleeping quarters. My mother, a girl of twenty, fresh from a comfortable London home, thought for a while it was a wonderful adventure. Dad, always clever with his hands, made furniture from kerosene cases, which his young wife stained to walnut-brown with Condies Crystals (permanganate of potash). But then, reality. Crop after crop failed. Boll-weevils. Grasshoppers. Drought, when water had to be fetched in 44-gallon drums by horse and dray. Then good crops but no market. Nothing but hardship. Eventually, they were to walk off the property, beaten.

So, despite the generational difference, I could identify completely with the stories told by these earlier North Queenslanders. I felt an Insider to their experiences. When they spoke of fetching water up from the creek, I could smell the sweetness of it, see the cut-down kerosene-tin bucket, feel the weight and the splashing on bare legs. I knew about Coolgardie safes, carbide lights, snakes in cupboards – we once found a carpet snake in the writing desk. And just as had happened to Florrie Toombs, Susan Gallagher and Olive Stallon I had been in an orphanage. For when our mother was bitten by a black snake, and in pre-antivenom times, was ill for many months, what was Dad to do with my brother and me but place us in St George's Orphanage near Rockhampton? The remembered bleakness of that experience made me feel a oneness with all these elderly Narrators, spellbound by their stories, and compelled to make them known, to give them their place in the history of the North, for they speak not only for themselves but for their generation.

My criteria for selection from the archive were that the stories should be 'a good yarn', convey something that would enrich our understanding of a period that is gone, and should embody something of the triumph of the human spirit in adversity. However, elderly people's taped reminiscences do not come packaged ready to present as written testimony. Often a story starts on Tape 1, Side 1 but does not get to the point until Tape 3, Side 2. Or does not get to the point at all. I transcribed the words as I heard them, often rewinding seven or eight times to catch a particularly elusive word or phrase. I gathered sections on the same topic together, and arranged them in chronological order in what was essentially a spirit of collaboration, always remaining faithful to the way in which the story had been told. All this was done with love, for after a week or ten days listening to the voice of each elderly Narrator it was impossible not to feel I knew and loved them for themselves.

I tried to select representatives of the various socio-economic groups; male or female, town or bush dweller, cultured or unlettered, hard-up or well-off, to build up a tapestry of an earlier North, hoping to take the reader back through time to identify with the courage and resourcefulness of this earlier generation.

There were some surprises. The magical quality of oral history is that it can provide fresh insights about our past which we would not be likely to gain from written or printed sources. For instance, who would have expected this intimate glimpse into the character of one of Australia's legendary figures, Breaker Morant, as related, quite fortuitously, by Florrie Toombs.

> Mother come out as an immigrant girl… and she got sent to a place called Duckbrook station. And who do you think was on the station breaking-in horses! Harry Morant! Yes! And she was in the kitchen one day working, and he come in… and he says, 'Nellie, when are you going to marry me?' And she laughed. She thought it was just a joke. She said, 'I wouldn't marry you! You drink too much!'[3]

One can only wonder; supposing Nellie had blushingly complied? Supposing the bush wedding had taken place? Supposing wee toddlers round the horse-breaker's hut? Might not Harry Morant have been content with his lot and not gone for a soldier to the Boer War? History would have been changed. But Nellie said 'No', and that was that. And one can only wonder what effect the drinking 'too much' had on the events that were to unfold on the African veldt.[4]

Another aspect of oral history is that it fleshes out statistics. Small incidents can speak eloquently of large issues. We know, for instance, that the infant mortality rate was high in earlier times, but Edward Cummings, who grew up on the Koorboora Goldfield near Chillagoe, brings this into sharp focus:

> There was very little known about medical things. There was no doctor. A baby would become ill… by the time the parents realise it was getting serious, the baby would die of dehydration.'[5]

And Susan Gallagher recalls the sense of community solidarity that sustained a family following the loss of a child:

> And my sister, the little one, Esther, she was three when she died. And mining towns are all the same; everybody comes in to do what they can and help... and the shopkeeper, he had a consignment brought up, come by pack-horse... and he gave the packing case for the coffin... and everybody walked to the funeral.[6]

Just so, in Henry Lawson's 'His Father's Mate', does a neighbour give a prized table so that a coffin can be made for a dead child. Of such incidents is the Australian saga composed.

Oral history adds the value of individual experience to text-book history. In the spirit of the old teaching maxim, 'One good example is worth a thousand words', the shared memories of Edward Cummings and Susan Gallagher have more impact on the reader than reams of infant mortality statistics. By identifying briefly with one human tragedy, we gain greater understanding of the community to which that person belonged. Especially is this so of the previously marginalised groups, women and children, in an era when there was no social security safety net to ease times of hardship or bereavement.

The interviews of the North Queensland Oral History Project capture something of a way of life at the point of its vanishing, a watershed moment. For in some respects, life in North Queensland had continued in an almost anachronistic fashion, after other more settled areas in the south had left the pioneering era behind. When Olive Stallon recalls her mother doing the family washing 'down at the creek; make a fire with two cross bars, down there, and boil it up'[7] she speaks for countless bush women. Other timeless practices were still current. Butchered meat was salted or shared with neighbours. Women supported one another during childbirth. Community support was an oft-repeated motif.

Another recurring memory is of homes built by menfolk from bush-materials; of ironbark with earthen floors watered to keep down the dust and with furniture improvised from saplings and corn-sacks. Julius Mathieson recalls that at Major's Creek his brothers and sisters sat on forms adzed from logs supported by forked logs set into the floor; an image made endearingly familiar by the cartoon 'Saltbush Bill'. The ubiquitous kerosene case was made into wardrobes, side tables, and store cupboards, sometimes with the addition of 'a bit of cretonne for a frill' in which case it was known, wryly, as the 'Laurel Suite', from the brand logo on the end of each case.

In these recorded life stories we catch echoes of some once-common usages before they vanish from the language. Although many of the Narrators of the North Queensland Oral History Project reported having left school at an early age, often at twelve or thirteen, their diction was clear and their grammar competent. Their use of 'done' for 'did' and 'seen' for 'saw' reflects speech patterns of the day. Sentences were constructed so that they started and finished, and conveyed the meaning that was intended. There were no profanities, very few expletives. The strongest form of emphasis was, 'My word!', or to really make a point, 'My word, Yes! Or, 'By Jove, Yes!

Some charming idioms were used: 'spare boy' (a teamster's offsider), wharf lumpers (waterside workers) marriage lines (marriage certificate); industrial terminology such as 'cut and shut' (tightening the steel rims on wagon wheels), and 'spiffs' (carded samples of embroidery threads); and everyday expressions such as 'favoured' (to take after), kak-hander (left-handed), 'brace of shakes' (immediately), 'give me the office' (let me know), 'hanging up his hat' (courting) and 'cove' (fellow). In many places, these have faded from our language.

It was not easy to work with tapes that had been collected years earlier by another interviewer. At times it was exasperating. Perturbing questions remained unanswered. So what did happen when Barbara Aitchison's little brother, 'the only one born in Townsville', drowned at Picnic Bay in 1904? And was Connie Hill's brother who 'died when he was fifteen' the naughty Ray whom we hear so much about? A gentle, 'Do you feel you could talk a little more about that?' might have elicited the full stories. And there will be few readers not vexed at finding they are never to know the outcome of Tom Kerr's gallant night ride to his dying wife's bedside.

One essential which every Oral Historian should bring to the interview situation is a sound background knowledge of the period under discussion, a lack of which is a barrier to entering imaginatively into the Narrator's world. Elderly people sharing their life experiences feel dismayed at ignorance of facts well known to their generation; that the Gallipoli landing took place in the First World War, not the Second; that thongs weren't invented until the 1960s, and so on. For example, right up until the 1940s many North Queensland families still had a 'billy cart' or a 'billy goat cart', a box on two wheels with wooden shafts used for countless household errands such as fetching groceries or firewood. In recounting her life story, Florrie Toombs had explained that, to earn sixpence a week for her school fees at St Patrick's Convent on the Strand, she ran messages for the neighbours with her 'billy goat cart'. The Interviewer interrupted with, 'Did you have a goat to pull it?' At this there was an interval of pained surprise. Then Florrie snorted, 'I was the billy goat!' For one moment there, she could feel herself superior to this Bright Young Thing from the University! Fancy not knowing what a billy goat cart was!

The Narrators were all children of the decade and a half which saw the dawning of a new Australian awareness. For the first time people who had regarded themselves as Queenslanders, Tasmanians or Victorians began to think of themselves as Australians. Integrated with this fresh sense of national identity was a mounting imperialistic fervour. The population of the newly formed Commonwealth in 1901 was just over three and a half million. Of these, 77 per cent were Australian born, 18 per cent British. In the years

1906 to 1913, a drop in the national birthrate led to an increase in immigration from the 'Old Country' with an increasing Britishness in the population. Schoolchildren were encouraged to see themselves not only as Australians but as 'citizens of the world's vastest and mightiest empire'.[8] Australia's destiny was seen as being as part of the British Empire.

To this new nationalism and loyalty to Empire was added a long-held sense of racial superiority. Many of the decisions of the early Commonwealth Parliament embodied the wish of the majority of Australians to preserve a predominantly European society in Australia.

In making these transcriptions I found a recurring problem was the use of what would be by today's standards, racist terminology. While I wanted my Narrators to tell their stories in their own words, some expressions they used fell pretty clangingly upon the ear of the modern reader. But in that earlier period of North Queensland history, terms such as 'blackfellow', 'Chow' and 'Jap' were part of everyday speech and were not intended to be derogatory or offensive. 'Gin', derived from an Aboriginal word for woman, was common usage.

When Fred King speaks of the gins at Bulliwallah he does so with respect for their unique qualities and with genuine fondness. 'Chinaman' was standard English at the time, comparable to the long-obsolete 'Indiaman'. Numerous 'Chinamen' are recalled with admiration not only for their ability to wrest bounty from the reluctant soil but for their medical skills in problems ranging from toothache to rheumatic fever. The English language is ever changing and such expressions are no longer acceptable. They are included to convey a sense of the period. Perhaps they signpost where we have come from in the long haul towards understanding and tolerance in our multicultural society.

Each of the elderly Narrators was speaking, probably for the first time, on to a tape-recorder to an unknown interviewer. You can sense the misgiving, the tension. Suddenly, they are not at all sure about all this. Oh! Dear! How did they ever let themselves be talked into it? The first answers are given as though to a tax inspector, formal, stiff, edgy. But before long memories come crowding, one image triggering another. Recollections tumble over one another in the delight of recalling long-ago times to an interested listener. They tell their stories in their own words, plain and unvarnished. I tried to remain faithful to the telling.

The reader will become aware of some repetition of incidents. Cyclone Leonta, in 1903, is recalled by nine Narrators. It was a shared experience, in the same way as the Japanese air-raids were to children of wartime Townsville. Similarly frequent was recollection of the loss of the *Yongala* in 1911. If people have been through these things they want to talk about them. It is part of their life story. I was not about to deny their memories to them.

The North Queensland of the Federation years was a region of scattered communities not yet linked by road or rail. Coastal vessels supplied the only means of communication with Brisbane. Inland, there were isolated pastoral properties, townships and mining communities dependent upon mail coaches, mailmen, and 'packers' who plied the rough tracks. Lumbering horse and bullock wagons hauled out the produce and took in supplies meant to last many months. The principal means of transport was still the horse. Oscar Crowther, of Belgian Gardens, could still recite a long list of station brands he had known as a boy, saying, 'Boys knew horses like they would know cars today.'[9]

Charters Towers, known fondly by its population of 30,000 as 'The World', was the largest centre in the north. Townsville, population about 10,000, was but a coastal outlet for the rich hinterland. Its streets bore a denuded appearance, most of the trees having been cleared in the early years to fire the boiling-down works, a process aided and abetted by herds of feral goats. Photographs of the period show picket fences surrounding trees planted in public places, such as the juvenile Moreton Bay fig trees and banyans on the Strand. Should the occupants of private homes cherish hopes of gardens and fruit trees they must perforce barricade themselves behind stout fences against the goat barbarians.

To give readers a sense of the period and to set the life stories of the Narrators in the context of a wider history, I have included as much contemporary material as possible. There is something about old newspapers that provides a Tardis on time. When, with your own eyes you peruse the pages that long-dead eyes have pored over, when you savour the advertisements and ponder the photographs, you find you are Then, not Now. In the Appendices are accounts of the celebrations of the inauguration of Federation – I trust readers will relish the importunate goat on the official dais in Charters Towers – of the plague in North Queensland, of Cyclone Leonta and the loss of the *Yongala*; news items that would have been on everyone's lips at the time. A book should be like a Christmas stocking, as stuffed full of delight and surprise as it is possible to make it.

The Narrators are ranked by chronological age: thus Mary Grimwade with her epic account of life on Cashmere station before the turn of the century leads the way, and the tail-ender is the youthful, seventy-three-year-old Edward Smedley. Their names are like the roll-call of some long-ago school class. Some of them would have been no little surprised to find themselves in the company of one or two their classmates.

I have loved preparing these accounts of a generation of North Queenslanders who previously had no voice, no opportunity, to tell their unique stories. In doing so I felt a deep sense of bonding with the Narrators and the need to make their brave, self-effacing voices heard. They have good things to say to us which should resonate to modern minds concerned at the wastefulness of our society. They spoke of self-reliance, generosity of spirit, neighbourliness, loyalty and trust, and of down-to-earth things; of 'making do, or doing without' or 'If you see a job has to be done, get on and do it, and make a good fist of it while you are at it'.

Although, in our modern world, we seldom pause to consider it, our present moment is fleeting and the future unpredictable. Not only do circumstances change but the very problems which seem so urgent change, too, and will doubtless be replaced by other, different sets of uncertainties. Although we cannot steer our course into the future by looking backwards, we may yet derive some insight about coping with the surprises that tomorrow may bring. As we face its perplexities and uncertainties perhaps we may gain from the quiet courage of those who have lived in and loved the North before us, and draw strength from their memory.

1 Abrams, Jeremiah (ed.), *Reclaiming the Inner Child,* Harper Collins, London, 1996, p.198

2 Pilot Hill, at the mouth of Ross Creek, Townsville, blasted away during reclamation for the building of the new wharves.

3 Florence Toombs; transcript, p.7

4 Three Australian lieutenants, H.H. Morant, P.J. Handcock and G.R. Witton were charged with the murder of Boer prisoners. Morant and Handcock were executed by firing-squad, 27 February, 1902. 'The Breaker' was the pen-name under which Morant had contributed poetry to the Sydney *Bulletin.* Following public outrage in Australia over this incident, the execution of Australian volunteers during the Great War was not tolerated.

5 Edward Cummings, transcript, p. 13

6 Susan Gallagher; transcript, p.4

7 Olive Stallon; transcript, p. 7

8 Crowley, F.K. *Australia in Documents,* Wren, Melbourne, 1973, p 207, quoting Sydney *Daily Telegraph,* 15 January 1914.

9 Oscar Crowther; transcript, p.17

Contents

1

Cashmere station, 1890s **Mary Grimwade**

A Hardier Type

Introduction

It is possible that we as a people have grown softer, more effete. Not many families of today would be willing, or able, to face the rigours of life on a northern cattle property which Mary Grimwade's family, the Kerrs, accepted as normal in the 1890s. Drying the beef on the back fence, making do with fat-lamps, carrying a revolver when unfriendly Aborigines or swaggies raided the meat-house, doctoring cuts and injuries with kerosene, and being ferried as small children, across a flooded river in a galvanised-iron bathtub are some of the remembered experiences which make this a classic story of North Queensland pioneering life.

Two elderly ladies were involved in recording these memories for the North Queensland Oral History Project, Mrs Mary Grimwade and her sister Mrs Sophie Huddy, so bonded that either was able to complete the other's sentence, or to speak in unison with her. Each would turn to the other with a, 'Do you remember!' to clarify, or emphasise a recollection, with gentle chuckles evoked at memories of family jokes over eighty years old: about Grandfather Kerr's patched and mended saddle, or the pet possum that met an untimely end at the hands of Jack the terrier, ('And Dad laughed!' the pained indignation is still in the voice more than three-quarters of a century later) and Mother's cockatoo, taught to swear by a waggish station hand.

Through it all shines the girls' love of horses: Jasper, on whom they all learned to ride and who carried the little orphaned cousin safely over that formidable range; Pippin and Whitefoot the ponies (although it is hard to understand why the parents would not have got rid of Pippin, inadvertently responsible for the death of their little son); Deceiver, who could clear a six-foot jump; Antimony, who rolled with Mary in the water of Return Creek; Bellman, who jumped over little Dorie at the sliprails without injuring her, and the inimitable Whisper, who performed the heroic feat of carrying Tom Kerr through the night to the bedside of his dying wife, and then 'lay down for two days' to recover.

Today, the homestead at Cashmere lies in ruins. To get to it you must follow the line of the old bullock-wagon road, through the dense rainforests of the Seaview Ranges behind Cardwell. The black chasm of Blencoe Falls yawns just as threateningly as when ten-year-old Mary rode that way over a century ago. Of the homestead itself, all that left is a scattering of corrugated iron, some buckled water-tanks, a blaze of purple bougainvillaea in abandoned garden beds, shards of willow-pattern in the grass, and a lone date palm on the stony ridge – the ridge to which Tom Kerr promised to shift the house 'when cattle come to £2 a head.' He was wise to do so. In the valley below is the youthful Herbert River, flowing swift and strong from the ranges and not far down the slope below the homestead is a *Eucalyptus alba* to the fork of which is nailed a board; 'Level of 1967 flood'. There must have been many such floods.Nearby is a group of five graves of the pioneering family, the Aitkinsons, who took over Cashmere in 1904. In his memoirs, *Bush Tales and Memories*, R.L. Aitkinson remembers Tom Kerr as 'the best horseman I have ever known'.

A Hardier Type

My family went in a dray drawn by five horses to Cashmere station in 1891, and my father was managing there for eight years. The house at Cashmere was an old-fashioned square house with verandahs back and front. I think some of the stumps had given way[1] and my mother wanted it moved up to the top of the hill because it was flat on top and you could see for miles. And my father used to say, 'All right. Wait till cattle come to £2 a head!' Beasts were about thirty shillings a head then. And he said, 'When they come to £2 a head I'll get the house moved.' And so it was moved up.

There were five bedrooms altogether. One side of the verandah was closed in and made into two bedrooms. Then there was the living-room. There was old-fashioned good furniture. It all belonged to the station and had been there for many years. And there was a very wide back verandah with the dining-table on, which we used in the summer. And of course the kitchen was away separate, as it was in those days, not indoors as it is now.[2] It was a big kitchen with a long oven, wood. There was a pantry attached, and the storeroom. The men's quarters were about fifty yards away with the harness-rooms. And there were a lot of fruit trees, young fruit trees, brought up from the Cue River and planted; orange, lemons and mandarins.

Grandfather Kerr had come from New South Wales, from Condobolin, overland, with just five horses. And when he came to a station he would never come inside but just camp out in the paddock. Might go in and get some meat or some bread, but that was all he ever did. Just went from station to station and that was how he came up to the North. He had a wonderful way with horses.

One night we were having our tea… must have been fairly early... and there were quite a few horses in the yard, and one of them was a real buck-jumper that they were saying had thrown everybody, pretty-well. And Grandfather got up from the table and went out and he was away for some time. And then Father thought, 'Gosh! Dad's away a long time!' And he went out, and here was Grandfather at the yards, trying to catch this buck-jumper! It was a big bad horse, a real man-eater, and it had a gammy leg and one eye. And Grandfather is trying to put his old riding-saddle – an old patched-up thing that you wouldn't give a penny for – he'd patched it up and patched it up for years – it was his favourite saddle and he wouldn't part with it. And here he was putting it on this great black buck-jumper!

Once, when the river was in flood, my sister and I were taken across in a tub. We were going into Herberton. Mother was pregnant and we had to go across in one of those galvanised-iron washtubs, with two handles. The men had to swim the horses. And in the first place, to get the tub, one of them had to swim the river to go in to the station on the other side, to get the tub and bring it back across the river. Everything had to be ferried across like that. We'd sit in that and not breathe.

John Oxley Library

A little girl in her cot on the verandah of a homestead, about 1900. The floorboards appear to have been hand-shaped with an adze. Taking advantage of its relative coolness, family life was often centred on the verandah.

I remember going across with my little sister Sophie in my lap. She was only about two. And I was dead scared. But one man put a saddle-strap round the handle and he'd clench that in his mouth. He towed the tub. My father was an excellent swimmer. He swam on the downstream side in case it tipped over.

We were eight years at Cashmere. We made our own bread and our own butter. We had a churn but sometimes if there wasn't much cream you used your hand. We made the bread just whenever it was needed. If it was mustering time we'd make it more often. Mother did all the cooking. She'd make a half a dozen loaves at once. Make a big batch in her oven, because the men who were going out, they'd take big hunks of bread and meat for their dinner-camp. She used to make her own yeast out of hops, which is like little dried leaves. Or you can pour hot water over the potatoes.[3] Sometimes the cork used to come out of the yeast! You put the flour in a big round dish, and salt it, and make a hole in the centre, and then pour the yeast in. And then put a cloth over it. Then it was kneaded again and cut into bits and put in the tins and put in the oven and cooked. It was lovely! With a lovely crust. And Mother used to make cakes, chiefly fruit cakes.

The men, if they were out for long, would take flour and make dampers. Father used to make the *best* damper! He used to put sultanas in it sometimes. And the puftaloons that he would make! He'd mix up a batter and put them in the frying-pan. Puftaloons are just like scones, only they're fried in the pan instead of baked in the oven, because we always had plenty of dripping. Puftaloons and syrup! We used to love them. That was a treat!

We used to make hop-beer. We had rum in from Herberton but it was only for an emergency. If the men came in from the cold or the wet they'd be handed out a tot of rum. But Father never drank. He wasn't a drinker at all. We used to get our big lot of stores every six months. Bags of sugar! Bags of flour! It came on packhorses from Herberton, seventy miles away. And seventy miles was a long way in those days.

We had no conveniences at all. We had only kerosene lamps, and candles. And sometimes fat-lamps. For a fat-lamp you get a tin, then we used to get a strip of moleskin from old trousers because it was so thick, and you stick it in the fat, and wait till the fat seeps up, and then you light it. And then it goes 'Ssss Ssss Sssss'. And a putrid smell mostly. But it did the purpose. If you ran out of kerosene there was no corner-shop to run to. You had to make do.[4]

And the toilets were big pits down the backyard. Toilet paper was newspaper. I don't know when I first saw proper toilet paper.

We had plenty to eat even though it was usually corned beef. Or dried beef. We always had vegetables grown on the station and plenty of milk and butter. And for fruit whenever any friends of ours would come up from the Murray River they would have an extra packhorse or two with mangoes or oranges.[5]

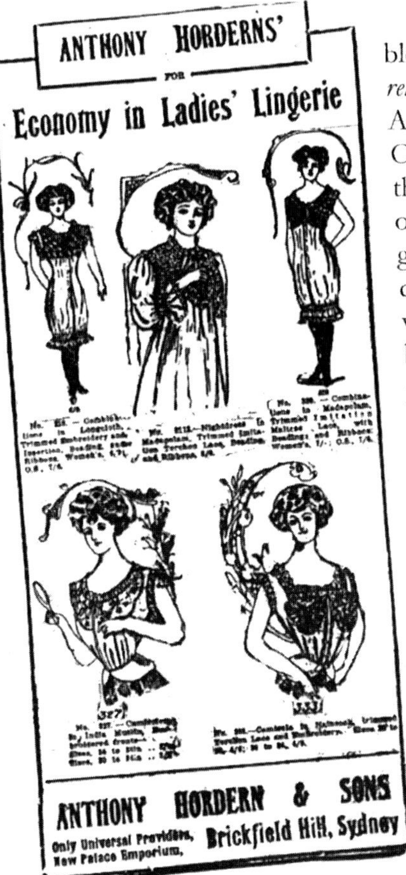

And whenever Mother ran out of vegetables she knew which bush ones to use. *Sida retusa*! Yes! *Sida retusa*![6] And the wild spinach. And sweet-potato tops, and pumpkin tops. Of course, you have to just bring them to the boil or else they go slimy. Those were our green vegetables. We children were given those. The men had to make do with dried potato. It came in square tins. They were cut up into tiny pieces and you poured boiling water on them and added a bit of pepper and salt.

And on killing-day, when we would kill a beast, Mother boiled down all the bones. She had two big boilers, out in the open on a fire. All the fat was rendered down because the men were always using fat, greasing their harness. The other boiler would have the bones and bits of meat, and they were boiled down to extract the juice, and Mother used to put that in tins. And so we were always able to have soup, or stews with a bit of taste. We only killed about every six weeks or so. And we used to dry the corned beef; rub the coarse salt into it, and put it out on the fence, and bring it in at night, then put it out again in the morning, until it was thoroughly dried. And we used to smoke some up in the open chimney, and keep the fire going there, and it was lovely! We only had fresh meat for two days at the most.

We had governesses teaching us, good, bad and indifferent. Two were really good, Julia Cronin, and Miss Davidson, who married Albert Bolanvada. We had a few books. But they were heavy, and packhorses could only carry so much stuff, because you had food, and goodness knows what else to pack in on the horses so we didn't have much in the way of books. The games we played were tiggy, and hide and seek; rounders, occasionally. Sunday afternoon we used to ask the stockmen to play with us. We were always happy.

Mother made all of our clothes, mostly loose things on a yoke. Except a few good things to go to Herberton Show. And once a year we got a Christmas dress, a made one from Allan and Starks. Two or three times a year Allan and Starks would send out catalogues, and you'd pick out this, that and the other, whatever you want, from there.

My sister and I were the first girls to wear a divided skirt for riding. Mother sent away for my sister's to Allan and Starks[7]. And then she made mine. They weren't long; just below the knee, something like culottes. We rode in the main events, hacks, and figure-of-eight. And I was riding at the Cairns Show once and they booed me all round the ring; 'Boo! Give it to a boy!' But I won Best Rider when I was four years old, or a bit younger than four.

We were very young when we learned to ride. So young that I don't remember. As soon as we were able to sit on a horse. It just came naturally. You were stuck on a horse; 'Now sit on the saddle and hold the pommel!' You didn't have the reins, of course. And the horses knew when there was a child there.They hardly moved along. The horses seemed to know as much as people. If you fell off they'd wait for someone to come along and pick you up.

And when I was round about seven, Dad and I went down over the range to Cardwell.[8] It was a terrific ride, through thick scrub, just enough room for a horse. There's a big gorge there. And there were big stinging-trees. If you went off the track you'd be likely to hit a stinging-tree and that was that. Some of the horses used to go mad if they were stung. You couldn't do anything. It just had to wear off.[9]

We went down to pick up my cousin whose parents had died. Her name was Edith Lees. She was eleven, and I don't think she had ever touched a horse in her life before. So she was put on a horse called Jasper, a horse we had all learned to ride on. And she rode over the range with us. I don't know how the girl did it. It was a terrible ordeal for her. It was cruel, but it was the

Frederick Charles Hall Collection

The Kerr children on Cashmere learned to ride 'so young that it just came naturally'.

only way to get her home. We stayed at Kirrama the first night. The second night we were home.

We had a weekly mailman used to deliver the mail round all the stations. It would take him a week to deliver and get back to Herberton. They were not supposed to swim a river or a creek in flood with the mail. But some of them used to. They used to tie it up on the horse's head and swim across. That's how the stockmen used to get across. They'd take off all their clothes and tie them on the horse and swim.

We used to wear big hats. And we were supposed to wear gloves out riding, but only cotton ones. If they were short of a man I'd have to help with the mustering. I didn't do a man's work, naturally, but I was there to help. If a beast broke away from the mob you had to go after him. We had ponies, very small ponies, Pippin or Whitefoot. They were only this high, and the bullock was that high! We bought them from a man that was travelling through with a mob of horses.

And when I was seven, the end of the world was supposed to be coming. And I was sent out to bring in the cows. And I was crying: 'I was sent out for the cows on my own and I'll die on my own with the cows!' Anyway! It never happened. That would have been 1894.

If we were sick we were taken into Herberton. It would take us three days to get there. And if we cut ourselves badly the only disinfectant we had was kerosene and then it would be bandaged up. Once, Peter Peterson, the fencer, was using the adze and he missed the log and it went through his boot and took the top of his foot off. He was working about a mile away from the house, but he came home. Kerosene, and bound up. And he was home for a few days and that was that. Good old kerosene! We had nothing else. And it did the trick. And when the stockmen went mustering, they always took their pocket-knife. And if ever they got bitten by a snake they'd cut it, and bleed it. That was the treatment. We had leg-splints and arm-splints and if somebody broke his arm, well, you splinted it up and that was that. My father broke his arm when I was little, and he rode in a race with that broken arm. We were a hardier type in those days.

We always had pets; birds of some kind. Mother loved birds. She always had a parrot. And Arthur Pacey taught one 'Good-bye! And bugger you!' As plain as plain. He used to go every night and say this to the parrot until he said it. Oh, Mother was upset.

And once we had a dingo pup for a pet, and we called him Tip. A beautiful animal! When he was a grown dog he followed us to Herberton. And on the way home, he was following the buggy, and some dogs ran out and frightened him. So he ran back to where we were staying at the hotel, and they didn't know what to do with him. And Mr Harding, Charlie Harding, took him and tied him up and he became savage and they shot him. Much to our sorrow, because we really loved that dog.

We had a couple of kangaroos. When they were tiny joeys they lived on milk, and after that they got bread and milk. And we had a possum, called Possie. And Dad had a terrier called Jack. And one night, Possie came up the stairs, and the terrier went like that! And that was the end of Possie! Of course there was a terrible commotion! A lot of tears. Oh, dear! And Dad laughed!

My cousin Cis and I used to milk the cows when the men were away out on the run mustering for two or three days. Sometimes the black gins did the milking. But we had poddy calves which used to be locked up at night, otherwise you wouldn't get any milk in the morning. The mothers might have died and we would feed the poddies. We'd put our fingers in a bucket of milk and let them suck the fingers and suck the milk up at the same time. We had one that we used to tie up and this time we tied it to the oleander tree and it ate oleander buds and died. We didn't realise they were poisonous.

And sometimes the blacks would come and steal a calf. They were really only looking for meat. Occasionally they used to raid the meat-house. That was down quite a bit away from the house. They'd get hungry but if you gave them meat they'd go away. Of course, you'd get the odd ones that were bad, but you get that in whites too, don't you! At times my mother used to have to walk round with a revolver round her waist. Only at times, if blacks or bad-looking swaggies were round about and the men were away. But if you showed them a gun, they'd go. We didn't have a lot of station blacks. Just a few. Old Judy, and Tiger. They were wonderful people.

We would get a lot of swaggies. There was quite a lot of tin-scratching going on along the creeks. Occasionally some of them used to take meat. But most of them were decent enough; they'd come for a bit of flour and sugar, then they'd move on to the next station.

On Cashmere there were no fences between the properties. Well, the stock from your property would come on to my property, and the stock from my property would be on yours. So once a year there'd be a big bang-tail muster and people from the different stations would come and look after their own. That was when you counted what stock you had. All the cattle would be brought in small mobs and put in a crush, and the hair on their tails clipped so that you'd know they had been counted. Our brand was XA9. We had our own people for the mustering. We didn't have to bring in outsiders. There was Will and Ted Lees. They were there, from young lads, on Cashmere, and Mr Joplin was there for a while as book-keeper. He was an English gentleman. And Arthur Henry was with us for a long time. Arthur Pacey. And others.

We girls used to go out on the run, to help collect horses. And one day we were riding out to a bore, and I was on Antimony, and as we were crossing Return Creek he just flopped down like that in the water! No indication at all that he was going to roll! Usually they give a bit of a paw.[10] But I had to ride all day in wet clothes and wet boots.

And, once, my father rode the seventy miles in to Herberton in eight hours at night. Mother was very ill. They thought she was dying. It was after my brother was born. And they sent this man, Paddy Mc——. He was a little bit soft, or simple. He was told not to spare the horses but to go right through to Cashmere. Well, he got to Woodleigh. Stayed there the night. Got to Tirrabella, unsaddled his horse; let it go. Mrs Garbutt – one of the Garbutts, of Garbutt Airstrip – she asked if he had heard anything of Mrs Kerr. And he said, 'Oh, Yes! I'm going to Cashmere to tell Mr Kerr that she's dying!'

And she asked him when he left. And he told her! So she got her son Jack to get a horse and go to Cashmere. Well, he did it in next to no time. And my father came back. And meantime Mrs Garbutt had sent word over to Gunnawarra to Mr Wilson, who was managing there. And he came across with two corn-fed horses which he was getting ready for the picnic races.[11] One horse was Whisper. My father was very pleased to see these two corn-fed horses. He rode the younger one into Hot Springs,[12] and then old Whisper on into town. Whisper lay down for two days, he was so tired. But Father did that on just a bush track, through the night.

And when my brother Jim was seven we were going into the Herberton Show when he had an accident. The Show was quite a big event and all the station people used to go in. And Jim and I were riding. He was riding Pippin. And I was riding Whitefoot. And we had to make a detour because there was another mob of horses on the road. And we had to go round through the bush a bit. Well, there was a gully, a wash-away, straight down and up. And Pippin jumped across it. And when we got up on the bank Jim said, 'Pippin did hurt my back.' And he complained of a headache all the time. Well, he died on the Thursday, the Thursday night. And was buried on the Friday. These days something could have been done about it but those days there was nothing they could do.

Herberton was the only place that had a Show for many years. And Mother and Father always used to ride in the jumps. They rode together in pairs. The show horses weren't looked after as they are now. They just took them out of the paddock and took them in. No training, no anything. Our father had a big black horse, Deceiver, a jumper, and he was the ugliest brute of a horse that ever was, a big, ugly, half-draught looking thing. Nothing to recommend him at all. A very ugly horse. But he could jump his six foot! Which was a record in those days. But Dad was the only one that could get him over six foot. When he was in the air, he'd stand in the stirrups so that there was no weight on his back.

I remember once at the Show, Dad was riding a chestnut called Limelight in the high jump. And Dad had his watch in his shirt pocket. Limelight hit top bar and was falling and as he was coming down Dad was feeling for his watch! Didn't want that to hit the ground! Everybody laughed about it! He was recognised as one of the best show riders in the North. He could get more out of a horse than anybody. He won a race once with a broken arm. He was a pretty rider, and a wonderful bushman.

He had another horse called Bellman, a jumper. And Bellman jumped over Dorie once. She wasn't much more than a toddler and she sneaked out from the back of the house to get to the stable. She was just at the sliprail when Dad let the horses out. And Bellman used to jump the sliprail, and there was Dorie right at the rail. And he jumped over her as well! Needless to say Dad put the strap round her then!

Cashmere was owned by a Mr Lewis who lived in Tasmania. When he died he left the property to his nephew who came up to Cashmere to look at the place, and he offered it to my father, but Dad didn't have the cash to buy it. My father then went to Woodleigh station. The stock had been sold to Gunnawarra, so my father then had to go out droving to buy extra cattle to stock up again. We were at Woodleigh for four years.

ST. PATRICK'S CONVENT.
TOWNSVILLE
PAROCHIAL AND HIGH SCHOOLS,
CONDUCTED BY THE SISTERS OF MERCY.

THIS Convent is beautifully situated on Cleveland Bay within sight of Magnetic and Palm Islands.

The Boarding School is large, well ventilated, and affords ample accommodation.

A University Class opened on the 18th, January 1892, obtained six (6) Certificates in the late Sydney Junior Examinations, taking a First Class in French.

The Grounds are carefully laid out, with provision for the children's recreation, and pupils have also the advantage of sea bathing.

The Religious and Moral training is strictly attended to.

The general course of study comprises all the branches which are required to pass the junior and senior examinations in the Sydney University For Teachers.—The examinations required by the Department of Public Instruction.

The School secured ten passes at the late examinations, Royal Academy of Music, London.

The New Term will Commence on the 22nd January, 1900.

Terms: University Class, Three Guineas per quarter.

Terms for Boarders: Thirty guineas per annum, including French, Drawing, Fancy-work and Calisthenics.

Extras: Pianoforte Tuition, Violin, Singing, Painting in Water Colors and Oils, and Dancing.

Entrance Fee: Two Guineas.

THE LADY SUPERIOR,
Convent of the Sisters of Mercy,
TOWNSVILLE.

And then in about 1903, I think it would have been, I went to the convent on the Strand in Townsville, St Patrick's. That was the idea in those days. You had twelve months away to finish your schooling. I went by train to Cairns and then by boat. I just had twelve months at the convent. We didn't go home for holidays because it was too far. Too much travelling in those days. There were about sixty or seventy boarders when I was there. Some were quite little, five or six or so, if their parents lived away out west. Then a lot came from the islands.

We boarders were allowed to go out for walks, along to Kissing Point. We used to bathe too, in neck-to-knees of course, at night. I was at the convent for [Tropical Cyclone] Leonta. We were not allowed to sleep in the dormitory because it was upstairs and it was swaying a bit. We had to bring all our bedding down and doss down in the study.[13] There was a lot of damage done around Townsville in Leonta but we didn't get to see much of it.

And then after when I was eighteen I was given a side-saddle, because Dad said that I was a young lady now and I had to ride sideways. Which was a load of rubbish!

1 No doubt the result of termites.

2 Detached kitchens were a feature of Queensland houses when wood-stoves and open fires were the only means of cooking. In the event of fire the rest of the home could be saved.

3 The fermentation of the potato skins formed a yeast-like raising agent.

4 For safety's sake it was necessary to put a layer of sand a couple of inches deep in the bottom of the tin to give it stability.

5 The Murray here referred to is the small river near Tully.

6 *Sida retusa* is a dark-leaved, knee-high weed which commonly grows around stockyards. As early as 1868, Walter Hill, the Government botanist, recommended that the only way to rid the paddock adjoining Government House in Brisbane of *Sida retusa* was to pull it out by hand. It has an extremely long, tough taproot. *Sida retusa* may be being confused with 'pig-weed' the succulent leaves of which were often cooked as a vegetable. Nearly half a century earlier settlers in the Maranoa District had been 'reduced to pigweed and fat hen which grew plentifully everywhere and were a good substitute for cabbage.' according to Mary McManus, 'The Early Settlement of the Maranoa District'.

7 One of many large department stores in Brisbane which specialised in mail orders for isolated families. The arrival of the glossy catalogues in the mail brought great pleasure to the lives of women and children on lonely properties. The 'feelers', small samples of fabric placed appropriately near illustrations, were an endless source of fascination.

8 Cardwell was settled as early as the 1860s as a port for the inland stations. Subsequently it was found that not only was the bay too shallow, but, despite government expenditure of £2000, the road over the range was 'constantly impassable during the wet season and often during other parts of the year to ordinary travellers'. It was 'infested with stinging-tree' and in some sections was so steep that the traveller felt his horse was 'walking on his hind legs while I had my face between his ears.' A. J. Boyd, quoted, in Gibson-Wilde, *Dorothy, Gateway to a Golden Land*, James Cook University, 1984, p.20.

9 The stinging-tree, once known by its Aboriginal name of gympie-gympie, has large, pale-green, heart-shaped leaves armed with stiff hairs which, on contact, deliver an agonising sting. One old bush remedy is said to be to cut a green twig of the stinging-tree, slice it diagonally, and rub the affected area with the oozing sap. It has the most virulent sting of the laportea species and its effect can be felt for weeks after contact. A bush poet, Bob McFadden described it in 1876 as 'a touch of Hell'

10 Most horses rake the bottom with a forefoot before rolling in water, giving the rider a chance to pull the head up sharply and spur them across.

11 There is an element of wryness here. Entries in Queensland picnic races are expected to be 'grass-fed'. However most owners will slip a little corn into their horses' feed on the quiet to improve their condition, knowing full well that others are doing the same. That the Gunnawarra horses had been corn fed greatly enhanced Bill Kerr's chances in the race against time to his critically ill wife's bedside.

12 Innot Hot Springs, a small township.

13 'The Sisters of Mercy Convent has escaped damage. In this it has been fortunate for much debris has been carried into its ground and some upon its roof. The convent schools have been badly damaged and will require considerable expenditure to repair them. The *North Queensland Register*, Monday, 16 March, 1903. See also Appendix C.

2

Ross Island, 1899–1906 **Ethel McLeod**

Threepences in the Pudding

Introduction

Ethel McLeod was ninety-one years of age when she recorded her story but the freshness of her voice was that of a young woman, such was her delight in bringing to mind the days of long ago; of being one of a large family where Dad's word was law, of school-days on 'forms' out under the trees or, 'in the shed', because of over-crowding, seventy children to a class; of evenings of content, singing around the piano; of study by lamplight to become a qualified teacher, of playing the organ at the Presbyterian Church.

There won't be many readers not taken by surprise at the anecdote of the whisky-laced Christmas pudding, in the recalling of which Ethel McLeod's voice took on the true whine of a discontented and disappointed child; 'We don't *like* it'. You can almost sense the exasperation of Mum and Dad at opposite ends of the long table, at the 'flop' of what they had hoped to be a special treat. The reader will possibly feel some exasperation with Dad for having been so liberal with good Scotch whisky. Perhaps, at the time, Dad felt a similar sentiment.

Ethel McLeod's story affords some historically interesting glimpses of an earlier Townsville, where steamers taking passengers to the south – there were no road or rail links – anchored in the bay and were serviced by steam tugs; a Townsville where flags were hoisted at the Pilot Station to warn inhabitants of impending cyclones; where children snitched rides on Victoria Bridge as it swung open to let coastal vessels up-river; where patients were conveyed to the hospital on a wheeled canvas stretcher; and a Townsville where Madame Melba could hold an audience spellbound in the School of Arts. Of special interest to anyone involved in education is Ethel McLeod's cameo-like account of the 'Babies' at Ross Island School chanting in unison to the utter distraction of their teacher, and of her own experiences as a Pupil–Teacher from the age of fourteen.

In later life Ethel McLeod was to give herself unstintingly to the service of her family, her four boys, 'all at the Grammar School', and her community, and would feel rewarded by the quiet praise of a husband's remark after afternoon tea, 'Well, we've made that cake look a bit silly, haven't we!' When asked about the Townsville of World War II she spoke of playing *You Are My Sunshine* for dances, and of thinking sharply 'You leave our kookas alone!' when American soldiers camped in the Botanic Gardens, now Queens Gardens, shouted 'shut up' at the kookaburras. Only briefly, with quiet pride, does she refer to the loss of two of her sons killed in action, one in the siege of Tobruk, the other as a pilot in a 1000-bomber raid over Germany. She has come to terms with the tragedy of those deaths, and now takes comfort in the achievements of a 'clever grandson', symbolic to her, that despite loss and sorrow, life in all its fullness, goes on.

❋

Threepences In The Pudding

Dad was in the police force in Bundaberg so we lived at the police station. We were there till I was about five or six and I can remember the nice big clean streets. Then we went to Ingham, by boat. I remember the journey because I had a doll as big as myself and another girl on board wanted my doll. She took such a fancy to it that I gave it to her. And when I went to my mother she said, 'Where's your doll?' And I said, 'I gave it to the girl.' And she said (Very, stern admonishing voice) 'Go back and get it at once!' And, Oh yes, I got it!

We came to Townsville when I was about ten. We lived at the police station down near the jetty, and went to Ross Island School, because it was an island then; it had water all round it. It wasn't South Townsville.

There was a little hill on the way to the jetty called the Pilot Hill and they used to have poles and a structure where they put up the height of the tides. It had flags, and a canvas kind of signal for the ships coming in. The Pilot Station was on a little rocky hill like the Cutting, like a rocky tor. We knew Captain Rawlmer who was in charge. But they did away with that little hill when they extended the jetty.

There was a swing bridge over Ross Creek that would open to let the boats come through,[1] the *Lass o' Gowrie*, the *Baratta*, the *Kuranda*, the *Seymour* and the *Mourilyan*. And when the boat went through and landed the people, they would make straight for Brady's Shamrock Hotel. Evidently they came from Ireland.

And boats used to go to Rooney's timber mill, further up the creek. Oh, but the port was busy those days! The ships were lined up along the jetty there. Before they built the second jetty ships had to wait right out at what was called the Lower Anchorage. The Harbour Board tug used to go out and take them provisions. One tug was the *Alert* and it would be tied up in Ross Creek, near the Metropole. I had a trip on it once because we knew the men on board. It was lovely going right out over the bay. They were big steam ships, passenger ships, anchored out. That was the only way to go down to Brisbane then.

And this swing bridge, one day – I shouldn't be telling these things against myself! – there used to be just a little part where you could jump on from the side landing. The middle was locked against all vehicles so nobody could go through that. But this little bit, before it would just close up, the children used to jump on for a little bit of a ride. We didn't see it as a risk. And this time, when we got to the other side, lo and behold, there was my Dad! And he said, 'Don't you ever do that again!' You can be sure I didn't! But the other kids still used to!

We knew that Dad's word was law. He only used to have to lift a finger up and we would behave ourselves. And Mum used to say, 'I'll tell your Dad!' or 'Wait till your father gets home!' And it was punishment.

My father was Scottish and my mother was German, but she had come out when she was a baby. A lot of German families came out long, long ago and they were good settlers. Some went up to Kuranda, and Atherton and went in for fruit-growing. During the war there wasn't much prejudice because they had been here so long and mixed in so well. They were just honest, hard-working people on the land.

In our family there were four boys and four girls. And Dad got £10 a month! But being in the police there were advantages; we got the kerosene and wood for the wood-stove provided and we didn't have to pay rent. So that would bring his salary up. But ten people living on £10 a month! We couldn't waste anything. If we didn't eat something on our plate we got growled at. But if we didn't want to eat something, we would take it off our plate and slip it along under the table. There was one brother, he would eat anything. He was always hungry. He'd eat it for us so we wouldn't get into trouble.

We always had fowls because you had to have them to supplement your food bill. You had the eggs and then you cooked them. I had a pet blind chicken I used to feed. It used to know to come after a meal to the front of the house and I'd give it its food.

The old Johnnie Chinaman used to come with his two baskets. You wondered how he could carry them, they were so heavy. He had a long pole, and his baskets would be one on each end, springy-like, up and down. In those days you could get a bunch of bananas for one and six. There were a lot of Chinese, but they were well behaved. They had their gardens. They used to say that they sent all their money home to China.

And Mum would wash all one day and iron on the next. We always had a roast dinner on a Sunday. And then there'd be the dripping with all the meaty gravy and salt and pepper for bread and dripping. And for puddings we'd have steam puddings, or bread-and-butter pudding, or rice pudding in a big dish that would go round a large family.

And at Christmas time, the Christmas pudding was put on the table, the whisky was poured on it, and it was lit. And when the whisky was burned away we were given our piece of pudding. Not one of us would eat it. 'I don't like it,' (whiney voice), we'd say. We didn't like the whisky taste! Oh, I wish I had it now! It was the whisky we didn't like. It seemed to go into the pudding. And there would be threepences in the pudding. In those days coins were silver and you boiled them all. And weren't you pleased when you found a threepence! And charms! Silver charms! There was a thimble for an old maid, and for good luck a horseshoe, a silver one. And a ring for a bride.[2] You'd put them in the pudding. They went in with the coins. We didn't have a Christmas Tree. We weren't that well off. But we might get something that you could wear, something that you needed. But for Christmas Dinner we had the traditional dinner as far as you could carry it out, the chook and the baked spuds and vegetables.

At school if you were to get a punishment you wrote down your punishment on your slate. And the headmaster had a lovely cane, and he would come round. And half the time you rubbed out some of your names. There was one girl, Mary Brady; she used to go to the convent. She really belonged to the Convent but she'd have a bit of a row there so she'd come back to the State School. And then back to the Convent again. Well, this day, she was bold and she put her tongue out at the teacher. So the teacher put down, 'Mary Brady was rude. She put her tongue out at me.'

And the headmaster says, 'Mary Brady, come out!' So Mary Brady comes out and she starts to sniffle. And he says, 'You were very rude, I believe. You put your tongue out at your teacher!'

DEPARTMENT OF PUBLIC INSTRUCTION.

ATTENDANCE OF CHILDREN AT SCHOOL.

PROCLAMATION.

By his Excellency the Honourable SIR SAMUEL WALKER GRIFFITH, Knight Grand Cross of the Most Distinguished Order of St. Michael and St. George, Lieutenant-Governor of the Colony of Queensland and its Dependencies.

Whereas it is enacted by the State Education Act of 1875 that the provisions of Part III. of that Act shall be in force in such parts or districts only of the colony as the Governor-in-Council shall from time to time notify and declare by Proclamation: And whereas it is expedient that the provisions of Part III. of the said Act should be in force throughout the colony of Queensland: Now, therefore, I, SIR SAMUEL WALKER GRIFFITH, the Lieutenant-Governor aforesaid, in pursuance of the provisions of the said Act, and by and with the advice of the Executive Council, do hereby notify and declare that on and after the First day of May, 1900, the provisions of Part III. of the said Act shall be in force throughout the colony of Queensland.

Given under my Hand and Seal, at Government House, Brisbane, this Eleventh day of April, in the year of our Lord One thousand nine hundred, and in the sixty-third year of her Majesty's reign.

By command,

JAMES G. DRAKE.

(L.S.) S. W. GRIFFITH,
Lieutenant-Governor.

GOD SAVE THE QUEEN.

(Extract from the State Education Act of 1875.)

PARENTS TO SEND CHILDREN BETWEEN SIX AND TWELVE YEARS OF AGE TO SCHOOL, UNLESS THERE IS A VALID EXCUSE.

SECTION 28.—The parent of every child of not less than six nor more than twelve years of age shall, unless there be some valid excuse, cause such child to attend a State School for sixty days at the least in each half-year.

Any of the following reasons shall be deemed a valid excuse, that is to say:—

(1.) That the child is under efficient instruction in some other manner.

(2.) That the child has been prevented from attending school by sickness, fear of infection, temporary or permanent infirmity, or any unavoidable cause.

(3.) That there is no State School which the child can attend within a distance of two miles, measured according to the nearest road ordinarily used in travelling from the residence of such child.

(4.) That the child has been educated up to the standard of education.

PENALTY FOR NEGLECTING TO SEND CHILD TO SCHOOL.

Section 29.—Any parent who shall neglect or refuse to cause any such child to attend school for the time aforesaid in any half-year shall on conviction of such offence forfeit and pay any sum not exceeding twenty shillings for a first offence and not exceeding five pounds for a second or subsequent offence, and in default of payment shall be liable to be imprisoned for any period not exceeding seven days for a first offence, and not exceeding thirty days for a second or subsequent offence.

And she goes, 'Snff! Snff'! And she says, 'It slipped out when I wasn't looking.' Well! We had to duck behind our slates!

And there was a gallery in this school for the Babies – the young ones just starting school. They had seats going higher and higher, a sort of gallery. And if one baby said something they all took it up in a chorus. And the teacher had

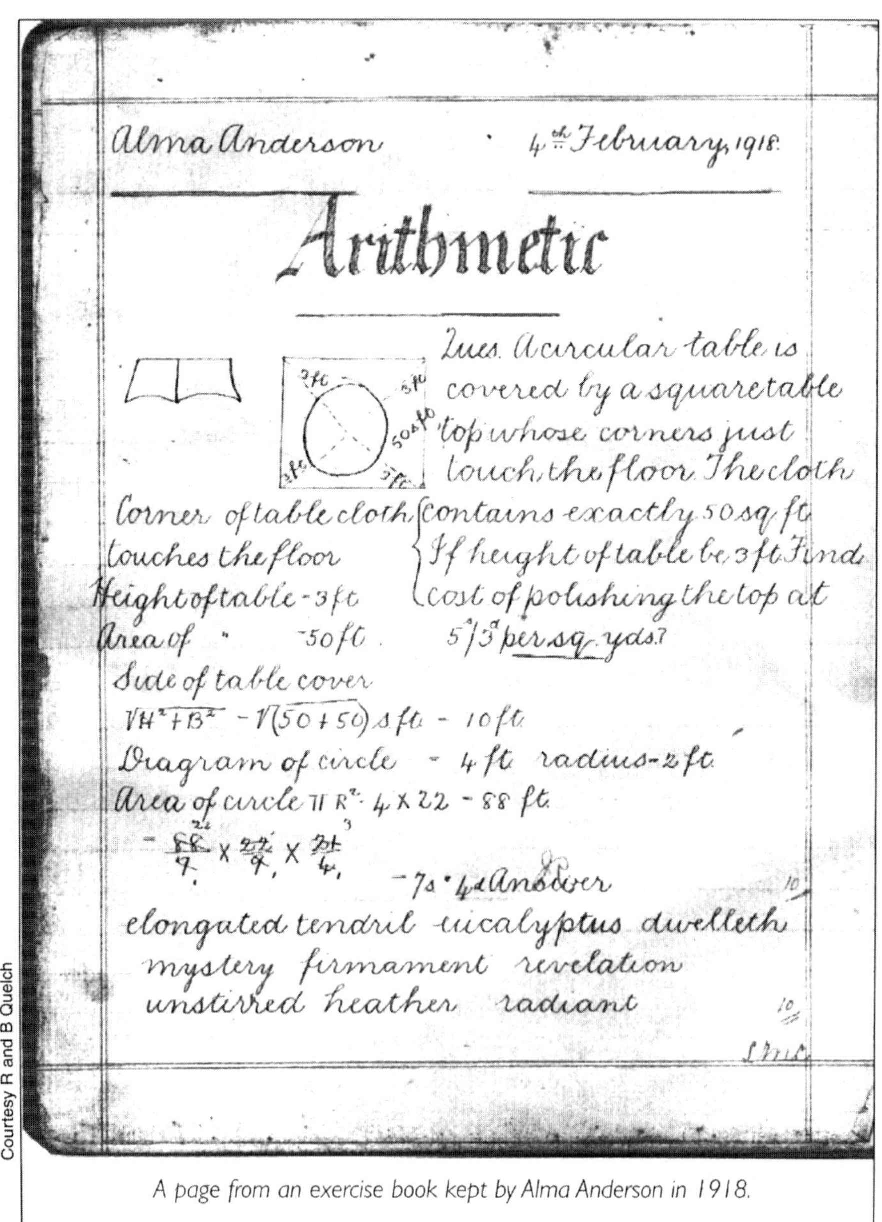

Alma Anderson 4th February, 1918.

Arithmetic

Ques. A circular table is covered by a square table top whose corners just touch the floor. The cloth contains exactly 50 sq ft. If height of table be 3 ft. Find cost of polishing the top at 5/3 per sq. yds.?

Corner of table cloth touches the floor
Height of table - 3 ft
Area of " - 50 ft.
Side of table cover
$\sqrt{H^2+B^2}$ - $\sqrt{(50+50)}$ s ft - 10 ft
Diagram of circle - 4 ft radius - 2 ft.
Area of circle πR^2 - 4 x 22 - 88 ft.
= $\frac{88}{7} \times \frac{22}{9} \times \frac{21}{4}$
- 7s 4d Answer

elongated tendril eucalyptus dwelleth
mystery firmament revelation
unstirred heather radiant

A page from an exercise book kept by Alma Anderson in 1918.

Courtesy R and B Quelch

been giving them a lesson about the elephant, and she said, 'Why does an elephant have short thick fat legs?'

And one kid says, 'Please, Miss, to hold its big belly up.' And the whole crowd of them took up the chorus '....to hold its big BELLY up!'

And then another day she's giving them a lesson about goats, and she's told them about Angora goats, and other goats. And she says, 'Now what's the name of a goat that has long silky hair?' Of course, she wanted Angora but one kid – those kids over Ross Island, they were up to the mark – he says 'Stinker, Miss.' (They called the man goat a stinker. And he earned it, too. Oh, it was an awful smell!) So this kid says, 'Stinker, Miss.' And then the chorus came. 'STINker, Miss!' Well, you've never heard anything like it! 'STINker, Miss!' from all these kids, fifty of them!

There were about seventy children in my class. We had different teachers, but we were all in the one room. Sometimes we could go out on the verandah, or sometimes go out under a tree. Or in the shed and have forms. In those days it was the Three Rs and more time was devoted to it. I didn't like mathematics. I used to like English. But the children knew they would be punished and it made them behave.

There was rivalry between the State School and the Convent. They used to call each other names. Only a tongue battle. There was never ever anything serious. In those days, at fourteen, when you did your education at the State

John Oxley Library

A sewing class in about 1905. At Ross island School the girls made 'samplers' and 'stroked their gathers to make them nice'.

School, you left school and went to work. And while you were at school you got discipline from the teachers, when you were home you got discipline in the home, and when you went to work you got disciplined from the boss. And kids were better people for it, and courteous! They had manners! Girls when they left school worked in their own home or if there were a lot of girls in the family some of them went out to domestic work. It was what they knew.

You didn't get much money and you walked everywhere. There were horse-drawn cabs, with four wheels, and the seats were opposite one another, and the hansom cab with the cabby on a seat way up outside. But ordinary people never engaged a cab.

There were mounted police, and Inspector Gailbraith in charge. He was a small man and once he was on this great big horse, and Mr Lowth had Lowth's Hotel. And Mr Lowth wanted to keep in good with Inspector Gailbraith, and he calls out (booming, officious voice): 'Inspector Gailbraith! You're the finest mounted policeman in this town!' Oh, but they had some splendid men and splendid horses. And the horses, didn't they know! They were disciplined! 'I'm doing my duty!'

The Black Maria, transported prisoners to the court house and back to the gaol. There was a gaol in town behind the court house, and there was another walled gaol down where the new Central School is, by the park. We had a cell at the police station on Ross Island, and sometimes a mother would bring a boy and she would say to my mother, 'Put him in the cell for a minute, Mrs McKay! Make him good.' So my mother would put him in the cell, didn't lock it or anything, and then the mother would say to her son, 'Will you be a good boy?' And, Yes! He was going to be good for ever and ever! So then he was let out. It was really only fun, but the boy would take it very seriously. He'd think, 'Well, I wouldn't like to get here! I'd better be good after this!'

In those days the ambulance transported patients on a litter. It was like a stretcher with four legs to stand it on and a canvas covering. There were two ambulance men, one at each end between the shafts, and they had to wheel it to the hospital. The money they got they earned! And it was very little. Mr Macintosh was one of the supervisors at the ambulance.

When I was about twelve I won a Masonic Scholarship; they were few and far between then. I was always top of the class except once when a boy cheated and beat me by one mark. I never forgave him. I went to the girls' secondary school. It was called the Church of England Girls' Collegiate School and it was on Melton Hill behind St James' Cathedral. We used to go down to the cathedral every day for Scripture. I was really a Presbyterian but I knew all the ritual of the Church of England.

Once, after some function we had there one night, Dad said he would call for me. I could have gone home with some people, but I thought, 'No, I'd better wait. He'll be coming all that way over.' And I thought, 'He'll be coming right over the bridge and up the hill and I won't be there. So I'd better do as I'm told. I'll wait.' But he didn't come. And he didn't come. He'd been called out on some case. So I walked from that Collegiate School, across the bridge, and all the way home, all by myself in the moonlight. And there was a crowd of drunken sailors I had to pass, but they never said a word!

And then Leonta came, and it was awful. We had to run from the school and across the road to a home owned by Mr and Mrs Dryborough who owned the Dryborough Foundry, over in South Townsville. And they housed us there that day and that night and the next morning we could go home. And, Oh! To see all the wreckage everywhere! It would break your heart. That was Leonta.[3]

I sat for Junior at the Collegiate, but I didn't go any further. The school folded up then, so I couldn't have carried on, even if I had wanted. There was the Grammar School but they only took boys then. The only school for girls was our school. Afterwards the Grammar School took girls. Effie Hartley, she was one of the first girls to go to the Grammar School. She was a clever girl.

I started pupil-teaching at Ross Island at fourteen.[4] We didn't have Domestic Science but we had samplers. We had to learn all the different stitches, how to do gathers. You had a long piece and you kept adding to it. And you had to gather the piece on and you had to stroke your gathers, make it all nice. And we had to learn to put a patch on, and do darning, and all the stitches; run-and-fell seam, top-seam, all by hand.

And when we were pupil-teachers we had to make garments, quarter-size. I made this baby's first long gown, every stitch by hand, the full length, those long ones that you tucked up to keep their feet warm. And a dress shirt for a man, quarter size. We had to do that for our sewing. All by hand. No machines.

Mum made lovely bread. And when I was a pupil-teacher at Ross Island School I gave a lesson on making bread. And I wondered why all the kids are sitting up and behaving themselves. And I'm punching away into the dough and I'm saying, 'You know, you've got to give it a really good punch to make it light'. And all this sort of thing. And all of a sudden I catch sight of… well, there was the headmaster, and another teacher from the West End School and they had been taking it all in! Oh, I did get ragged about it!

The only form of entertainment was every night, quite content, we'd get around the piano and sing a few songs. We used to have picnics down at Kissing Point. We all took our own food. And sometimes in the Botanical Gardens.

There was a rowing club for ladies. Jessie McQueen, she was the head of it, and they'd go out in Ross Creek, just for exercise. You could hire these rowing-boats. We would land up at the end of Ross Island; there was quite a big space there for games so we'd take our own supper and play games there, usually rounders, or twos-and-threes, they were favourites, and afterwards row back again. Sometimes we'd have moonlight trips to Magnetic Island on the launch, singing all the way there and all the way home. Oh, it was nice!

There was the Stanley pictures at the back of Lowth's Hotel. Open-air. I used to like that.[5] And there was the Olympia, too. Silent pictures of course.

I played the organ at the Presbyterian Church I was the last one to win a gold medal – it was supposed to be worth £5 in those days – it would be 1912. First of all a boy won it, George Duncan. Then another boy Douglas Campbell. They went to the Grammar School. And then I won it. I was the first girl to win the gold medal for the Senior Sunday School Examination for Queensland.

I suppose you would say we were a musical family. I played the church organ for ten years and so did my sister Mavis. And another sister played the banjo-mandolin. I used to play for weddings in all churches, not just our own. The favourite one to play when the bride came in was *The Voice That Breathed O'er Eden.* At the Presbyterian Church there was a bell up in the steeple and a little old lady, Mrs Stevenson, used to ring it and she wouldn't let anybody else. And oh, it was a strain for her to get it going, but once she got it going she was right. My Dad was on the committee for the church hall, and he pushed a lot for that.

Frederick Charles Hall Collection

Ethel McLeod's police-constable father was paid '£10 a month and brought up a family of ten on it'. He was stationed on Ross Island.

At that time, all wedding receptions were held in the home with tables on the verandah. You did all your own cooking and the centrepiece would be the lovely wedding cake. You didn't have beer at all. You had soft drink or a cup of tea.

We used to go swimming on the beach. And then once man walking along the beach, the shark came right up on to the sand after him. And another man, he was in swimming, and he tried to get out but the shark came right up after him and took him. And there was a another young man about eighteen taken over at Arcadia, at Alma Bay. But everybody used to swim here on the beach, running the risk. And there used to be a lovely long shelving beach, with lovely fine sand.

I didn't go out very much when I was a young girl because I had study to do. I had to get through my exams. Once, Madame Melba came to the School of Arts[6] and the policeman on the door let my two sisters in. And I'm on my own in the house next door – we were living in the house next to the police station then[7] – and I'm there studying, and they come home and tell me that the policeman let them in and that they saw Madame Melba and they heard her! And I missed out on that. I could never forget it!

And I went through the exams. until I became a Classified Teacher, and I could be sent anywhere then. They didn't transfer you before that. I taught at the old Central School, on the corner of Oxley and Mitchell Street, until I passed my Classification. And after I was classified I was sent to Ravenswood.

1 Victoria Bridge opened in 1889. The steel sections of the opening and closing mechanism can still be seen inside the modern canopied walkway.

2 The set usually included a silver button signifying bachelorhood and a money bag for wealth. Great hilarity attended upon the finding of one in a slice of pudding. In most families the charms were collected after the meal, and washed to be reused in following years.

3 'The Girls' Collegiate School was unroofed so that the inmates gladly took shelter under the hospitable roof of Mr Drysborough. who resides nearby… Owing to the damage done at the Girls' Collegiate School arrangements would be made hereby [sic.] tuition would be carried on at the Jubilee Hall.' North Queensland Register, 16 March 1903. See also Appendix C.

4 Under the pupil-teacher scheme, children of academic promise were offered positions as apprentices under the supervision of a fully trained teacher. They were assessed annually by School Inspectors and were required to study in their own time to pass the examinations necessary for qualification as a teacher.

5 Houldsworth, Marion, *The Immigrant Boy: A Townsville Boyhood, 1912-1918*, Townsville, 1997. Joe Clark, who as a boy of thirteen worked the sound-effects at the Stanley Theatre, gives a graphic account.

6 Now the Arts Centre in Walker Street.

7 A new police station had been erected at the corner of Sturt Street and Stanley Street in 1876.

Building the Macrossan Bridge, 1897 **Elizabeth Hinspeter**

On The Burdekin

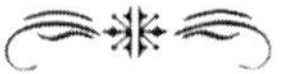

Introduction

This story evokes in the reader pangs of regret at not having been part of the excitement of the days when Charters Towers was the booming gold-town known affectionately as The World. The second largest city in Queensland, bustling with social and commercial life, it had a population of nearly thirty thousand. Horse-drawn vehicles crowded well-made streets, the ornate Stock Exchange was thronged, and mine whistles shrilled. There were splendid banks and shops, a School of Arts, and a world-ranking School of Mines. There were any number of Benevolent Lodges, a Show Society, and a Jockey Club. Brass bands and superb choirs competed fiercely for musical honours. 'The Towers' was still in its heyday in 1900 when Lizzie and Mary, the sisters in the story, in starched white dresses, flounced hats, and 'special shoes and gloves', giggled and flirted their way through picnics, surprise parties, and Sunday School Anniversaries, and, on Sunday afternoons, joined the promenade in Lissner Park where Lizzie was courted by her future husband, Joe.

At the beginning of the audio-taped interview the sentences are very brief, with frequent pauses. A frail elderly lady – Lizzie Hinspeter was ninety at the time – was being asked to peer back across the years, to remember things she had perhaps not consciously thought of for decades. She has had a very busy and fulfilling life – the firm of Hinspeters is well-known in the north – childhood now seems so very long ago. But gradually the images begin to form in her mind's eye. It is as though she is viewing some sepia-toned archive footage and reporting back on it to us. 'We had a bark hut'; 'We didn't build it'; 'It was already built'. She is deep in reverie for a moment as the memories come flooding back. Yes! That was the way it was! Like a piece of tapestry, stitch by stitch, she builds up the word picture. We begin to see the bark hut that 'Mother was quite pleased with', the five little children being bathed in turn in front of the great open fireplace, the washing days down by the river. We want to give those dreadful Heary boys the shaking of their lives for their boisterous pranks, all the while struggling to keep a straight face at their antics. The little bush school, the excursion trains of trippers down from The Towers to see the great bridge under construction; Mother doing a brisk trade in home-brewed ginger beer. It is all made clear to our imaginations.

The explorer Ludwig Leichhardt had camped close to the site of the future rail crossing of the Burdekin on his expedition to Port Essington in 1845. The railway connecting Townsville and Charters Towers was built in 1882. Large numbers of men worked on the line so the construction camps which sprang up at intervals beside it were like small townships, each with several licensed tent-hotels. The high bridge, on which Father worked, was completed in 1897. It replaced a previous low-level crossing which had been regularly washed out by floods.

A special kind of stout-hearted womanhood is represented by Mother in the story. We can be glad for her that she becomes 'one of the first white women to walk across' the newly completed bridge, 'on two planks'. Half a century later, in 1948, having read far too many schoolgirl stories for my own good, I was foolhardy enough to run away from boarding-school in Charters Towers, and as part of this adventure, had the experience of treading, in the light of an early dawn, across this bridge on the same 'two planks' as Lizzie Hinspeter's mother had trodden, the flood-bowed paper-barks in the bed of the mighty Burdekin seeming very far below. In transcribing Lizzie Hinspeter's story I felt that I had reached out and touched hands across the years with this brave bush mother of long ago.

On The Burdekin

We came up from Brisbane to the Burdekin. Father worked on the Burdekin Bridge the whole time that it was being built. Our family… I had three sisters and two brothers; my youngest brother, Reg, he must have been born while we were there. We was there all the time the bridge was being built.

We went to school there. It was a one-teacher school, most times a lady teacher, and not above a couple of dozen children. We had Primers then; Primers One, Two, Three. For a while I was in my sister's class, but then she got put up. She was always smart. I remember – I'd only be about six I suppose – once the teacher left my sister in charge to be teacher. She was two years older than me. And I didn't do as she told me. So she reported me. And the teacher said to me, 'Look here Lizzie! If you don't do as your sister tells you, I'll… chop your head off.' I thought that's what she said and I was terrified.

We had a bark hut. We didn't build it; it was already built when we got there and we shifted into it. Made out of bark, all stringybark; big sheets of it, with a wire band round; not exactly wire, an iron band. And there were shutters to put up. There were four rooms and the kitchen was round the back, with a chimney, a square chimney and an open fireplace. It was a hard-swept floor, ant-bed. It had curtains, and just an ordinary wooden door. And the rooms were partitioned off. Mother was very happy with it. We were all comfortable. It was one of the good-looking places on the Burdekin. Mostly the others were tents.

Then there was a lot of typhoid going around. My Dad had typhoid. Mother had typhoid. My mother and I, we went into hospital for six weeks in The Towers. Mother and I went in on the same day, and came out the same day. And she and I, we were just out of hospital, when my brother had it. There was a lot going round. The sanitary conditions were dreadful.

When I was in, we were all schoolmates in the one ward. They had to close the school. It was the sanitary conditions. Dreadful! When we first went there, honestly, all they had was deep pits, with a seat across. That's all we had. They had to fix it all up after we all had typhoid. They had to fill them all in. Then they put in the pans and the men would have to come round and clean them.

We used to buy water by the barrel, a shilling a barrel. The barrel was horse drawn, and the wheels would only be about that high; four little wheels and the barrel on it; and you'd order your water by the barrel, and he'd come round.

For getting bathed, it was all in the tub, one after another. To heat the water there was this great big square fireplace at the back of the kitchen, wider than the door, and open at the top. It had fire-bars to stand the kerosene tins on. And first Mother heated the water up in the kerosene tins on the bars and

Frederick Charles Hall Collection

Sunday excursions by train were a popular diversion in Elizabeth Hinspeter's day.

then she put it into the big tub. But, on washing day, Mother would go down to the river, to the Burdekin and we used to go swimming.

To keep the food Mother had one of those safes with netting on the side of it. We'd stand our butter on an enamel plate, in a big basin, with perhaps a plate over the top, and put a sweat-rag over it, with the ends down in the water on both sides. My Dad used to get sweat-rags given to them free so we had a lot of them, and we used to wet them and put 'em over the top hanging down into the water and it kept your butter lovely. We managed to keep everything cool like that. We never had oily butter. And for a cool drink we had waterbags, the canvas ones, hanging in the shade.

My mother was a good cook. We had good food. Lots of meat and vegetables. The vegetables must have come down on the train from The Towers or from Selheim. We didn't grow our own. Our backyard was all swept clean with not a bit of dust, or anything! And of a night-time, Dad would play his concertina and people would come and dance! (Laughs, in remembering.) Dancing on this big place, clean and hard. Not exactly parties… get-togethers. Not just friends, anybody. You knew everybody there on the Burdekin. We were fairly close to Selheim, as well. Selheim was a lot bigger then than it is now.

Of a Sunday, all the time the bridge was being built, there used to be excursions out from The Towers; people would come to the Burdekin for

Frederick Charles Hall Collection

Photographed at a picnic, perhaps a Sunday School outing, a group of women, dressed in their best, partake of tea and biscuits beneath a bough shelter. Such affairs were fondly remembered by Lizzie Hinspeter.

the day and to see how the bridge was getting on. And my mother would make her own horehound and ginger beers and she would make cakes and scones. And we had our flag; it was made of calico, plain calico, and it was tacked on at the front of the house, and on it was, 'Refreshments'. She used to sell her soft drinks to the Sunday excursions! You never hear about excursions, nowadays![1]

And I want to tell about the Heary Boys. The Hearys had the hotel on the Burdekin. The boys all had horses. And this is the honest truth. We would get let out of school, and as soon as we were out, these boys'd get on their horses and chase us. And we were terrified! That happened every afternoon! Once those boys were chasing me, and I ran into the hotel yard. And I didn't know where to go! And I seen the lavatory! And I ran into the lavatory! And the horse's head came in! And I stood on the seat of the lavatory, right on the back! And here was the horse's head, right in!

And what was worse! One day, the wind had knocked a tree down, and it went right over a gutter [a deeply eroded gully]. This tree'd fell right across. And I seen these boys coming and I ran and got to that tree and I straddle-legged over that tree, and I got into the middle over that gutter! And I was sitting on the middle of that tree, and he came under me with his horse! And he had his whip up here trying to hit my legs! And he was there on his horse! Oh, I'd like to see them boys now! (Fiercely.)

Something like that happened every day, coming home from school. We were terrified! We were always complaining!

We had had lots of goats. And the kiddies. Oh, yes! Everybody got their turn at milking goats! We all had our billy goats to ride, just sitting on its back. I had my own, a big billy goat; it still had its horns, big ones, but it was a quiet old thing. And we used to have races! We'd tie the grass across the little paths for the hurdles, and race them over. Sometimes one would go to run into the house and we'd have to get it out. Goats will eat anything. Dad would often kill a kiddie for meat.

We stayed at the Burdekin until the bridge was finished. It took quite a few years to build. Father wasn't a carpenter. A plumber was his trade. His name was Edward Tuff Richardson. Tuff was his mother's maiden name; E.T. Richardson. He was a fine-looking man. He had a straw boater, with a band around it, a corded band. And my mother, she was one of the first white women to walk across the bridge. She went over it on two planks.

When the bridge was finished Dad joined the railway and we shifted down to Townsville, and I went to West End School. In 1901 I got a Gold Certificate. 'Regular and Punctual Attendance'. I'd gone the whole year and not missed a day! I used to do that, regular. It wasn't for my good work! Though I wasn't a dunce. I'd have been eleven then. My sister was always the smart one. She had plenty of brains. West End School was where I first met my husband, Joe. We

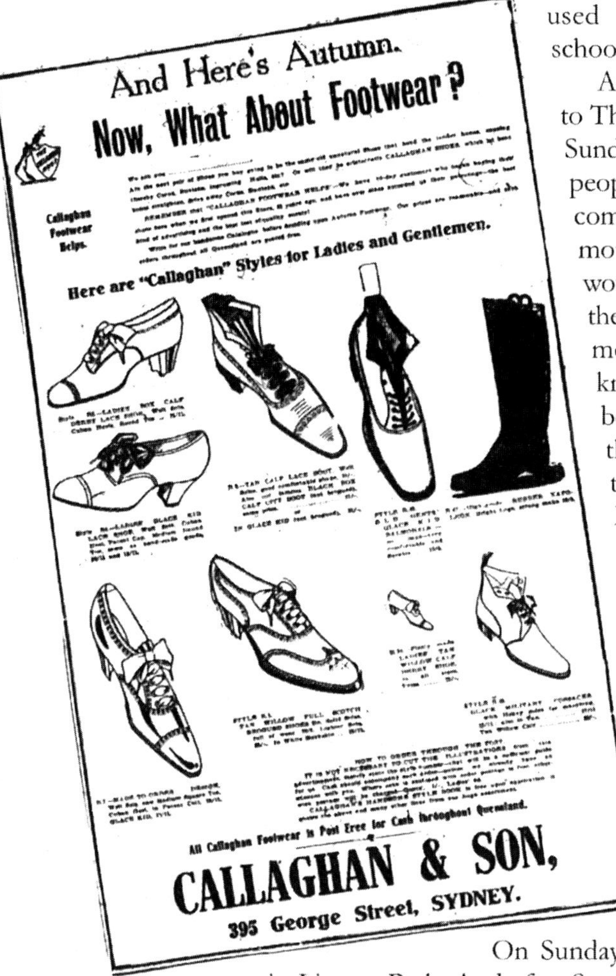

used to walk home from school together.

And then we moved up to The Towers. And the first Sunday we were there the people from across the road come over and said to my mother, 'Mrs Richardson, would you like me to take the girls to church this morning?' They didn't know where we belonged, you know, but they struck the right thing. We were Methodist. And they took us to church. And when we come out they told us what time for Sunday School. And I said to my mother, 'You'd really think that you'd met them all before, they were so nice!'

People on The Towers, they were lovely.

On Sunday afternoons the band was in Lissner Park. And after Sunday School we used to go and listen. They had a Bible class of boys and girls, a large class, and after we came out we'd all go to Lissner Park for a walk. And we would walk right round the band rotunda, and the band would be playing in the centre. And then we'd go home for tea, and most likely take some of our friends home for tea too. And after we had tea we'd go for a walk down the railway line. And leave my mother with all the dishes! And then we'd go back to church.

And at the Sunday School we used to have Anniversaries every twelve months, and at one Anniversary my sister was Queen of the Flowers. And we all had to represent flowers. I had to represent some tiny little flower, a forget-me-not, or something like that, and I had to buy artificial ones, there weren't any fresh ones. I borrowed a long skirt because, of course, we were still in short dresses. We'd have been about fourteen or fifteen, maybe sixteen. And we used to have a lady come in to make our frocks for three-and-six a day.[2]

We sung in the church choir. And one time there was a piece in the paper that there had been 'a Service of Song in the evening, and a quartet was sang by Mrs Williams, Miss M. Richardson, Miss L. Richardson and Mr J. Hinspeter.' That was my boyfriend! 'And it was excellently sung!' (Breaks into delighted laughter.)

Joe was four years older than me. He worked down the mine, The Brilliant! The Brilliant Deeps, but only for a very little while. Then he did a little bit of striking for the blacksmith. And he was in the Fire Brigade, a volunteer, in the uniform. Then he had a delivery van and he would cart furniture, or anything like that. And the Fire Brigade used to use his horse. The horse used to stand under the harness and they'd drop it on to him. Then off they'd go to the fires![3]

And we used to have Surprise Parties. Once we went to the Williams's. Mrs Williams, she was the wife of the mine manager. She said, 'I'll have to ask my husband if you are welcome.' And she come back and said, 'He says you are all very welcome.' So we all went in.

And Friday nights was Town Night on The Towers. Everyone was up the street. They'd close the main street, and the main street had quite a slope, and you would just see nothing but a sea of heads, walking. Friday nights! It was lovely! The Towers was a booming place then. They called it The World, and, really, it deserved it.

1 In the days before individual car ownership, Sunday Excursions were a pleasant aspect of life. As many picnickers as could squeeze on board, with picnic baskets, rugs and billy cans, would climb on to an 'Excursion Train' – or wagon, bus or boat. On tray-back lorries passengers dangled legs over the side. To while away the time everybody sang. In the late afternoon, to signal departure time, a warning toot on the whistle might be given, or a resounding clang on an old plough share to summon revellers for the journey home.

2 About 70 cents. This represented quite a fair day's earnings, as the sewing-lady would be given a midday meal and provided with cups of tea and cake, and gossip.

3 Joe was a volunteer firefighter. Horses like Joe's would have 'the harness dropped on them from above' before they went dashing off with the Volunteer Fire Brigade until 1916, when the first motorised fire engine in Charters Towers was purchased.

Pajingo, 1901–1909 **Violet Allingham**

Two Days Into Charters Towers

Introduction

The voice of ninety-year-old Violet Allingham, who recorded this story, was feathery with age, so her words in parts of the recording were extremely hard to catch. Sometimes the tape would have to be rewound time and time again to catch a particular word or phrase. Even so, names or phrases were often indecipherable. 'We had to be very careful with kerosene because it wasn't very plentiful' for example. How many pressings of the rewind button did it take to get that! But the genuine pleasure when the meaning suddenly became clear! And the regret, and sense of loss, when despite repeated efforts, a passage had to be abandoned. One felt it may have been perhaps a perfect gem of information lost for ever.

However, in Violet Allingham's story we are given an insight into life on a drought-stricken property in the early years of the twentieth century. The family could not have bought Pajingo at a worse time. The drought of 1903 crippled many. The fat-lamps are a telling detail of the extremes of hardship to which the family was reduced in those first few years.

How we sympathise with poor book-loving Mother! Her one pleasure was reading, yet, once daylight had faded, there was little chance for her to indulge it. Did she never find herself wondering what she was doing in the harsh North, so far from family and friends? And wonderful Father! When first we hear of him he is 'in a bank in Scotland'. Yet we see him, pitting himself against one of Queensland's worst droughts, with waterholes dry and breeding-stock perished, mustering with the help of his little ten-year-old daughter, battling on with the determined courage that posterity can only admire. Fred King, whom we meet in Chapter 11, stayed overnight at Pajingo with his family, on their way to take up Bulliwallah. He remembered Violet's father, Adam Black, as, 'One of the finest men I have ever known'.

Happily, in the mode of a satisfyingly good story, all ends well. Pajingo rides out the drought and becomes well established and prosperous. Violet marries the son of another property and their children are, in their turn, sent off to the very best boarding-schools in the South. Finally, we learn that a grandson has taken over the running of Pajingo, and doubtless finds that, nowadays, it is but the briefest journey by car 'into Charters Towers'.

❋

Two Days Into Charters Towers

My mother wrote a book about the pioneers because she had come out to Winton in the very early days.[1] She came from Victoria, and she was shocked to see the hardships that a lot of those pioneer women endured. No-one knew anything of what they had done helping the men to open up the country. She had great respect and admiration for the women who had gone out there before her, so she decided to write about them. That would have been about 1900 so I must have been about ten.

I was born on the 11th March 1891, at a station called Elderslie outside Winton. It was a stone building, built of stones off the property. My parents pioneered Elderslie.[2] I don't think there was even a Hughenden in those days. That shows that they really were a long way out.

Mother was born in Scotland, but she came out to Victoria as a very young girl. She was educated at a private school. She loved reading and liked to keep abreast of the times. My father had worked in a bank in Scotland.

Mother didn't have to help with the outdoor work on the station because, in those days, help was a good deal easier to get than it is now. Every station had a cook, and, as a rule, before a cook left she arranged with a relative, or a friend, or somebody, to take over her position. And of course, there were a lot of Aborigines that lived there, in what would now be called humpies. They used to come over to the house and sweep up the leaves and do odd jobs like that.

There were a large number of Aborigines about in those days and they just lived on what they could get hunting kangaroos and possums and things. There were hundreds of them. They lived on the station wherever they could get good water or find a good waterhole.

Mother was very fond of some of the old black women she had working for her. One was named Judy. They did the washing and the sweeping. One or two of them helped in the kitchen. Of course, they had little ones, so they'd be about the place too. But they would all go away later on in the afternoon when they had finished their work and join their families in the camp.

The humpies they lived in were mostly made of bark. They'd get the bark off the trees. They didn't have axes; but tomahawks... the kind that were made of stone; no handles on them. To sharpen them they'd grind them against another stone. I was very small, but I remember them doing it.

After Elderslie we lived on a property outside Pentland, called Lolworth. I think it was owned by Dalrymple and it was a timber house. After that we shifted to Kynuna. Dad was in partnership with Mr Dalrymple, and it was his ancestor that Dalrymple Shire was named after. But we didn't like Kynuna. It was drought-stricken all the time we were there.

And then my father bought a place called Pajingo outside Charters Towers. That was in 1901, because he took delivery of the place on 1st July 1901. And it was drought-stricken right up until 1903. That was the worst drought, I think, that Queensland has ever known. It wrecked not only my father but everybody else that had a station.

I remember it well. In those days the waterholes used to be permanent, and yet they all dried up. And nobody had any windmills or wells, so when the creeks dried up, well, that was the end.

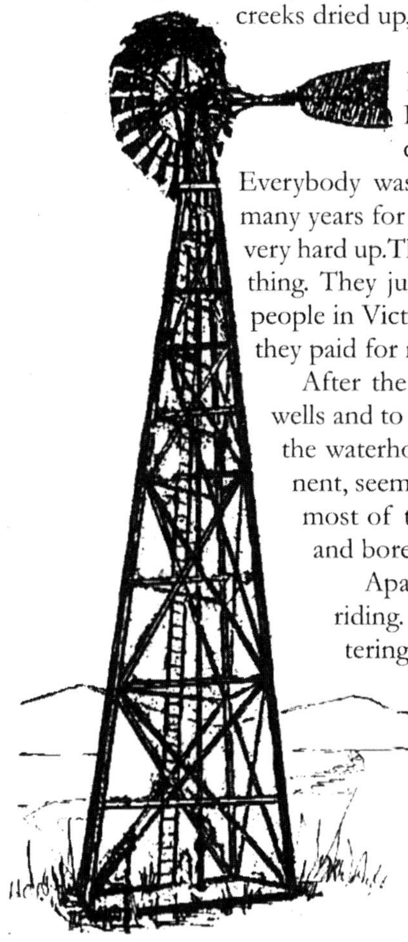

At Pajingo we had cattle. All around Pentland and Charters Towers was cattle. But after the drought there was hardly a couple of hundred head of cattle left. Everybody was in the same predicament. It took many, many years for the numbers to build up again. People were very hard up.There was nothing to sell. No bullocks or anything. They just had to do the best they could. Mother's people in Victoria helped her a little, I think. In later years they paid for my schooling.

After the 1902 drought, people began to put down wells and to put up windmills to tide them over. Most of the waterholes, which until that time had been permanent, seemed to have pretty-well silted up. So after that most of the stations depended entirely on windmills and bores.

Apart from lessons I used to like to go out riding. I'd go out with father to help with the mustering. We'd take corned meat and bread. Tea, of course. And there'd be the men, the musterers who were helping on the place. There were no cattle-dips. That was before the ticks came. They weren't a problem then. I think it was about 1900 that the ticks first began to show up. But we didn't have to dip in those days, just brand them.

There were brumbies on the property but the camp horses were handled quietly and never got away to mix with them. I had my own horse, my favourite, a blue one. I was very fond of horses. I lived on them before motor cars came. We relied on them. When we went to town Mother and Father would ride in the buggy and I would drive the spare horses for the buggy. It was sixty miles into Charters Towers. It would take a day and a half to go in and the same again going back. The first day we'd go about forty miles. We used to stay a night on the way with friends. We only went into town two or three times a year. Might go for the Show. And perhaps if Dad had some business to attend to, Mother and I would go in with him. And as long as I can remember we would stay at the Crown Hotel. Some people might take their own camping gear with them, or stay with friends. But we would stay at the Crown.

And when the rains came and work would stop on the station we would sometimes visit other properties. Or they would come over to us. Neighbours who were far out, when they were going to town, would come and stay the night with us. And then the next night with someone else on the way in. And the same thing when they were coming back from town.[3]

Frederick Charles Hall Collection

The Black family took up Pajingo just before the onset of the terrible drought of 1903. Ten-year-old Violet loved to help her father with the cattle work, as confident in the cattle camp as the little girl pictured here.

A big wagon-team with horses used to bring the rations out, but he only came every four or five months or so. Flour and sugar and things like that, we used to buy them by the sack. They'd be put in a big storeroom with an iron roof, or a bark roof in many cases, and walls of bark. Once they were put in there they were safe enough.

We always had good vegetable gardens but it was a rare event for us to get English potatoes. We used to grow sweet potatoes and pumpkin, and tomatoes, plenty of tomatoes.

For meat we killed our own and salted it. There were no refrigerators. We only had fresh meat for a day or two after killing. You couldn't keep it any longer than that. But corned meat could be made into fritters and curries and stews. But we had a meat safe called a Coolgardie safe and it was considered quite an invention. It had wire netting round the side, and on the top there was a big galvanised-iron dish, and we'd put water in that. Then we'd put bags around it, and the water would seep down the side. It was surprising how cool it kept things. We kept things like butter in there. But it wasn't any use for meat.

For lighting at night we relied upon fat from when the cattle were rendered down into tallow.You put the tallow in a tin with a bit of old moleskin cloth and burn the end and you'd get a light. When things got better after the drought there was kerosene but you had to be careful using it because it was expensive. It came out in four-gallon tins. And, oh, those tins were a boon to the housewife because you could make them into buckets, and all sorts of things. Everybody did. Kerosene tins were invaluable.

There was a big open fireplace, and there were drums with boiling water for washing-up and for cooking. I would have been ten or twelve years old before we had a stove. Before that we cooked in camp ovens. An experienced cook could make cakes and scones as well as stews and roasts in a camp oven. They make beautiful fruit cakes. You build the ashes and the charcoal round them. Then, of a night time the grown-ups would sit round the fire playing cards.

I only had one brother, Archie. He was four or five years younger than me. My mother taught us our lessons. There was no Correspondence School in those days. But mother loved books and she tried to give us a fondness for them. If we got a present it was always a book. I could read really well before I went away to school.

Mother made all her own clothes. Everybody did in those days. She made mine; bought the material in Charters Towers; and Archie's shirts and trousers. She made Father's shirts; blue they were. My mother loved reading and she would get the *New Idea*. It was a great event and, oh, we used to look forward to it coming. I think it was every fortnight in the early days. It would be three weeks old by the time we got it. But that didn't matter.

We got our mail by packhorse from Charters Towers. It was round about 1915 or more before the mailman started coming in a buggy. And as long as I can remember, even when I was a tiny child the *Register* came, the *North Queensland Register*. When the mail came they would open the *Register* and it had this lovely pink cover. What was in it didn't interest me, but I thought the pink cover was beautiful.

Then afterwards, when I got to about twelve, they sent me down to Melbourne to boarding-school to the Presbyterian Ladies' College. I went down on the boat. There was no other way to go. I was there a couple of years. I didn't come home for holidays because Mother's people were in Victoria and I could stay with them. We did writing and arithmetic, the Three Rs. We were taught deportment. At home we were taught how to behave ourselves, but at the school we were taught which knife went with what, and so on, in the dining-room. We had starched pinafores and petticoats, and hats with ribbons on. And black stockings. I was grown up and married before I ever went without stockings on. And I *never* remember my mother without stockings!

Archie used to help Father a lot around the place. They'd go out for days, mustering, with just hard rations, camped out. Later when he was about ten or twelve he was sent to Townsville Grammar School. That was in the very early days of the school.

The first meatworks up here was on the Burdekin River where the railway crosses at Selheim.[4] The bullocks were sold on the property, so much a head, then they were driven in. It was the best part of four or five days to deliver

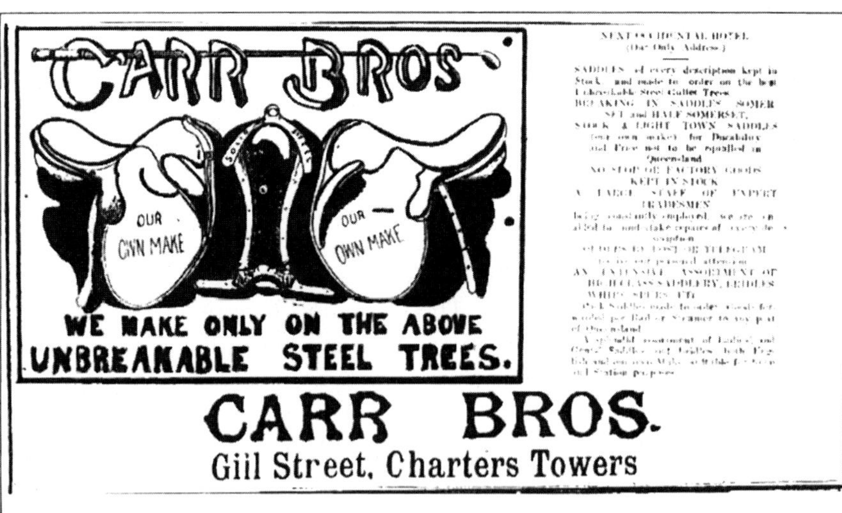

This was a regular advertisement in the NORTH QUEENSLAND REGISTER during the first decade of the twentieth century. It would have been very familiar to most of the narrators in this book, who depended on horses as their sole means of transport.

them. When the mines in Charters Towers began they used to sell bullocks straight to the butchers' shops. They'd send a buyer out and a bullock was sold, £5! £7! Dear me, it was the talk of the district! We'd only been getting a pound a head!

Once the ticks came you had to dip your cattle all the time, otherwise the ticks would kill them. That meant that you had to keep your men. You couldn't let them go. They had to be on the job all the time. There were quarters for them. Managers were always respected. To be a manager then was more important than it is today.

And the blacks had their camp well away from the place. At Pajingo we only had one or two blackboys at different times. There were no black women there. I think by that time the Government had more of less taken over and sent them all to reserves. And, my word, the poor old things! Most of them were dead in no time. They were accustomed to having a free life and just wandering about and doing what they wanted to. Being confined was the end of them.

And after I left boarding-school I returned home to Pajingo and stayed on there helping my parents until I was married.

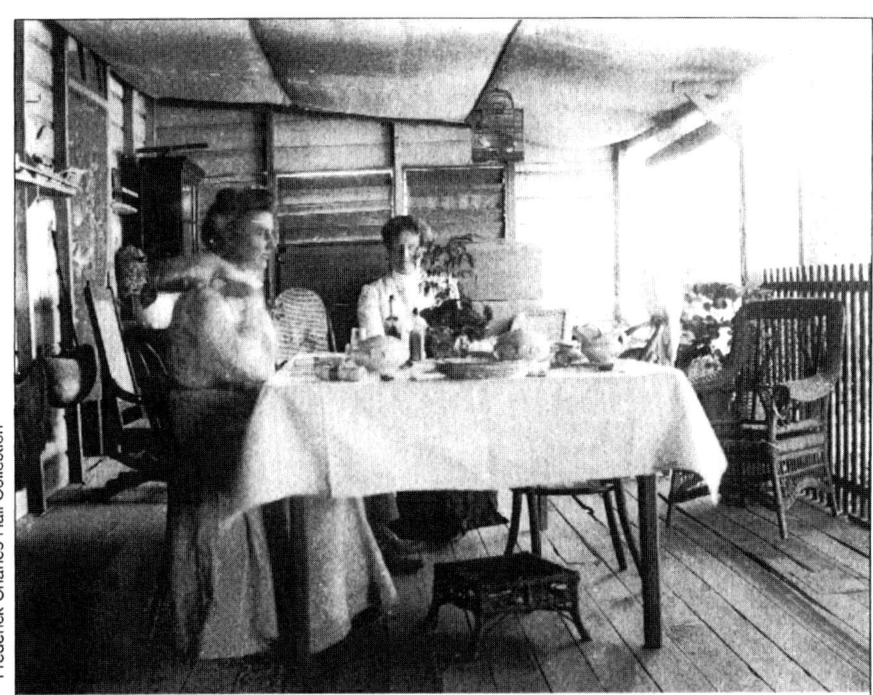

Frederick Charles Hall Collection

A homestead verandah, the table beautifully set for dinner. A sulphur-crested cockatoo perches on the back of one chair and another is on the shoulder of the woman at the left.

1 Black, Jane; *North Queensland Pioneers*, N.Q. Newspapers, Charters Towers, 1900.
2 A contemporary reference to Elderslie in the *North Queensland Register* of May, 1901, reads: 'HORSE SALES… beauties in the shape of horses for the sale which is to be held next month, some of the finest draught-horses and mares that ever looked through a collar, and remind the writer of the very fine draughts bred on 'Carrandotta' years ago which old carriers round Winton, such as "Lock" Jim Glisson and others used to shift mighty loads of wool off 'Eldersly' and other stations in that district.'
3 In Chapter 11, *Born to Floods and Droughts,* Fred King relates that his family stayed at Pajingo on the second night of their journey to take up Bulliwallah.
4. Possibly a small-scale operation set up initially to cater for the needs of workers on the building of the bridge, the Burdekin Meatworks at Selheim had opened in 1895. The following incident indicates the difficulties of the life-style in transient work-camps. 'Michael Murray proceeding against Hock Miller at the Police Court on Thursday for alleged malicious injury to a pig. Mr Wynn Williams appeared for the complainant, and Mr R. J. Gair for the defendant. The evidence for the complainant was that the defendant had broken the head of a pig belonging to the complainant, thereby killing the animal which was about 20 yards away from the defendant's tent, near the Burdekin Meatworks at the time. For the defence it was alleged that the defendant was much annoyed with pigs about his tent, and on finding several inside the tent one day, picked up a stick and struck one on the back as it came out, crippling it but not killing it. The case was dismissed with costs against the complainant.' *North Queensland Register,* 19th. February, 1900. In Chapter Five, Susan Gallagher relates that her father had to keep the flaps of his tent laced while he was working at his mine shaft or 'the dingoes would get in'.

The Palmer Goldfield, 1892–1905 **Susan Gallagher**

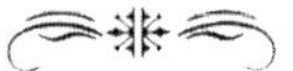

Introduction

Who has ever heard of Maytown these days? But once, in its heyday, Maytown was virtually the capital of the Palmer River goldfield. And who has heard of Limestone. These, and dozens of similar places have disappeared, not only from the map, but from human memory. Limestone, where our story begins, was the last field of the Palmer River rush. Three tiny hamlets, Groganville, Quartzborough and Harbord, each little more than a cluster of makeshift huts and tents, made up the Limestone field. At Groganville there was a police camp, a telegraph station and a post office from 1887 to 1895 and a population of one hundred and eighty whites and one hundred Chinese. By 1900 the field had already declined and the total population was down to eighty. As Susan Gallagher, our Narrator tells us, 'There's no Limestone now. There's not even where it was'. But she vividly recalls her early childhood there, and the hardships endured by her mother, possibly archetypal of the women of the North's gold-rush days.

The changes we witness in poor 'Mum'. First glimpsed, she is a newly arrived immigrant girl, laughing and chattering in Irish brogue as she and her friends scrub the cottage in Cooktown in preparation for the arrival of the Mercy nuns; the happy gigglings of a group of girls conscious that they are doing the virtuous, church-approved thing. Somehow this gives them a sense of being still in touch with the values of home, now far away across the sea for ever. Next, we see Mum as a young married woman on arrival at the diggings. 'She never got such a shock in her life' – possibly an oft-repeated phrase in mother and daughter conversations in ensuing years – expressive of the dismay at finding herself in the godforsaken nothingness of tents and makeshift camps that was Limestone. Mum was to endure nine years of living in a tin humpy, cooking over the open fire, bearing successive children without medical aid, burying one of them in a packing case. Then, defeated, the little family struggles to Maytown, taking only what they can carry on the long walk. We see Mum, grown bitter with the loss of girlish dreams, 'very strict', 'strapping Charlie all the way up the hill' over a bit of discarded chain; Mum, eyesight failing with recurrent blight, that fly-borne scourge of the bush, 'worse because she had to look after the rest of us', her husband oblivious to her sufferings in his obsession with gold. Then, release! The journey over the range on a borrowed horse (the kindness of that neighbourly offer!), rest and recuperation in hospital, and, finally, triumph! Persuaded to make the move to Cooktown for the children's sake, she sees them lined up on the convent verandah to be quizzed by the nuns. Eyes that had been dim, shine with joy at the pronouncement, 'Esther! You have taught them their catechism!' The years have not been wasted, after all.

Today if you drive in to Maytown, and you would need a four-wheel drive vehicle and good reserves of fuel, food and water to do so, you will find that little remains of a town that once had twelve hotels, two newspapers, a variety of stores, a lemonade factory, two banks, a court-house, school of arts, a police barracks, school, and population of 252 whites and 422 Chinese. Now, all that remains is a scattering of bricks under a bloodwood tree where the baker's shop once stood, remnants of flagstone kerbing in what was once the main street and a dereliction of battery machinery shrouded in rubber vine. Over all hangs that vast silence that seems to brood wherever man has expended fervent energy and moved on.

No-one in that once bustling little town, not the magistrate, nor the police sergeant nor newspaper editors, and certainly not the schoolteacher, would have dreamed that perhaps the most telling account of life there was being stored away in the memory of the barefoot daughter of one of the least successful of miners, old Joe Gallagher, and that Maytown would live, in years to come, through her eyes.

Maytown Girl

My mother was an immigrant out from Ireland on the boat, a real New Chum. She came out in 1886. Cooktown was a big harbour then, a natural harbour, no trouble for overseas boats to come in. And what they had in Cooktown at the time was the Immigration Depot, that's where she was in. The convent wasn't ready. They'd worked it out that the convent would be ready when they came, but the people who was doing it had no idea what the conditions would be like; the wet season had come on and they couldn't get the timber in, or nothing else.

So she got employment in one of the hotels. People'd come up to the Immigration Depot and get them and take them for work. And my mother was one of five women that got a cottage ready for the first nuns that came to Cooktown. And they cleaned the cottage up, and scrubbed it up and went round from this one and that begging for something to loan the nuns, till their convent was ready. Those nuns, Mercy nuns they were, come straight from Ireland.

My parents were married in Cooktown. Dad was a good bit older than Mum. Looking for gold; always gold, Dad was. They went straight up to Limestone, about seventy-five miles from Cooktown, on the Palmer Goldfields. Mum never got such a shock in her life when she got there. I was born in Limestone, a mining town, well, a village really. There's no Limestone now. There's not even where it was. It's all bush.

I can remember Limestone. I was only four years old when I went to school, but they took me because the numbers decreased a bit, and they took me to keep them up. It was what they called a Provisional School.[1] The building was mostly galvanised-iron. It was only a one-teacher school; a woman.

Our house was… they used to get the logs and split them in two and make the walls with that. We had an ant-bed floor. Ant-bed, you know, gives more wear than concrete. There was a bedroom, and then there was, like, a front room, and the next part was long, the full length of the house. And in that was

Frederick Charles Hall Collection

When Susan Gallagher's mother arrived as a bride at Limestone, on the Palmer River goldfield, she 'never got such a shock in her life'. The photographer, the Rev. Frederic Charles Hall was compassionate enough to wait while this miner's wife, near the windlass, hurried to change into what would have been her best dress for the carefully posed photograph.

the stretchers Dad made for us to sleep. The windows was a framework made of timber and a sheet of galvanised iron and then you had a stick to poke it up.

You see, in the mining, they had no tools. All Dad had up there was a pick and a shovel. The bucket, for the fellows that went down the shaft digging, was a bullock's hide, stitched up, to cart the stone to the top on the windlass. They had a windlass at the top. And when they got down there so far, there'd come the water, and they'd have to give up. My father, if he was alive today, he would tell you, there's more gold in Maytown than was ever took out of it!

When we were at Limestone my mother used to cook on two bricks, a couple of bricks, and bars across an open fire, outside the house. Now, beds, I'll tell you what we used to have. They used to get the timber, and they'd make the structure of a bed, perhaps as high as a chair; slats across; then you get the unbleached calico, and make a mattress and fill it with grass. Same for a pillow. We had blankets. You had to get them up from the south, from T.C. Beirne's. Come up by a fellow with a dray. You could count on your hands anyone who had some sort of conveyance. The general public, though there wasn't that many there, all had to walk. We walked to school; we walked home. Everywhere.

And for water, you had to go down to the creek with a kerosene tin. Kerosene always come in tins in those days, and you'd wash them out, and that was our buckets. Usually the people that went out of the house that you went into – they'd had enough of it and gone – they left everything that they had. They couldn't carry it! You leave your things when you left.

My mother was an excellent bread maker. About every third day she'd have to make the bread. She set the batch in like a big wash-basin. And the other people that was there before us had left a couple of tins and a colonial oven. It's about two foot long, and on the sides there were slits, where you put in the plate, with the batch on to cook, and you lit the fire on the top and you lit the fire on the bottom. She had that out in the open. She got to be an expert bread baker. When we went to school we had the bread and jam, and honey. And treacle.

We had fowls and we had goats. The ground didn't grow vegetables. It was a mining town. Some people, they tried to grow pot-plants. But nothing was a success. Limestone was, well, I don't know what you'd call it; it was a real wilderness! A real poverty-stricken place! Having the goats, we had the little ones, the kids. My mother could never kill a goat. Oh! No! I don't think Dad was much good at it either. But there was a Chinaman that lived near us – he never went down the mines; he did the alluvial stuff – and he used to kill the kiddie goats, and he'd skin them and clean them, and all. And we'd give him half a goat. And that kept him in meat, too. While we had the goats we could always say we had a bit of meat. Most of it would be salt meat.

We had mostly sweet potatoes from places out a bit that the Chinamen grew them. They brought them in their baskets. So of an evening we'd have the meat and mostly potatoes. There was the table, a home-made one, and forms, that two or three could sit on.

Everybody had a galvanised-iron house. There was one store; a man, there; he was like, the general store. And he taught us a bit of everything. And my little sister, she died in Limestone. There was no doctor or anything. There was no nurse, or anything. Just a handywoman. And my mother paid the price of never having proper medical care, until she died. She had Josephine. I come second. Then there was Esther, the little one that died. Then there was Bid. She was the youngest. Bid was ready for school when we went to Maytown. She'd be five. And I'd be seven. There's only two years between us.

And the little girl, Esther, she was three when she died. And mining towns are all the same. Everybody comes in to do what they can, and help. They all help one another there. And the shopkeeper, the fellow that had the little store, he had a consignment brought up, come by packhorse, and there was a case, it was fairly long, and not very wide. He gave the case for the coffin. And somebody wrapped a sheet round it, a white sheet. And everybody walked to the funeral. There wasn't a priest. He came once in three years. Once in three years! Every three years he did the round and he'd come with the mailman. The mailman made his round about every fortnight; came on horseback. The priest came from Cooktown; and they had a railway line to Laura. From Laura the priest'd pick up a horse to go with the mailman.

A train went up to Laura from Cooktown twice a week.[2] There was a railway bridge put in, and the only thing that went over that railway bridge was the engine that tested it. Never a train passed over a new railway bridge! A very bad government. My father, he was a learned man, my father, and he said, if they only had a government they would have opened up the north years ago.

When we shifted into Maytown, we walked it. Dad was going to the mines in Maytown. It was seventy-five miles, I remember that.[3] And when we camped at night the mosquitoes were bad, and what you do then is, you look around to see if there was any horse manure about and make a smoke fire. We carried nothing. We left everything at Limestone. Had to. We had to walk and we couldn't carry it. We were young. When you left Limestone, you went on this way; you always struck a miner's camp. It was the nature of the bush that they'd put on the billy and give you a cup of tea. We took two and a half days, as I think, to walk it. When we started off we had the bread. And the rice was boiled and we put honey on it. Dad had his tools. He had to carry them, a pick and shovel. And, like that, we got to Maytown.

There was a bit of a place that somebody else had left. It was deserted. And their bedding and things were left. They couldn't carry them. We went into that. We were better off in Maytown. Improved from Limestone. After we came, my father would be away all the week. Come home at the weekends.

The women would be more in the town, but the men would be working further out.

There was quite a few Aboriginals. They had big camps. People weren't frightened of them. They all spoke English because they never knew any different, because the miners were there. The babies were born, and they learned to speak English, and that was that. There was no trouble.

They never went to school or anything, but as we grew up, you get to know them; the womenfolk. Oh, you knew the menfolk too, but it was the women you know properly. And sometimes you'd miss one of them for a while. And you'd say, 'Maggie, where's Tilly? I haven't seen Tilly for a long time.'

And they'd say, 'Oh, she bin tumbledown.' She'd a' died. But she might have been hit on the head with a tomahawk! See, there was nobody there to say whether she was killed, only one policeman and a blacktracker. The policeman was a middle-aged man. They never sent a young policeman to those places. They tried to get a mature man. Dad says at one time, he was out bush, and this policeman pulled up with this black gin on a horse. Her hands were

Frederick Charles Hall Collection

Susan Gallagher recalled that when they walked into Maytown 'There was a bit of a place that somebody else had left... We went into that.' Though this is only a bark hut, the yard has been swept clean. In the foreground, a pile of washing waits to be done.

strapped. And he come over to Dad's tent, and he said, 'I don't know how we're going to manage it but I want your help.' Dad said, 'Whatever I can do, I'll do for you. I'll put on the billies and make a cup of tea.'

And the man said, 'I'll have to unloose her hands, so she can drink the tea.' Dad put on the billy and got it ready. He had plenty of bread, because Mum was a bread baker. He give them a bit of a meal; a tin of pressed beef. So they fed the woman, and the policeman had a cup of tea, too. Then he said, 'I'll have to carry on. We'll be there in Maytown either late tonight or in the morning and I'll hand her over.' The police patrol had six hundred miles to look after.

Another time a policeman had this Chinaman that he'd arrested. And he went into the pub. I suppose he thought the Chinaman would be all right while he was in. But he stayed too long. When he come out, no Chinaman! And he was looking around, looking around to see if he was anywhere about. And he saw another Chinaman coming with his baskets. And he says, 'As long as he's a Chinaman, that's all I wanted!' And he met the Chinaman on the bridge, threw the baskets and the bamboo over into the river and grabbed the Chinaman. The Chinaman kept saying, 'No savvee! No savvee!' He didn't know what it was all about. And the policeman says, 'Oh, shut up, you bugger! You'll find out when you get to Cooktown!' He got six months! And his garden was left until he come back. The policeman used to laugh! He'd say, 'I didn't care which Chinaman he was as long as he was a Chinaman!'

Blackfellows are lazy, the men, not the women; but the men are. Lay in the camp all day. They didn't exert themselves. The women used to wander round from house to house and they'd want to do something, and you give them something, bread or a bit of tea or sugar. And if they didn't bring home enough to feed the blackfellow, he belted her. They et different food, the Aboriginal. They et snakes and goannas and that. Dad said one time he was finished with his cooking at night, and the ashes were there, and a blackfellow came along and he said, 'Yupella yu bin pinish cookim?' And Dad said Yes, he was. And the blackfellow, he said, 'Mepella cookim long pire long yu?' And Dad said he could. And he pulled out of this bag a great big goanna and killed it and cooked it in the ashes. And Dad said he couldn't use that fireplace any more for the smell of goanna oil.

But they was never any trouble to the townspeople. They all seemed to know, well, the miners are here, and they've got to make the best of it. Everyone was very friendly.

When we went to Maytown we were three miles from the school. See, Maytown was the centre, and then out a bit there was Mount Louisa, and The Ida, little places that had a few people. But anything that was there was in Maytown. And we had to walk to school in Maytown and walk home. When the wet season was on, you couldn't take your lunch because you couldn't get the flour. Mum would try to have enough put by to carry us over the wet until the first packer could get through, but oftentimes it happened that there was no packer for weeks and so no flour. So then, at dinnertime we used to have to run home for dinner and we'd have rice and milk.

My father worked at different mines. One time he was at The Queen about four or five mile from where we lived. And when we come home from school, I was the best messenger. I used to always run. I was more dependable than Josephine, although she was older than me. She didn't like doing those jobs, running out to the camp. And Mum'd have the bread ready to take to Dad. By the time I got home from school – we left school at four o'clock – I had to walk out three miles to where we lived, and then I had to walk three miles or more to where Dad was working; to take the bread. And Mum would have cooked the meat, the salt meat. Mostly there was two mates and they worked together. They had a tent and cooked out in the open. They'd put up four saplings, and lay the one sapling across it, and tie the tent to it. The tent was one that you laced the front of. They had to, or the dingoes'd come and eat their food when they were working if they didn't have it secured.

Anyhow, this day I was going out. It was four o'clock before we left the school and had to walk the three mile home. And from there I picked up the bread and meat that Mum had cooked and I'd start off to go to The Queen. And I'd go along. I never had any fear of anything. But one night, it was just starting to get dusk, and I was coming back from Dad's. He never kept me, either. He knew I had to get home in the light. And I was coming along the track, and in front of me stood a great big red dingo. A wild thing, too. And I didn't know what to do. And I just bent down and picked up a couple of stones and I threw them at him. And he fled into the bush. A dingo will never tackle you on his own. That's where the saying comes from; to be a dingo.[4] But if he'd had his mates with him, he'd of torn me to pieces!

When the men were away the women had to battle along; take their washing down to the creek, and do the washing with a scrubbing brush and a board. For the house we'd have to have a kerosene tin and carry the water up. But those gins, they'd say, 'Me carry-im water! Me carry-im water!' And you give 'em something, something to eat.

We lived in several different houses in Maytown. If Dad was at The Comet, we'd be there. Later on he was at The Ida, and there was a house empty so we'd went into that. They were all better than the one at Limestone. People leaving Maytown, as they got a bit of money together, well, there was no way of carting furniture, so they left it. You never had to be shifting furniture. Whatever you had it was left behind. In Maytown, Mum had a Crown stove. It was much the same as the Colonial stove, but it had legs on it, and the top was open and you could put your boiling-pans on it. Women used to chop their own wood.

Sometimes there were dances. There was a bit of a hall at one of the hotels; for music just a concertina. Those miners were good dancers. My word! The waltz, the barn dance. Square dances. There were a lot of single white men, and they were a different class of men; a different class of men that go out in the wilds like that!

There was a gold battery at Maytown, and this man at the battery, probably he could take what he liked out of the quartz he crushed. You could never be certain what you were getting. This man had a dray, and my father and his mate, they'd be crushing, say, this week, when they had enough quartz, they'd get this fellow to take it. He always had a boy, and they'd load it on to the dray and take it in to the battery. And Dad, whenever he was getting the crushing done, he used to sleep in the battery. He'd just lay down on the floor until the crushing was done. But this man had the say of what gold was there. They sent that to the bank in Cooktown and the money was sent back up to the fellow that did the crushing. And he paid the miners. Nobody had any say.

Some miners there would sell their gold to the Chinamen. The Chinamen always had plenty of money. Those that come out from China couldn't speak a word of English, but they soon learned. There was three Chinese stores in Maytown. The Chinaman, he never dug a hole. He never dug a mine. But he did fossick for gold. And there was plenty of it. He fossicked in the creeks. And everyone of those Chinamen that I knew, they used to take a trip home to China. The Chinese were very friendly. People liked them. And in those places people had to like one another. And for this reason; the Chinese had the store. And you couldn't pay your bill for your groceries until you put your crushing through. And then you pay the Chinaman. And he'd wait.

The butcher was a local man. He had his own place, and reared the cattle to kill. There was a father and a couple of brothers. And there was a sister, and she come out to our place one time, and she could sew. And Mum got some turkey-red material, a print, and she made a dress for Josephine, and m'self and Bid. And she put feather-stitch around the collar and goodness knows what, and, oh! I thought I was Queen Anne! Swell!

My mother had a go at making us dresses but she wasn't much good at it. But you could buy them from T.C. Beirne's down south. We had to send for them, send down the measurements. For shoes you put your foot on the floor and then you put the lead pencil round to get the size of the shoe. We always wore hats, big hats. You always had a hat because it gets very hot.

And one morning, there was a woman out at The Queen. Now she was four miles away from our place. And she had twin sons. And she had just a handywoman come to her. And she charged her. Twin boys, and they arrived all right, and the old woman that was the handywoman, she went and got drunk. And through the night, the babies were a couple of days old, and the mother had to get up and attend to the babies and she caught a chill and she died. And this gin come over from the Queen and she said to Mum, 'Mumma Chapman bin tumbledown.' That's how they said die. 'Mumma Chapman bin tumbledown.' Mum questioned her and she said, 'Are you sure? Are you sure she tumbledown?'

'Eh-eee! He bin tumbledown pinish.' So Mum walked over to see what she could do over there. She was dead all right. There was no such thing as a doctor. There was no such thing as an undertaker in Maytown. There was nothing medical.

There was no such thing as a dentist. I had my second teeth, of course, big strong teeth, too. And I had this toothache. Oh! And anybody who had toothache and suchlike went to Chapman the blacksmith at The Queen to get their tooth out. And he had a pair of pliers. And I went out to get m' tooth out. I couldn't stand the pain of it. And he just said, 'Open your mouth!' and he'd pull out the tooth. Great big strong man he was. Sometimes we used to use creosote. It burnt the tooth out of your head.

I'll tell you about my father, too. This was in Limestone. Once he was coming home and his face was out on one side. Oh! Swelled up! And he was crossing this little creek and a Chinaman was washing for gold, washing the gravel, getting the gold. And he said to Dad, 'What sa matter? What sa matter?' And Dad said to him, 'Oh! Bad tooth. Bad tooth!' And the Chinaman said, 'Me lookee.' And he looked at Dad's tooth and it had a big hole in it and an abscess. He said, 'Me fixim.'

In those days matches were always little wax things in tin boxes, Vestas; wax matches; and you had to strike them on the box. So he said, 'Yu come long me.' And he went over to his hut, and Dad went with him. And he took a match out of the box, took the head off it, and he dipped it in opium. Dad wouldn't have cared what he put into it. The Chinaman always had opium. Always had opium. I don't think it was so widely criticised then. The Chinamen always had it. And he dipped the bottom of the match in the opium. And he put it in the hole in the tooth. And it took the pain away altogether. The swelling went down. Dad died ten years later and he still had that tooth in his head.

The whites never bothered with the opium. If you ever went past a Chinaman's hut when he was sleeping or in his tent – he always slept on a very low mattress, and he had a… they used to call it a Chinese mosquito-net.[5] But the thing that the putty was in, it was full of smoke. That was the opium. The smell of it hung around. It's a heavy smell, not an offensive smell. It wouldn't hurt anybody that's not smoking it!

The blacks used to hang around the Chinese huts for the opium. They didn't buy it. They had other ways of getting it. They used to have their gins with

Consumption

It Can be Cured.

There is no doubt about it. Begin early, take out all impurities from the system, enrich the blood, and recovery is certain. If your child is thin and pale give Ayer's Sarsaparilla at once. Consumption only attacks the weak.

Mr. Alfred G. Stevens, of Parnell, Auckland, N. Z., sends us the photograph of his daughter and says:

"My daughter Emily, 17 years of age, was in a very low state. She could not sleep because of her violent cough. Two doctors said she was in the first stages of consumption. She was so weak she could not go out by herself. A friend induced me to try

AYER'S Sarsaparilla

In less than two weeks our daughter could sleep well at night. Her mother and I would go into her room at all hours of the night, it seemed so good not to hear that awful hollow cough. She raised great quantities of blood, yet notwithstanding all this I can now say she is entirely cured."

Take Ayer's Pills with the Sarsaparilla.

Prepared by Dr. J. C. Ayer & Co., Lowell, Mass., U.S.A.

them. There was a sprinkling of half-caste children around the town, that had a good dash of Chinee in them.

For medicine, you always had Epsom Salts. And pain killer. It was a reddish mixture in a bottle, good for everything. You'd rub it on a swollen joint or put it on anything. And there was Dr William's Pink Pills, and Beecham's Pills. They were for stomach or anything. The pills were mostly taken for bowels. Actually there was never anything that you could say was a really serious disease. If there was a broken limb or anything like that, they had to make for Cooktown. Someway or other somebody would come to light with a horse.

Nothing was discussed with us girls about how babies came. But we all went to the one school and this one would say, 'My mother had a baby last night.' And that would have been the first we knew about it. We all of us knew when the babies arrived. And perhaps some that was a bit older, or wiser, or listened-in more, would say, 'My mother's going to have a baby.' And we learnt it from other kids. But we wouldn't dare to question Mum. And she wouldn't tell you! Mum was strict. The strap was always there and she used it all right. Now my brother, Charlie, he wasn't school age, but he was getting close to it, in Maytown. And he wandered about. And this butchers', they had a hut further up the road from us, up the hill a bit. And one day Charlie come home, dragging a bit of a chain, two foot long. And Mum said to him, she said, 'Where'd you get that?' And he said, 'Up at Tom Graham's.' And she said, 'Did you ask for it?' And Charlie said, 'No. He wasn't home.' He just saw it out in the yard and he brought it home. And Mum said, 'You're taking that back!' And Mum got him, and she strapped him up the hill. And when they got up Tom Graham was home. And he said, 'Aw! What'd yer do that for! It's rubbish! Just rubbish! He kin have it!'

And she said, 'That's just what he won't have!' And she wouldn't allow him to have it even though the man give it to him after. She was very honest and she brought up two honest men.[6]

Looking back on my life, I have never had a holiday. Never. In Maytown, and later on in Cooktown, when school holidays come, I used to go to one of the hotels and do the scrubbing and cleaning. And I got four shillings a week. I'd have been about twelve.

Mum got the blight real bad.[7] It used to go round every year. Every one of us got the blight. But Mum got it the worst because she was looking after the rest of us. And she got cataracts, but she didn't know what they were. She was going blind. And a man in Maytown, he had his daughter down at school at the convent. And the holidays were coming and he knew Mum wanted to go to Cooktown and she had no way of going. So he said, 'I'm taking down the spare horse to bring Minna home. You can come down along with me.' And Mum said, yes, she'd go. And away she went.

And when she got down to Cooktown, the people that had the hotel that she worked in when she come out from Ireland when she was young, oh, she was very friendly with them. They were like sisters, you know, and this woman, she said to her, 'Now, Esther,' she said, 'What are you going to do with that family! They're growing up. What are you going to do? They can't get work an' they can't be taught anything.' Dad had one set thing in his mind, and that was to find a reef, the one that had the gold.

And this Mrs Lane – she was one of them that was cleaning the house for the nuns when they came; they were all mates – she said, 'What are you going to do with that family?' And she said, 'Why don't you come down here to Cooktown; get them all down here. They'd have the Catholic school…' Not that my mother didn't teach us the Rosary and the Catechism. Gawd! I used to hate to think of it. We'd start the Rosary, and Mum'd say the Rosary and she'd have all the trimmings in the world, someone was sick, and someone else was sinking, and she'd be praying for them. Always religious. So's m' father. There was no priest at Maytown. My sister, she was three years old when he came, and to baptise her he had to bend down and baptise her on the floor. She was terrified of 'im! She didn't know what he was going to do to her! But I can tell you, my mother baptised her well and truly before that! She did it herself! I can repeat the catechism. Had it drummed into me from babyhood.

And, anyhow, when Mum went down to Cooktown with her eyes, she was in the hospital, must be three weeks. No! Must be longer! And Dad was up in Maytown, and we was all up in Maytown; Josephine and I, we carried on and did what we could. And this Mrs Lane said to Mum, 'Now, you write and tell Joe that you're not going back to Maytown! You're not going back!' And she said, 'Your eyesight's no good. It's taking time. And besides, you've got to study the family. If Joe's studying the gold, let him study the gold. But you're not going back!' And she said, 'We'll help you down here.' And of course, that wouldn't suit Dad. So he gave up the gold. And it was those people and Mum that forced him out of the gold. He'd be there now! If he was livin'!

We all went to the convent. The boys too. They was younger than us. They got girls from everywhere: from outside of Townsville, from outside of Cairns, and they had ones from the Gulf and Normanton . They were boarders. They come from everywhere. The convent was growing all the time and they had to build another place. What they did was they put all the boarders in the new building and the day-scholars were in another building; but in the one grounds.

It was a shilling a week. And they took you, even if you weren't a Catholic. The nuns, the older ones that were there, were the ones that come out from Ireland first. And Mum was one of the five women that cleaned up the cottage getting ready for them. And of course, when we all got down to Cooktown on the Monday, we had to be carted up to the convent. And one old nun there said, 'Esther! Did you teach the children the catechism?' And Mum said, 'Yes. I think I did.'

And in the meantime another old one slips away and brings back a threepenny catechism, and she lines us up. And she picked out a question and Josephine answered that. Then she picked out another one and I answered that. And she picked out until she got us all in. And she said to Mum, 'Esther! You have taught 'em the catechism! Heh! Heh!' And on the Tuesday morning Mum wanted us to go to school, and we had to go. I'd have been thirteen. It was 1905. Jim would have been five. And Charlie would have been nine. And Bid, she's after me.

And when the school holidays come, I went to work; working in the hotels and that. But I always wanted to sew. I didn't want any of these other jobs. And there was one woman in Cooktown, she was a dressmaker, a professional. She was an Irish woman, too. And she used to take girls. And somebody said that this Mrs Wallace said that she would like another girl. And I told Mum. And Mum said, 'Oh, You're a bit young. A bit young. You'd better have another year at school.'

And I said, 'I don't want it.' And so we went up and saw Mrs Wallace, and she took me on. The first year I got nothing because I was learning. The second year I got half a crown a week. I was just going on fourteen.

1 One to which, if the parents provided the building, the Education Department supplied a teacher.

2 The railway station at Laura was on the Cooktown side of the river. The bridge was built, presumably to extend the line further into the interior, but never used.

3 Perhaps there is confusion here with the previously given distance of Limestone being 'about seventy-five miles from Cooktown'. According to Colin Hooper, the authority on North Queensland's abandoned mining settlements, Limestone was about twenty to thirty miles from Maytown, a more likely distance for small children to have walked in two and a half days.

4 Term of contempt for a person considered to be treacherous.

5 A reference to opium smoke. Opium was smoked in a long-stemmed pipe with a small, flat bowl.

6 Later in the tape-recording Susan Gallagher expands on this theme. As an adult, Charlie worked as an accountant at Rooney's mill in Townsville. He became aware that a senior staff member was pilfering large amounts of stock and selling it on the quiet. Charlie did not like to report the man, but, instead, handed in his own notice, telling Mr Rooney that there were things going on into which he would be advised to look himself. Later, Rooneys' mill went bankrupt. At the final sale Mr Rooney came up to Charlie and said, 'Charlie, if I had only listened to you this would never have happened'.

7 Trachoma, commonly known as sandy blight.

Majors Creek to the Somme, 1895–1917

Julius Mathieson

Battlers

Introduction

'Julius Albert Mathieson,' he answers softly, hesitantly, yet precisely, when the Interviewer asks his name. It is the voice of one of 'one of nature's gentlemen'; that of the shy little boy from Major's Creek, south of Townsville, who remembers that, as second youngest in the family, he 'most often slept in the big double bed with Mum and Dad', yet who would grow up to fight at Pozières, one of the bloodiest battles of the Somme.

Julius was one of a family large enough for him to forget the names of two brothers as he counts them off for the interviewed recording. 'Oh,' he says, 'I left two behind!' And counts again for good measure. 'Where we all slep' I'm sure I don't know' The family home had been built by Dad from timber felled on the property. The seats around the table were squared-off logs on forked stumps set in the dirt floor, 'Saltbush Bill' style.

Major's Creek is an area south of Townsville off the Charters Towers road near Woodstock. It was on the road south before the highway was re-sited east of the mountains. Now little except the harsh voices of crows disturbs the dry, empty silence.

Julius's description of troubled relationships with the local Aborigines probably amounts to little more than episodic stone throwing between the Mathieson boys and the boys of the local tribe. The reality would have been scarcely more threatening than the stone throwing and name calling that once took place between children of State and Roman Catholic schools, taunting one another along Townsville's dusty streets with ritual exchanges of 'Proddy Dogs!' and 'Cattle-ticks!'. The perceived threat is very real to the children involved and Julius's voice is solemn with remembered fear as he recalls, of the local Aborigines, 'We were only small numbers compared to them.'

The father's heroic struggle to make a go of the property and the eventual loss of all hope is conveyed in the words, 'In the end he gave in. We left Major's

Creek when I was about seven or eight.' If Julius, the second youngest, had been born at the farm as had his oldest brother who had never been to school, it is possible that his parent's struggle had lasted over twenty years. Twenty years of hardship and blighted hopes. All to end in failure. As Julius says of his father, 'He had everything. Fires. Droughts. Cyclones'. Not to mention the recurrent disappointment of finding the year's crop unsaleable. The discussions that ensued on the father's return home after a fruitless journey by dray to Townsville must have been bitter, for Julius to be able to recall, eighty years later, the final straw of the 'dumping fee'. One is reminded of the passage in Steele Rudd's *On Our Selection* when, finding the cheque for the year to be a mere £12, 'Dad chewed on a straw and stared thoughtfully into the fire'.

Some readers may wonder at the inclusion of Julius's wartime experiences, as he was in 1915 in his early twenties, but his adventures are told with such boyish ingenuousness: the diving naked from the troopship in Colombo harbour, the gunning for rats at Ypres, even the wonderment at finding himself to be the only one in his trench hit by the fragment of high explosive, that they form an integral part of his youthful experiences. Julius is archetypal of the generation who as boys enlisted for the great adventure of war and did their growing up in the mud of the Somme.

Battlers

My father had this mixed farm at Major's Creek, at Woodstock.[1] And times were bad. He had cyclones. He had bushfires. He had droughts. He had everything. And Major's Creek, when Dad took it up, was a very deep creek, but in the time of [Tropical Cyclone] Leonta, the sand came down and filled the creek up as it is today. It spoilt the creek. I remember the flood after the cyclone, because I was put in a kerosene case, out on the front, and I sat there and I could watch the logs coming down. My parents had eight children, and I was second last. I was born on Major's Creek, in 1892.[2]

Dad built the house himself, out of logs. Felled the timber himself, river gums. He had an adze to shape the logs so that they could fit. There were push-up shutters. At one end there was a big chimney, and you'd hang your corn beef up in there and get it really smoked. We had a camp oven that Mum used for making her bread and dampers. And we had big cast-iron saucepans. You'd have a rod across, and you'd have hooks hanging down. You'd have a big cast-iron kettle hanging on the middle and you've always got hot water.

The fire would be going all the time. Put a log in. The whole neighbourhood was full of timber. You'd never run short.

Most of the furniture was kerosene cases. You'd hang cretonne over it for a curtain, over the top, or over the front. And it looked very elegant, too. You could place the kerosene cases different ways. You could have them on two stumps. You could have them that way [horizontally] And you could have one that way, and two up on either end. [in the form of a dressing-table] and draped with sort-of curtain. They were called 'the Laurel Suite' (remembering pleasurably the family joke) Laurel was the brand of kerosene. Those kerosene cases were very useful.

For seats, you'd go out and get a couple of tree-forks, and you'd bed them into the floor... the dirt floor... and these were cut off to carry a plank, or you'd use the adze and square a log off for bench seats, forms, round the table.

There was the bedroom, and the dining-room and the kitchen. We had one big double bed, and I was more often in the double bed than anywhere else. I used to sleep with Mum and Dad.

There was Brother Bill, he was two years older than me; and then there was Don, he was three years older than Don; there was Herman. I forget their ages. There was Betty; there was Jack; and there was Chris. Oh, I left

Frederick Charles Hall Collection

Julius Mathieson was the second-youngest of a large family farming at Majors Creek, south of Townsville, at around the time this photograph was taken.

two behind; there was Hilbert, he was the youngest, then me. That was the family. But where we all slep', I just can't tell you.

We never went short of food. We killed all our own meat. Our own steers. Because when they killed, there was a vat for salt beef... corned beef. And that's what we lived on until it run out. We'd kill, and with our surplus we'd supply round-about. And we had fowls. We had a fowlhouse but they perched mostly in the mulberry tree, not very far from the house on the bank of the river. There was a covered-in lavatory, down the back yard. It'd have a bit of bag, a corn sack, for a door.

No shoes. We didn't know anything about shoes. We'd bathe in the river. At that time the river was running. You bathed when you felt like it. We had no trouble getting the water. When the river stopped running, we just had to excavate the sand a bit, and there was pure, clean water all the time. Like a soak.

Sugar was bought by the sack. Flour was bought by the sack. Bacon by the side. A lot was got by the shotgun. We were close to Serpentine Lagoon so there were always ducks. Not so many fish. Plenty of eels. We skinned them and boiled them, but, ah, they'd have a very weedy taste.

Mum had washtubs, galvanised-iron tubs. Us boys used to use them too. We'd find out where a wild-bee nest was and cut it out and get a tubful of comb. Then that had to be put into a sheet and hung up and it would just drip into the tub, and you'd bottle it for honey.

We had kerosene lights. One shaded lamp that was hanging from the ceiling down to light the inside of the house. And others, with a lamp glass on top, and hurricane lamps.

Mum had an old sewing machine, a hand model. She used to make our clothes. Father's had to be tough clothes, more of a dungaree kind. They had to last. They had to stand up to hard wear. Mum, if she went to town, had the cheapest of the cheapest clothes. Oh, she had no luxury. No, fear!

We had one neighbour, within half a mile and the next neighbour was about five mile. And there was only scattered farms here and there; Habbricks and Petersons. Mr Habbrick lived there alone. We were only kids you know, and Peterson, he's always ready to help you in any way, he gave us horses each, and we rode anywhere we wanted to go. So we thought, 'Oh, well, we ride up and see Habbricks'. And, apparently we rode through his rose garden. Didn't he come out and perform! Told us to get out! And the dogs! They were savage, so we got out and we never went back to Habbricks' anymore! We were afraid of the dogs.

The local Aboriginals, they were Trouble! Oh, by Jove! Yes! Yes, my word! See, there was the Serpentine Lagoons, two of them, the top end, and the lower end. And Cummins, they had the cattle station. There was a big lagoon, a long neck, and then it opened out into another big lagoon. And between the two lagoons there was a big camp of blacks. We were only small numbers compared to them. And the road from Woodstock Station to Majors Creek, was just a dirt road. And the blacks, they knew we had to cross that little neck, and they'd stone us! (laughs with remembered apprehension) They were black and we were white.[3]

Or they used to come down, that's the young fellows, they'd come down and raid our corn. Dad, he had a big Snider.[4] A breech-loading gun. About the

John Oxley Library

Marbles was ever popular. This photograph is dated 25.12.1914, so a bag of marbles may have been someone's Christmas present. Three men are as absorbed in the game as the boys and one of the group is a girl. From the attitudes of the players, the game is possibly 'ringie' in which each player 'dobs in' an agreed number of marbles and tries to win them back, along with those of the other players, shooting with a favourite taw.

size of a shot-gun. It would take anything you could ram down. It was a muzzle loader, see.

So, he used to pull out his Snider. 'The Snider' Dad used to call it And he used to load it with a cap, and a flint, and powder. The cap and the flint was put in, and he poured the powder in, and then they rammed it with paper. Or anything they could ram in. The more you rammed in the bigger the charge. Dad wasn't game to hold it to fire it. So he'd strap it on to the side of a tree, and got on the other side of it with a string, and pulled it. And, bang! She went! And the blacks they'd run for their life! He wasn't actually aiming at them. Oh, no! Just in the air. It was just to frighten them away from the corn with the noise.

Sometimes they would want to trade. Aw, yeah! They'd come along and they'd want tobacco or sugar. They'd have a big barramundi. They had their own fish traps, made from rushes, all interwoven. Shaped like a… Cone shaped! And in that channel, that linked one lagoon to the other, there where the road was, there was only a very narrow channel, and that's where they caught the barramundi. Because the barramundi, wherever there's a flow of water, they go with it. And they had these cone-shaped traps in there and that's how they caught them.

Mum wasn't frightened of them. She had no trouble with the blacks, as far as that's concerned. Dad would often have to go into town and leave us there, Mum and the family. He'd go to town; might be in town for a couple of days. Mother never went to town, or not so very often. In those days money was very scarce.

There was one Aboriginal, he wasn't with the tribe at the lagoon. And I never knew the tribe that he come from. But in his tribe, whatever happened, he'd been hamstrung. The sinews at the back of his legs were cut. And they formed underneath him. And he used to slide all the way, with just his hands. Never knew what he did to get that done to him. But it was a common sight to see him along the road, going into town. You'd see him anywhere, sliding along on his hands. Charters Towers Road, anywhere.

There was an old dialect lady[5] used to come. She wasn't an Aboriginal. She was a white woman, well educated. She'd travel from here to the Burdekin, to the Towers, Ayr. And how she got there nobody knows. She was called Annie Baggs, and she used to stay at a place over from ours, allowed to camp in one of the sheds. And then she'd disappear. Nobody'd know where she'd go. Oh, for years she might just turn up. Nobody'd know where she'd been, where'd she go. Lived on what she could get.

Dad would take his stuff into town or to the railhead at Woodstock. Pumpkin, potatoes, corn, that was his chief. He had a horse and dray. It'd take him nearly all day to get in and back. Sometimes he'd do all right. Depends on the market. Sometimes he'd go in and there'd be no demand for whatever he had. There'd be a slump in the market. Tomatoes, well, it was only a matter of time; those things start to decay. And they'd all be dumped. And Dad'd be charged a dumping-fee. So, that's a year's work, you might say. (Voice is tinged with sorrow at the remembered dismay.)

In the end he gave it in, and we came to Townsville, and he worked in the railway on the links; laying the lines and tending to the sleepers. Wages was £2 or £3 a week. Our neighbour, Habbrick, he bought Dad out. Dad's holding adjurned [sic] Habbrick's. So all that he had to do was work our ground the same as his.

I'd have been about six or seven. I started school at West End. The older ones... brother Jack, he had practically no schooling, and he was too old when we come into town. But he was clever, he taught himself carpentry.

Very soon after we come into town, my Dad got to hear of this place in Hermit Park that McQuague was about to sell and he bought it right away. There was a saltpan and a row of houses and ours was the last one. It was all cedar, all the architraves, all the windows, all the doors, all the skirtings, all cedar. Beautiful, it was. I think he paid about £250 for it.

And there we saw the first mudcrab we ever saw in our lives. A big one, standing there with its claws up! We didn't know what it was. But we knew about shanghais! We were pelting it with our shanghais. But it got back into the saltpan.

Friday night, when the shops were open, we'd walk into town. Flinders Street would be really crowded. It was more of a dirt road, Flinders Street, and, when it was dry and no rain you could walk up and down. But when it rained it was a quagmarsh![16] The mud was inches! And we had tins, such as ox-tongue tins, and we'd put a hole in them and strap 'em on to our boots, and we'd walk across on the tins. Oh, the mud! Look! They had to have sweepers there, to make a passage so you can go across, otherwise you fill their shop up with mud and they didn't like that.

And you'd walk up to the Post Office and down to Lowth's, up and down again. Then into McCrea's and you'd have an ice-cream or a soft drink, and away you'd go, home. I met my future wife down at Sandy Crossing, one Sunday afternoon. These two girls, they knew we'd be there and they always used to be there too. Just a Sunday afternoon walk. That was the usual thing. The girls were never much allowed out on their own. Mixed bathing was something that was not allowed. It was out of the question.

We built little flatties, and we rowed from Sandy Crossing right down to Gordon's Creek and we'd camp down there. And we sailed a little twelve-footer that Jack made over to the island. He made a good job of it, nice decking done with inch b' inch, and top edges chamfered to make a V running all the way round. Looked all right! We took her to Magnetic Island and, oh, we thought we were just it! It was a big feat to get to the island. Before we come home, we got up on the hill and cut the top off a pine tree and lashed that on top of the mast. We were proud of ourselves!

And in the holidays we'd mostly go out to Majors Creek and camp. We'd have a tent and go shooting and climbing. All those hills, we scaled the lot of them, around there.

From West End School, I left and started work at Rooney's mill. I was about thirteen, fourteen. I started as a floor boy, and after a while, when I was about sixteen I suppose, you got promotion. You got on the benches, and you

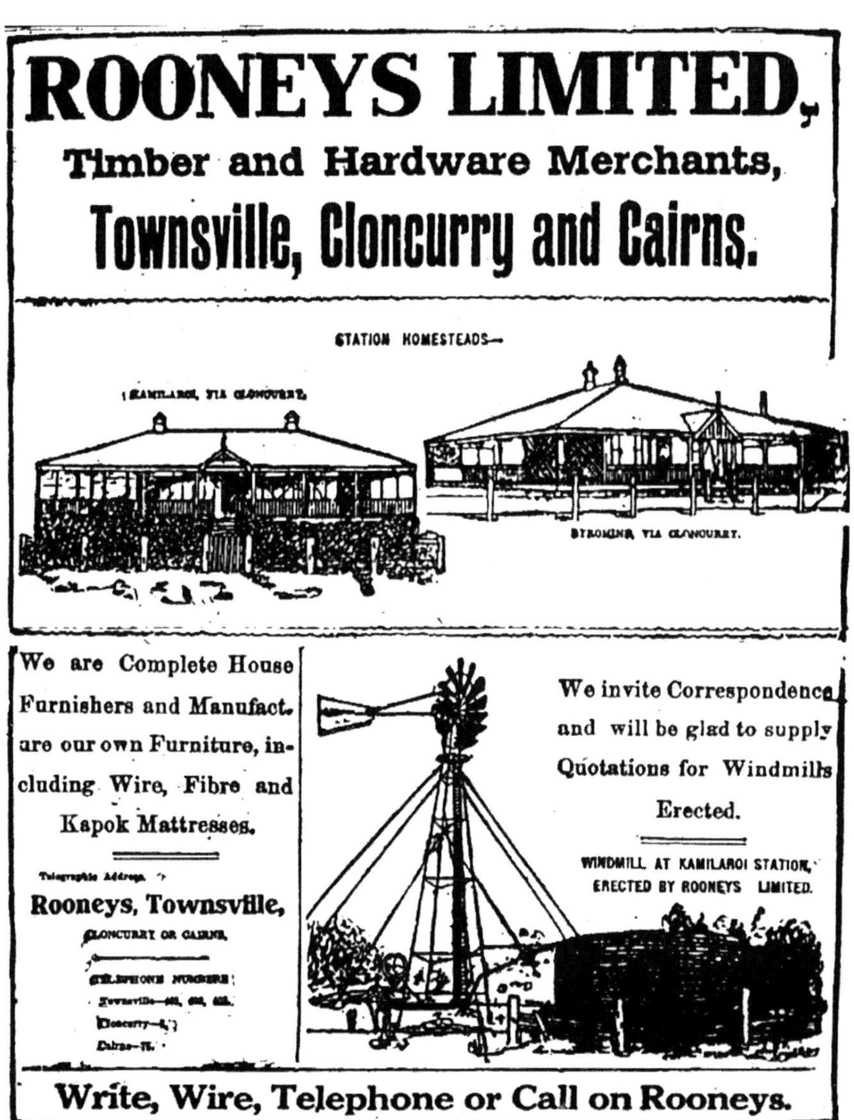

were supplied with a kit of tools. All joinery. Mostly assembling doors and sashes. Cleaning them off. The usual run was pine for the doors and cedar for the sashes, and anything special, we'd have maple and cedar and bean tree.

And the *Clyde* and the *Scout*, they were two big sailing ships. Usually they were towed in by a steam motor. But at times, when the wind was favourable, they'd come in with full sails set. And to see those sails on top of the mangroves... (his voice breaks with emotion) If I'd only had a camera! If only I could have taken pictures. Remembering it to myself won't transplant it to anyone outside. It was beautiful!

Ah, yes! You can talk about these things but no-one wouldn't believe... a big sailing-ship coming up through Ross River. Yes! They had the ships loaded with logs and they came from Innisfail and Tully. They'd come down with these big logs. And at the mill there was a wharf, and they used to winch these big logs up. There'd be a stack of great logs on the wharf. Then in the mill we had this big, about five-foot diameter, circular saw. You don't see them very often, big saws like that. Then we had what they call the breaking-down saw. And then there was one, like a nest of saws, that would cut the log up into planks. The mill was steam driven, and all the shavings and all the offcuts, that was all used in the boiler. Rooney's was a big mill.

It was right alongside the bridge... There's the bridge that runs across, well, just from there that adjurns [sic] Rooney's mill. The whole block was Rooney's mill. They had a wharf there. No logs came on the northern side (via Herveys Range) It all came by boat.

Chapman's had a mill there, too They used to raft their logs. The *Swordfish* used to come through Victoria Bridge. I only saw that bridge open once! To allow the *Swordfish* to go through. Well, the *Swordfish* would come up... there was a gut-way into Chapman's, and the *Swordfish* would unload the logs and they would lash 'em all together, spike 'em all together and then they'd have a motor to tow them round to Rooney's mill. It'd start at the beginning of the tide. And as the tide gained so the motor launch would get speed to drag the logs along. But if it hit the bottom! That was the end. They'd have to wait till next tide. If it was big tide in the afternoon, well, they'd have to work the tide all night.

If they had too many logs up on the ramp they couldn't handle them, so they leave 'em in the water. While the logs're in the water they wouldn't split. The ends split if you took 'em out and they dried out too quick. But while the log was nice and green it was easy to cut. If it dried out too quick even the planks would split. They'd have to put inch b' inch pieces on the ends, nail them on; stop them from cracking.

They had a big timber rack and trolleys. They'd be loaded up with timber and they'd be taken to where the various different sizes of timber were, and stacked to dry. Rooney's in those days, was the supplier of the all western districts, all the northern districts.

There was old Mat Rooney. He was the chief of them all. He went down one time to Maryborough buying timber and Mrs Rooney with him, too. And Cecilia. And during Leonta, on their way back, the *Yongala*[7] was wrecked. Off Flat-top[8] they run into bad weather. The bad weather increased until they hit the Whitsunday Passage. And those days… I don't think they had wireless. And the *Yongala* got into trouble and they didn't know where she was. There was no distress signals. Nobody picked up anything. She just disappeared with all hands. They were all drowned. And eventually, when the Americans were here in the war, they spotted her behind Cape Bowling Green when they were flying over. They weren't the first. Butler, on Magnetic Island, he said all along he knew where she was. Yes, all those years there were terrible tragedies, 1911, 1912 and 1914. There was the *Yongala*. There was the *Titantic* [sic.] and there was the First World War.

I was on the trade at Rooney's until the war broke out. There was three of us, Jack McShirring, myself, and McTagney. We all decided we'd enlist. We'd arranged to meet at the barracks, North Ward, straight opposite the hospital.[9] But I was the only mug that went. The other two just didn't turn up.

When I went overseas I was attached to the Ninth Battalion. *The* Battalion! We left Brisbane, Pinkenba, about June or July, 1915. We were on this troop-ship, the *Arcadia*. And we sailed to Melbourne, to Adelaide, to Fremantle, to Colombo. And at Colombo, they kept us out in midstream. There was about two thousand troops aboard, and we got a little bit fidgety, so we got down on to one of the barges, and we all stripped off and got into the water. And there was a hospital ship just across the way, and there was nurses and doctors and here we were all stripped off, in the water. And Arthur Doig, he was one of my pals, we pretty-well went through the whole business together, he thought he would do something good. So he climbs up the boat. Gets on the boat deck and gets out on one of the life boats. And he done a swallow dive! Nothing on! And it was absolutely perfect! (His voice still ringing with admiration.)

Well, we left Colombo, and we went to Port Said and we all got Egyptian money. But the Egyptians, they were cunning. They'd come along; they'd have a handful of money. And if you wanted to change ten shillings, well, they'd give you about two handfuls of coins, like that. Because molines and quarter molines, there'd be something around nine or ten to a penny. So you can imagine what you got for your ten bob.[10]

We got mid-Mediterranean, escorted by torpedo boats. And the escort spied something on the horizon. And our boat was ordered to do zigzags. We couldn't do a straight course. We had to go all out, in case of the submarine. The escort picked up a ship's boat. They'd just been torpedoed before we came along. We got into Marseille and we unloaded there. And the escort, she took off straight back out again and scooted straight away. They didn't hang around, because of the submarine.

And from Marseille, we got on to a train and went right across France. We came up to Le Havre. We stayed there for a few days and we were transported over to England. And from Southampton we went to Epsom Downs and we done our five month training there. And from there we went from Folkestone across to Boulogne. And from Boulogne we went to what was known as the Bull Ring.[11] That was the absolutely final training. And after the Bull Ring we were drafted off to our battalion.

Well, our battalion was in a very quiet sector up around Ypres.[12] We joined the battalion there at what they call the Railway Dugouts. From there we went up to the line. You'd only hear a machine gun, no shells. There was no shells at that time when we were holding the line. It was Hill Sixty.[13] It was a very quiet sector. Rats were very big and plentiful. What we used to do was we'd put a bit of our cheese on our bayonet and put it on the parapet. And the rat would come up and he'd start nibbling. Well that was the end of the rat! And on our way back, it was that greasy and slippery, with the mud, and being pitch dark, you couldn't see where you were going. You couldn't stand on your feet! But we'd have our bayonets fixed and we'd charge rats as we were going out.

Anyhow, we got back to our Railway Dugouts. And we were transferred from there down on to the Somme to a place they call Albert, just on the outskirts of Pozières. Pozières was the first initiation of the Australian soldiers.[14] Oh, it was a battle! We was up against the Prussian Guards. And the Prussian Guards had this close-fitting helmet with the coat of arms, the spread-eagle on the front. And after that battle, the majority of them[15] all had a helmet. (His voice breaks at the remembered carnage.)

Then, there was Mocave Farm,[16] then what we called Smokes Trench, and Sugar Refinery. We were at Albert and the Germans were at Bapaume. So for twelve months or more, that ground between Bapaume and Albert was just honeycombed with shells. There was a big forest area, Mametz Wood and Polygon Wood. And there wasn't a stick left standing! Not a stick!

I got a slight wound in the leg. I was in a shell hole and there was a bunch of us, and this shell, HEs we called them, high explosives, come over us. And I was the only one that got hit. (The voice still conveys the astonishment of it.) I looked at it. I tore my trouser leg and had a look. I didn't think it was worthwhile going to the aid post for. And the corporal says, 'Did it bring blood?' I says 'Yes'. He says, 'Go for your life! Go back to the aid post.' And I got back to the aid post and things started to happen. Oh, it swelled and pained. Because HE is deadly poison. If you have a splinter of HE and if you don't get attention, you're gone.

Anyway, I got to the aid post and orderlies and a doctor come round. And the doctor would classify you as so-and-so, depending how serious. Then the orderlies would say, 'This wagon. That wagon'. Anyway, I got to the First Australian General Hospital. The AGH. And we were all placed in beds. And the doctor done his rounds. And he come to me. And he went away and he come back with his bag and he started to extract the poison from me knee. I says, 'Is it serious, Doctor?' And he says, 'Oh, yes. If it had been another few hours you'd have lost your leg.' So I was in the AGH quite a while and then I was sent over to England, convalescent. After, I was sent back to France again.

Then when it was all over, there was the Victory March! We were in Hyde Park, in London, the whole pile of us in divisions, assembled there. And from there we were to march to the front of Buckingham Palace. And there was the King! I was as close to the King as near to that door. Oh! We thought we were made! We were proud to be so close to the King. Well, we marched past Buckingham Palace and then back to where we started again. But then the trouble was we didn't want to go back to camp. We all wanted leave. A stupid way of doing it, but we all sat down. We wouldn't take an order from any officer. So the officers got together and they managed to get leave for the weekend for us. And we were happy.

I met a few North Queensland fellows over there. One was Talbot Heatley. And there was Inglis-Smith; he got killed, poor chap. Then there was Trotter and Arthur Doig. Him and me we were good mates. Anyone from Townsville or The Towers, we always stuck together.[17]

1 The Woodstock district is named after Woodstock station, the lease of which John Melton Black applied for in April 1862, and was granted the following year.

2 Thomas Major was possibly the first European to climb Mt Elliot, in the 1860s, when John Melton Black was investigating the Cleveland Bay area prior to the settlement of Townsville. Dorothy Gibson-Wilde, in *Gateway to a Golden Land*, James Cook University, Townsville, 1984. p 25, quotes Thomas Major's *Leaves from a Squatter's Notebook:* ' What a lovely prospect was now open to our view'.

3 The 'trouble' with the local Aborigines was in all probability merely the sort of stone throwing and name calling that exists between rival groups of boys in any community. Relations between the adults were obviously amicable as Mrs Mathieson felt confident to remain on the property while her husband was away.

4 *Encyclopaedia Britannica,* Volume VII. 'Breech-loading firearms made all muzzle loaders obsolete soon after 1865. Most armies changed from muzzle loaders to breech loaders without adopting entirely new weapons. Muzzle loaders were converted by cutting off the rear of the barrel, threading it and screwing it into a new single-shot action. The British calibre .577 Snider was of this type.' Of this very old weapon of his father's Julius adds later in the tape, 'I had that old gun for years but it was put up in the rafters and the white ants got to it and ate the stock.'
5 The intended meaning is probably 'derelict'. Annie Baggs is also mentioned in Diane Menghetti's *I Remember Charters Towers* and by other narrators in the North Queensland Oral History Project. It seems Annie Baggs has made a niche in the lore of the North more firmly established than that of many a more decorous matron.
6 Not in the dictionary, but very onomatopoeic.
7 Julius is confusing the loss of the *Yongala* in an unnamed cyclone of 1911, with Cyclone Leonta which had occurred in 1903. See Appendix C.
8 Island off the mouth of the Pioneer River at Mackay, behind which vessels anchored while passengers and cargo were taken to and from shore by lighter.
9 Alice Chapman recalls: 'Every Monday night, the boys that were going to the front were lined up in front of the Town Hall. And they'd march from the Town Hall over to the jetty wharf to catch the boat to go away. There were no trains. And we used to follow them over and wait till the boat pulled out to wave them goodbye, and sing, you know... "When you return you'll find me waiting here..." And one time I felt something touch my shoulder. And this boy, a lovely boy he was... Bob O'Brien, he was a windmill erector with Southern Cross... he'd thrown down a tin matchbox. And when I looked inside there was a message telling me where to look where he was standing. I thought that was lovely! And it wasn't long after that I picked up a newspaper and I see where he's been killed in action.'
10 Before decimal currency was adopted in February, 1966, Australia's currency was the same as that of England. £1 (one pound, of 240 pence) = \$2; 10s. (10 shillings) = \$1; 1s. (of twelve pence) = 10c; 1d. (one penny) = 1c, 2c. Coins had familiar names: A pound was a 'quid'; a shilling was a 'bob' or a 'deener'; sixpence was a 'zac'; threepence a 'tray' or 'trizzy'. Prices of quality goods were often quoted (pedigreed livestock always) in guineas. 1 guinea = 21s.
11 A notorious staging camp, scene of a later insurrection.
12 Holt, Tonie and Valmai, *Battlefields of the First World War*, Pavilion, London, 1993. p.93. 'Rain has turned everything into a quagmire and the shell holes are full of water. The debris of war is lying about. Broken guns, limbers, horses, blown to pieces. But very few human bodies, for they have all been swallowed up in the mud of this horrible sector.' (Diary of a sergeant in the Light Somerset Regiment). It is remarkable that seventy years later, Julius recounts none of the horror of Ypres, merely the boyish sport of trying to kill rats.
13 Hill 60 had been mined in April 1915, with great loss of life to the enemy.
14 Op. cit. p. 77. 'The high point of Pozières Ridge was bitterly and bloodily fought for by the Australians. Over the month of August 1916, three Australian divisions hammered towards the high ground. In 45 days they launched 19 attacks and lost 23,000 officers and men. Australians fell more thickly on this ridge than any other battlefield of the war.'
15 The sense of the phrase is that the Australians had each souvenired a German helmet.
16 Mouquet Farm, known to the troops as 'Mucky Farm', was regarded as a key to the capture of Thiepal.
17 The names of Julius Mathieson and some of his mates are recorded on the Roll of Honour at Townsville West School.

7

Brandon, 1905–1914 **John Walker**

A Chance of Taking Articles

Introduction

John Walker gives us a window-on-time glimpse of life in the opening years of the twentieth century, on a dairy farm and a sugar farm at Brandon. He describes getting up before dawn to fetch the cows in, sometimes on mornings so cold that stubbing a bare toe on a piece of cow manure, brought youches of real pain. He laughed in the telling, recalling, 'You think your toe is coming off!' The remembered pain could have been only yesterday.

We see family life where economic survival depended upon the boys taking their share of the work-load. After riding horseback to and from school they helped with the milking or made 'chop-chop' for the horses' fodder – taking care not to lose a finger in the process; heavy and demanding tasks for eleven and twelve-year-olds.

Many of the farm practices which John Walker describes have become obsolete. Cane from the farms of North Queensland is now cut by huge mechanised harvesters and delivered to the crushing mills in short lengths. Until the 1960s it was still being cut by hand in seven- to eight-foot sticks. When the audio-taped interview was conducted, John Walker was over eighty-five years of age, and had spent a lifetime in a successful legal practice, but as he talks, the physical actions involved in cutting cane come flooding back in his memory: '…you run the back of your knife up and down the stick to remove any dead leaves… I could almost go through the motions now!' he exclaims with pleasurable satisfaction.

The description of loading the cane at the railway is of historic interest; the backing of the loaded tip dray up on to the 'Chinaman', or dirt-filled loading ramp, of the kind which were once a feature of northern railway sidings. We can perhaps detect, three-quarters of a century later, a touch of discontent that there was another method of loading, involving the use of a hoist. To boys hard at work loading cane under their father's vigilant eye, anything that represented a lessening of the hard labour involved would have seemed enviable.

But boyhood was not all work. There was fun to be had, too. Cricket and football on the dirt pitch at school, wallaby shooting for the price of the skins, trapping bandicoots, fishing for barramundi, and nights at home when the washing-up was done, of singing round the piano. But the highlight of the month was the school dance, beneath flaring carbide lights, always with half an eye on the girls, who could astonish small boys by transmogrifying into fully grown women, overnight, as it were, by appearing in public for the first time with their hair done up and 'their skirts down to their ankles'.

John Walker's later experiences as an office boy in Townsville are included for the details he gives of the period. Like Julius Mathieson, his war service was integral to his boyhood and growth to manhood, but is included mainly for the warm tribute he pays to the valued role of the women of the period.

⁂

A Chance of Taking Articles

I was born in Townsville in 1895 but until 1905 we lived in Cooktown. My father was working at the bank. I had a brother a year younger and two other brothers and two sisters. The first schooling I had was with two little old ladies called the Misses Cloasey. Then I went to the State School. There were two, a girls' school and a boys' school. There were no black children in the classes the way there are today.

There was one family with seven boys and we all used to play together. And there was a butcher's family and he had five or six. We made boats and we used to sail in them in a little creek called China Creek running into the Endeavour. Sometimes we didn't have much freeboard but that didn't worry us. We had a lot of fun.

Monday. February 26th 1900 NORTH QUEENSLAND REGISTER

In A Tight Corner

SERGEANT MAHOOD AND TROOPER HUBBARD RESCUE TROOPER PARKES UNDER HEAVY FIRE

There was a doctor there, had three boys. They used to tell us... show us... how they could 'make stone burst into flame'! They'd get a tin and stick a few lumps of carbide in... put a bit of water in, and... Whhissht! Up she'd go! We thought that was marvellous!

There were over twenty hotels in Cooktown at that time. It was entirely cut off from the south; there were no roads or no rail. Only steamers. The AUSN had the *Wodonga* and the *Wairema* which used to come... and then there were the *Lass o' Gowrie* and the *Kuranda* and the *Mourilyan*.

For holidays we used to go out on to a cattle station about fifty miles west; friends'. And they had an itinerant teacher – a government teacher. He'd stay a fortnight there, and children from other stations would come in, and then he'd go to the other stations and we'd follow him. School under the mango trees! After school we'd go and have a swim in the Macarthur River. We had a whale of a time.

We used to go out with the bigger boys shooting wallabies and fishing in the Macarthur. We used to shoot Torres Strait pigeons, big black-and-white things. We snuck up to the tree and got underneath them. Phhut! And we'd skin the wallabies and the station would sell the skins.

In 1905 my father left the bank in Cooktown and we went to a dairy farm near Brandon. We didn't own it, only rented it. It had been a cattle station, Lochinvar station, and it had an old homestead, with a big grapevine over one side of it. The homestead would be about half a mile from the railway siding, about halfway between Giru and Ayr. And it would be, I suppose, six hundred-odd acres. It had been Cunningham's bullock paddock for fattening bullocks. There were big mangrove swamps but that was all right because there were plenty of wallabies in there. We used to go shooting wallabies and kangaroos and possums and we'd get a couple of shillings for a kangaroo skin and about a shilling for a possum skin. We'd go fishing for barramundi. You're not very far from the coast, you know, Brandon isn't. It wouldn't be more than a dozen miles, from the Barattas.

We had plenty of bandicoots on the dairy farm. We used to catch them with a box, a stick under it, and a bit of meat or something for bait. And the bandicoot would come along and, whisss! But if you didn't get there quickly he was out! He'd dig his way out. They mainly come out at night. We'd get the

skins and we'd peg them out on the ground with bits of fencing wire. Then we'd get a pea rifle and the bandicoots'd come up for the skins at night and they were easy mark! We'd do this to get a few bob to spend. We'd sell the skins to Wilcox and Moffat in Townsville. We wouldn't get much for them; a shilling, or eighteen pence or two shillings. If we got two shillings for a skin we reckoned we were doing all right! We were never bored when we lived in the bush. We made our own fun. There was nothing to covet or be jealous about.

Of course, the dairy farm is slavery, there's no doubt about that. There were no milking machines. My father and brother and I used to milk about thirty or forty cows every morning. And then we would separate the milk. We had a Millot separator. Then we would take our skim milk over to feed the pigs. At first we used to send the cream to the butter factory at Ayr. Later on we made butter ourselves and sold the butter. So I learned to do quite a bit there. We used to let the calves run with the cows and shut them up at night, amid loud cheers from the calves! And only one day, Christmas Day, we left the calves out. That was the one day off. The only day off in the year.You didn't milk the cows at Christmas.

You didn't bother much about shoes in those days. Shoes! By golly! We'd go out in the morning to get the cows in and you'd stub your toe on a piece

John Oxley Library

Children of Brandon School about 1912, many dressed in their best clothes for the important 'school photograph'. Older boys are wearing unaccustomed ties, while at the front, some of the smaller boys are in sailor suits or lacy 'Little Lord Fauntleroy' collars.

of hard manure, in the early morning. Awhh! Gee! You'd think your foot was coming off! Very few boys wore shoes to school. Girls more than the boys. For boys khaki was the favourite thing and a schoolboy never wore pants below his knees. I didn't wear long trousers until I was thirteen or fourteen.

At home we had carbide lamps which were like two cylinders, one inside the other, with a nozzle on the top. The water was on the outside and the carbide was on the inside, and the water used to drip in, very slowly, so the carbide lamp would last you all night. They gave a good light, too! But sometimes you would be just in the middle of something and the carbide would cut out. Then you'd have to go outside and start it all over again. There were also hanging lamps, kerosene, with a big shade over the top and a glass bowl with a round wick inside. Or mantle lights. These had a little bit of silk called a mantle, and you had to light the mantle and the mantle had to be burnt through before it could become incandescent. And you'd get one nicely 'cooked' ready to go, and a moth or a beetle'd come along and if it happened to hit it, bang goes your mantle, and that'd be tenpence!

And there was the Primus stove. It had a tank made of brass for the kerosene, which the housewife kept brightly polished. There was a burner with a little cup round it and you put methylated spirits and lit it, and that heated your burner, and inside the burner was a little pipe with a hole in it. And once you'd heated your burner you started to pump. Right! And you pumped up your tank to get enough pressure to squirt the kerosene through. And up she comes… if you're lucky!… and you get a real good flame! But you always had to have a pricker.[1]

At night we used to read. Or we would play cards or dice games, Ludo and things of that nature. Mother was a very good pianist and we had a piano and we would gather round the piano and sing. Pianos in those days had a little holder on each side to hold a candle, and whoever was playing lit this candle. There were always plenty of friends to stand round the piano and sing. That was a lot of our entertainment. The family and friends. A real sing-song; *Way Down Upon the Swanee River* and *Annie Laurie* and *The Bonnie Banks of Loch Lomond.*

We went to school in Brandon. We all had ponies. We rode them in and put them in the school paddock. Most of the children had ponies. But when we first started we used to go into Brandon in a spring cart with an old mare called Biddy, and going home we could let the reins go and Biddy would take us home. You could go to sleep on it.[2]

There were families all round there, all with youngsters, and we made our own fun. We had a little cricket team and a little football team; just an ordinary dirt pitch in the schoolground. Our schoolmaster was a very fine chap. He went to the war and was killed.[3]

There used to be really good school dances. Everybody would be there; the girls all sat along one side and the boys on the other. We danced the

Mazurka and Barn Dance, the Gypsy Tap, and the Boston Two-step. When girls were growing up they went from a child into long dresses at about sixteen. One day they'd be going out with short dresses and then next they appeared on the scene with dresses to their ankles. They were on the market then for a husband!

We used to be sent to Sunday School. The Presbyterian Church, there was no minister, so we used to go to the Church of England. They used to give us little tickets at Sunday School. You got six of these tickets and you got a bigger one. And you got three of these and you got a big one that you could stick on the wall. We used to value those. And once, they did they did up the Church

John Oxley Library

Children on their horses ready to ride home from school about 1908. All are double-banking younger siblings. All sit their horses with accustomed ease and brief years later would be of the right age to join the Light Horse, as John Walker did. The older boy on the centre horse appears to have his hat turned up in the style of the troopers who fought in the Boer war.

of England, all blue and white and it had lights installed. There were about a half a dozen along each wall, kerosene lamps with a reflector behind the glass which was polished tin, round, about as big as a big plate, and it fitted into a slot at the back behind. It reflected the light and magnified it and, oh, gee, you'd think you went to heaven straight away!

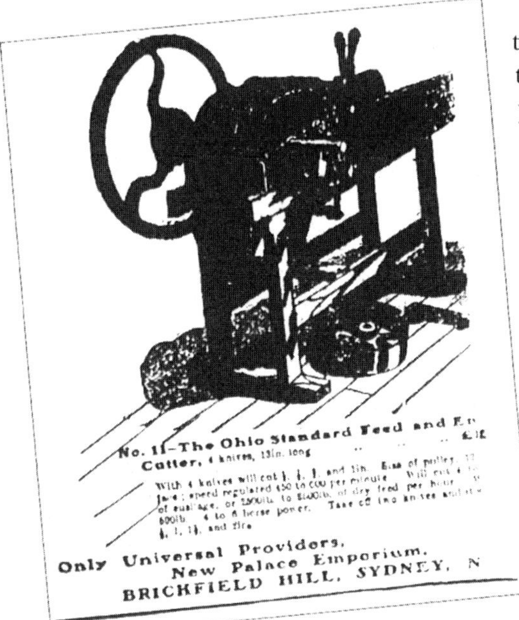

So that was the sort of life they lived on those little places in those days. Then after about five years on the dairy farm we gravitated into sugar, on a sugar farm at Brandon. And that was hard work. There was only my father and myself and brother. The cane farm was harder work than the dairy farm. And you didn't get very much for cane then.

There were no tractors. It was all horses, beautiful big Clydesdale horses – oh, lovely ones – and at a place called Klondyke, which is about two or three miles on, they had big stables, and these horses were all in teams, kept together, beautiful to look at; usually bay, with white feathers on their legs. Lovely glossy things. And they'd go into the stable at night, knew where to go, and they were groomed, and fed. They would feed them on chop-chop, and oats, and they used to fortify it. And these fellows would go out and they would work in the field all day. Each ploughman had his own team, and they'd take them out and they'd plough furrows that were dead arrow-straight. Beautiful! This was not on our farm. Ours were a bit lighter. We didn't have any Clydesdales.

Chop-chop is cane tops just cut with the chopper; sometimes they'd put molasses on it. They didn't burn cane in those days, not at that time. They only burnt cane when they discovered Weil's Disease, oh, some years later. And then they had an outbreak. It is supposed to be transmitted by rats in the cane and so they adopted the practice of burning the cane and that fixed the Weil's Disease.

Making chop-chop for our horses was the job my brother and I had to do before going to school every morning. Well, at the top of a stick of sugarcane there's a fan of leaves. Suppose your cane stick is six, seven foot; well, you cut it off down at the ground. You'd cut it by hand. There were no machines. It was all back-breaking work. You cut your stick of cane and with the back of your knife you rake off the dead trash and throw it out. And then another stick like that, see, and throw it out. You cut, slash and run the back of your knife, the cane knife with a hook on the end, up and down to remove the trash. All the green tops go on to a heap for the chop-chop. I can almost go through the motions now! The stick of cane goes onto another heap to be picked up later.

So you'd take the spring cart out and get a load of cane tops. Then you'd bring your load back and you tip your load of chop-chop out in your yard, and put the old horse away and the cart. Then we had a chaffcutter, with the handle on, and we'd run the cane tops through the cutter, chop, chop, chop, chop, chop, like that. And sometimes you'd put molasses on it. That was the horses' feed.

Well, that's doing it by hand. But then we got a horse-gear. That was a big improvement. A horse-gear was fitted to a beam, and you fixed your horse to the beam and he used to walk round and round. He gets used to it. And this operated a cog wheel that was fastened to your chaffcutter. This spun the chaffcutter and all you had to do was feed the chop-chop in and look out you didn't put your hand in. Which was easily done! The cane tops are going in all the time and you could forget. And if you forget or get distracted, off comes your finger, quick smart!

Eventually we got a little engine, a Mynx and Weeks kerosene engine; this would be about 1907. And it used to tick away and blow smoke rings, beauties! Once she was started up, pop-pop-pop-pop-pop! Beautiful smoke rings out the top! And that took all the heavy labour out of the job. It was wonderful!

We'd take the cane to the railway siding by tip dray. A tip dray is one which when you want to unload, you pull a lever and it tips. They could be backed up on to the loading bank at the siding – that's a construction we used to call a Chinaman, a bank with logs, and you back up on to it – back it up to a log so it wouldn't go over. There'd be a railway wagon underneath, a cane wagon, two ends to it and open at the sides. And they'd tip the dray up and the cane'd fall down. The cane lies across and they'd put a chain over and fasten it down tight so it wouldn't slide off on the way to the mill.

In some places they had a hoist and instead of tipping the cane they would hoist it and drop it in. That was an improvement. But in our day we had the horse and tip dray.

The first plough Dad had was a mouldboard plough with a pointed piece of steel that goes down into the soil and turns the soil over. It wasn't a stump-jump. Oh, No! *You* jumped with the plough! The mouldboard had a sort of knife, called a coulter, down the front, on a beam. That disposed of roots to a certain depth; it would cut them. But later on then, he got disc ploughs.

The first motor vehicle that we saw at Brandon would have been about 1905. It was a motor van built for Cootes who were in the milling business, and they drove down from Townsville in this motor van to Brandon, and it was Patrick's Day. There were plenty of Irish Catholics on the Burdekin; Hoeys, and Kellys. Lots of Kellys! They always had a great sports meeting on Patrick's Day. Footrunning. It was an institution. Professional footrunning, for prizes. A friend of mine he went in once; he used to do a bit of running, but he said, 'No more! Too crooked for me!' They started the race then called them back, and it upset him and he lost the race. He never ran again. And this motor van was there and they were giving the kids rides for sixpence in the grounds. It was a novelty. Yes, in the delivery van. So St Patrick's Day was a big day in Brandon.[4]

From the cane farm I got a job as cadet clerk in the CPS office at Ayr. I wanted to get into the public service. And I was sent to Townsville. There was a Police Magistrate, a CPS officer and about three or four clerks. I was the junior. Many a night I used to go into the office and work just to keep my job up to date. No thought of overtime. I was boarding in Mitchell Street, with another chap; his mother owned the house and we boarded with her, and I used to walk in over the hill. There was a little shop and I'd buy a packet of biscuits on the way in and eat them walking home. That would be my dinner. At weekends we'd go chasing the billy goats around on the Hill, or pinching a few guavas from the back of the Chinamen's gardens.

Townsville then was pretty primitive. Public transport was horse buses. Flinders Street was just a succession of potholes. And in the wet weather the potholes'd be full of mud and they'd go 'swhhisht' 'swhisht' on the footpath. You'd be splattered in mud. And the boys used to stand on the back seat of the bus, trying to get a free ride. The bus driver'd – he had a big long whip – and he'd whip behind. And there were horse cabs; a rank in Stokes Street and another one in front of the Great Northern; a dozen or so lined up, nosebags on the horses. Nobody rushed in those days. The *Bingera* was the mail ship. She was a steam turbine. Every Monday morning, regular as clockwork, you'd see her coming in.

Bikes were scarce. I bought a bike on time payment, half a crown a week! I used to ride that bike to work. I had a carbide light for it. All you needed was about half a dozen lumps about the size of your fingernail, and then you turned the water on and away she went! They were good lights, too. I biked down to Ayr one time. I dropped in on my parents and they were greatly surprised. I was very proud of myself, too, but I went back on the train! Put the bike on the train. The road wasn't a road then; it was a track. And that was so for a long, long time. Very little traffic. There were very few cars. The first car I remember seeing here in Townsville was a French car owned by a doctor.

And I was a member of the crew of an eighteen-footer, *Satinita*, owned by Fred Satini, who was assistant manager at Allen's.[5] They used to anchor the boat on the seaward side of the old Victoria Bridge! I was the youngest so I used to have to wade out, water up to here, and pull her in. Never mind about sharks! We used to have races in the bay, but they'd handicap the big boat out of contention. But we got a lot of fun out of it. We'd go over to Alma Bay and throw a net over and catch whiting, or round to Cockle Bay and get thick-lip bream, then jump overboard for a swim. We didn't worry about sharks.

And then I was offered a chance of taking Articles with a prominent law firm and I was articled to George Suthers for five years. I'd never been to a school other than a country school. I'd never done Latin or French or algebra or geometry which were all compulsory subjects. So I went to the Grammar School at night after work to get coaching to get through my Prelim exam. Roland was the headmaster, and he was a character. They were all very well liked. Dunster, he took me in languages, and I had to do two languages and two maths. And I'd never seen any of them before. But I had a pretty big thing at stake so I ploughed into the work.

I did some training in the militia in the Light Horse. We used to have a camp at Easter at Kissing Point, the Infantry, the Light Horse and the Artillery; a Training Camp, about eight days.[6] And the CO would recommend those to go to Officer Training School and I was sent down to a camp near Duntroon. We played the cadets from Duntroon at rugby and beat them. I was a front-row forward. Then we were sent overseas. My second brother, the one a year younger than me, he served in Palestine and I served in France with the Infantry.

These days people don't realise what your mother meant to the family. I know that when we were on the farm, my mother used to make all our bread. She made all our clothes, and she had, what, five kids then, and she ran the house with no help at all. Being a housewife was a full-time job. Those women thought nothing of it, and took pride in everything they did. Mum had a vegetable garden and that was her only recreation! She'd look after the chooks and collect the eggs. Your mother was the tower of strength in the family. She was the mainspring! I didn't see my mother again after I went to the war. She died when I was on the boat on the way back.

1 A small implement with a needle-like spike of fine wire. It was wise to wriggle this into each of the holes around the burner to ensure an even flame before lighting the methylated spirits in the cup.
2 Such journeys to school were not without their hazards. The *North Queensland Register* for 7 April 1911, records: 'Stanley, second son of Mr J. Bell, had a miraculous escape from death this morning on his way

to school. He was riding in a wagonette from Wondecla when he slipped and fell between the wheels. He was caught in the wheel but the driver pulled up instantly and saved crushing the lad. He received a deep gash in the shin-bone, thigh and muscles of his left leg . He was attended by Dr Macdonald and is progressing well.'

3 Ernest William Spreadborough, 31st Battalion, Killed in Action, 4 June 1915, France. He taught at Brandon from 1904 to 1914.

4 Peake, John Henry. *A History of the Burdekin*, Burdekin Shire Council, 1951. 'In the heyday of its career, Brandon was the chief sporting centre, for it had a large number of big-hearted Irishmen, and some keen contests were waged in the main street, where the tossing of the caber, foot-running and hop-step-and -jump were indulged in.'

5 Samuel Allen and Sons, founded 1872, a noted North Queensland trading company.

6 Alice Chapman recalls: 'Every year they had an encampment at Kissing Point and of a Sunday we'd all go down, dressed up in our best. And, oh, the band would be playing and it was beautiful to see. All the local boys that were in the army were all in camp. This would be about 1910.'

8

North Ward, 1901–1911 **Barbara Aitchison**

To Get To The Beach, You Had To Climb The Sandhills

Introduction

The voice has the gentleness of a well-brought-up little girl 'never allowed out at night', from an era when 'all entertainment was in the home'. There is delighted recall of 'games... puzzles round the walls... sitting in a ring' and of course, music; everyone singing round the piano, followed, perhaps, by *The Grand Old Duke of York* up and down the verandah'.

Eighty years after her childhood has ended Barbara Aitchison can still recall, and sing with a lavender-fragrant sweetness of tone, the little songs that the children of her day sang as they marched into school. It is likely that there is now no-one still living who would recall these songs. The tune of *The Cat Came into School One Day* was very like that of *There was a Farmer had a Dog and Bingo Was His Name-o*. As for the catchy ditty, *Wait Just a Little While in Townsville,* Barbara Aitchison tells us that the head teacher at Belgian Gardens, 'wrote it', but Mr Tuffley possibly had echoes of *As We Were Marching Through Georgia* in his mind as he did so. The lines

> Shout, Boys, shout! Hurrah! Boys, hurrah!
> Won't we have a lovely time when riding in our car
> Round the Hill we gaily spin, people popping out and in

celebrate the fact that motor cars were just making their appearance on the streets of Townsville. Harry Page had brought the first car, a de Dion, to Townsville in 1900. Modern children might sing similarly about journeying by spaceship or yellow submarine with little expectation of ever actually doing so. In the early years of the century, 'driving out round the Hill' was a popular way of celebrating, but the driving was done in horse-drawn vehicles. Another Narrator in the North Queensland Oral History Project, Francis Valenta recalls that after a wedding, the guests would 'drive out round the Hill in their sulkies' by way of celebration.

The lagoon in which Barbara Aitchison's brothers swam in 'seven feet of clear fresh water' was Hambeluna Lagoon, the banks of which had been the site of the original encampment for the settlement of Townsville in the 1860s. Dorothy Gibson-Wilde quotes Rowe's description of the lagoon:

> The beautiful clear water was surrounded by lofty trees whose branches interlocked overhead and on hot days its pleasant shade made it a most delightful spot.'[1]

The lagoon later became known as Comerford's Lagoon after the family who 'had the big dairy at the back'. We can only regret that this beauty spot was eliminated in the name of development. The 'lofty trees' were felled for timber and the depredations of mobs of semi-wild goats finished the job off. The lagoon was filled with sand from the sandhills which Barbara Aitchison remembers 'behind the beach' and the land sub-divided for housing.

Barbara Aitchison also describes her life as a shop assistant in Townsville's then most prestigious store, McKimmin and Richardson's; the uniforms of starched white blouses, and long serge skirts 'to the ankle', the ribbed stockings (in Townsville's heat!) and the hair tied back with a black ribbon. Today's shoppers might find themselves envying the thought of a Head Girl who had to be summoned to ensure that a customer was satisfied before leaving the store.

To Get To The Beach, You Had To Climb The Sandhills

I was born in Gard's Lane, behind the Crown Hotel, in Charters Towers, 9th November 1893. My father was a plumber and he was mayor in 1895. We were there when the Milginiva mine blew up. We were all in bed and everybody just rushed out into the streets in their night attire. I thought, 'Oh! Gee! It might be the end of the world coming!' But it was only the mine blew up.

Father had his own business, a tinsmith's shop. It was made out of corrugated iron, and we lived next door. My grandmother had a grocery shop, The Cardiff Store, because they came from Wales, at the top of High Street. When they came out from Wales it took 'em a whole week in a dray to get from Townsville to Charters Towers. They were very clever old people because they could not read nor write but they ran a shop. I used to read to them. I served in the store behind the counter; all groceries and lollies. And they lived there on the premises. The store was in the front, like.

I was going on for nine when we left Charters Towers and come to North Ward. We went to the Central State School. Mr Caldersmith was the headmaster. Mrs Caldersmith, she was the headmistress. And he had the Boys School. And he liked music; tonic solfa. I used to think, Oh! Gee! This tonic solfa! Now I play the piano, and it's mostly tonic solfa! Yes! Any note on the piano is 'doh', and you can play it from there.

There were two schools, the Girls School and the Boys School. You were five, you went to the Infants School, and then when you were seven you went

1 Gibson-Wilde, Dorothy; *Gateway to a Golden Land*; James Cook University, 1984, p. 37

to the Girls School, and the boys went over to the Boys School.[1] And where you sat in school, say you were in the front seat or the second seat, well, in line, you stood in your place. And the music would start and we'd sing:

> The cat came into school one day,
> Shoo! Shoo! Go out, black cat!
> The teacher chased it round the room.
> Shoo! Shoo! Go out, black cat!

[Tune similar to *There Was a Farmer had a Dog; Bingo Was His Name-o.*] Then, when you came to your seat, you stayed there, see! We had slate pencils and slates.

And there used to be a lolly shop over the road in Oxley Street. We used to run across from school there. Mrs Caldersmith used to say Oxley Street was the only street that ran north and south, from the top of the hill down. And the lolly shop was there on the corner. Oh! Lollies! You could get two peppermint sticks for a penny. You'd get raspberry bars for a penny. You'd get two big licorice sticks like that, for a penny. You bought them separate. They was just handed to you. Boiled lollies. You used to get six a penny. You'd get a lot for threepence (laughs with remembered delight).

Frederick Charles Hall Collection

Sunday School picnics were much looked forward to. At Townsville these were often held in the bed of the Black River. The game in progress here is twos and threes. Couples form a circle, with one of the couple standing behind the other. A chaser tries to catch a runner, the runner darting in and out among the couples or running to the front of a couple if she is in danger of being caught. At this, the person at the rear of the couple must run.

We lived in Warburton Street. It was a brick place, on blocks, very low on the ground, with two mango trees at the front, and pot-plants, two by two, on the verandah. There was only four houses there then. And Comerford's big dairy was at the back. Sometimes when they finished milking the cows, we'd have a go.

And myself and my sister we walked to school with the orphans from the orphanage every morning. They used to pass our place, nine o'clock. And they'd walk all the way home for dinner, back again, and all the way home, four o'clock. And we were allowed to walk at the side of the line, not in the line, but the side of it.[2] Where the new Central School is now, well, the gaol was there, and from there, right down to the orphanage was nothing.[3]

In the 1903 cyclone we were at school. It was very windy but we went to school because we loved going. It was hard to keep us home. Even in the rain we'd go off with umbrellas. And it was very blowy in the morning. And we'd just got into school, really, about nine o'clock, and the wind got worse. And there was a little house up on top of Melton Hill, it blew right over. And Dad must have thought, 'Well, I'll go and get the two girls'. And he came down for us, for my sister and I, and of course, we hung on to him all the way home. We had to lie flat on the ground and sheets of iron going over us. And in Cook Street we were hanging on to the corner fence for grim death, my sister and I, and we wore Japta hats in those days, and our hats went. 'Go and get our hats!' we said. And Dad shouted, 'Leave the hats! We've got to have our life! Never mind the hats!'

And the Grammar School boys, they were running through the park to the orphanage, laying on the ground and then up again and off.[4] And we just got home when the back of our place all went, so my father and mother, they gathered blankets around us and over we went to the orphanage. And that night at the orphanage, there were a few hundred people, Chinese, blacks and whites, and we all slept on the floor all night. In

[Tropical Cyclone] Leonta, North Ward got really badly blown.[5] I think the 1903 cyclone was worse than Althea.

We had a nurse girl to look after us children and a woman to do the cooking. I don't think my mother did much cooking. And later my sister did the cooking on a wood stove. We used Pott's irons to do the ironing. Everything, all your underclothing was starched. We used to wear what was called combinations; well, the frill at the bottom would be all starched. And your petticoats, oh, a lovely deep frill of embroidery. And they had to be starched too. And your pillowcases. Packets of Silver Star Starch; and little blue bags.[6] And there was Kitchener's Kerosene Soap which was made in West End.

We used to go on the North Ward bus, the old horse buses. They used to take us from the stables, along Eyre Street, down to the Queen's Park, around along the Strand, around the Customs House and into town for threepence, a penny for children. And you'd ring the bell and they'd stop anywhere. They didn't have a stopping place. If you wanted to get out here, he'd stop and he'd stop next door again. The bus would seat about twelve; six each side on a seat and the driver and three on the front seat. The owner, he was Charlie Beale. He did all his own work, kept his men there, them that worked for him, boarded them in. Down the end of Cook Street to Landsborough Street; diagonally there, that was the stables.

They used to let us have a ride round to Mitchell Street of a Friday night. Friday night the shops were open till nine o'clock. My sister and I and our friends Nellie and Grace used to go across and help them wash up the dishes to get a ride around on the bus. We had good times when we were children though we were never allowed out at night.

The only thing we ever got taken to was the circus! They didn't come to town that often, maybe once a year. The name began with a W… Wirth's! You went over the Causeway and somewhere there it was on the left. They had a big tent. Elephants! Once – I'd have been about fourteen – we went and they used to feed the elephants just about half-past four and it was a wonder some of us weren't knocked down with them, they rushed for their feed!

When we first came to Townsville, down at Rowes Bay, there was all dark people lived there; in tents. And where the army is now – the barracks, Jezzine – that was a golf course. A lot of the boys used to go round and carry the caddies for the men. My brother was one of them. There used to be a rush down there, who'd get the sticks. Sixpence for the afternoon they were paid.

And in North Ward, there were what you would call identities. Annie Baggs,[7] she'd have a bag in this hand and a bag in that hand, and she'd have a few cats. I don't know where she lived. But she could play the piano very nicely. She came into our home once and she'd play the piano beautiful!

And then there was Fat Mary. Oh! she was a big woman, about fourteen to sixteen stone. She wore long dresses. No shoes and socks; barefooted all the time. She used to just yabble to herself. And then there was Mad Jackson. He was tall and he was a bit silly. And there was King Billy. He wore a big brass plate round his neck on a chain, and it had 'King Billy' on it. But they did you no harm; no harm at all.

In those days Cape Pallarenda was called Cape Marlow. There was nothing to get around there; no bridges or anything. When the tide was in you had to wade through the water. And out there was where they used to take all the nightsoil. Take it and bury it, with a big horse and cart. The Common was at the back and there used to be two windmills; a small one and a big one. And we used to go out there for picnics and, oh! lovely pie melons used to grow on that land! There was nothing there but bush. We used to go with Mrs Anderson, she had a friend worked in the orphanage in the hospital; they had a little hospital there for babies and everything, and a Miss Williams, she was the matron, and we used to go with them.

Right around the hill there was no houses, only the orphanage. Once you got around into German Gardens, as it was then, there was only four houses on the right-hand side, Anderson's, Price's and Molloy's, and the Bishop's Lodge was on the hill. And right around there was no houses right till Stagpole Street. My brother used to go over the hill by a short-cut to Belgian Gardens School.[8] The headmaster was Mr Tuffley. He composed a song; *Wait Just a Little While in Townsville* (Tune similar to *Marching Through Georgia*):

> Shout, boys shout! Hurrah, boys, hurrah!
> Won't we have a happy time,
> When riding in our car,
> Round the hill we gaily spin; people popping out and in;
> Wait just a little while in Townsville

There was three Chinamen's gardens in North Ward. There was Lee Wing, and then there was Ah Say down towards the end of Eyre Street. Lee Wing took a cart around. Ah Say, he had a basket on a pole. He come twice a week. He was a good old Johnnie. He used to come to next door's, and one day she'd make a cup of tea for him, and the next time it'd be us'd make it for him. And Christmas time! Those Johnnies, they used to bring you big baskets! Crackers, and watermelon! Ginger! Oh, yes! In the china jars. Everybody got that. And a lolly-stocking and crackers for the kids! And fruit! They brought you this big basket. It was beautiful! They were marvellous, you know, the Johnnies!

And we used to get everything delivered in those days. The butcher used to come round for orders. And the baker came round with a cart.

And of course there was the big lagoon and to get to the beach you had to climb big sandhills. The boys used to go down to the lagoon of a Saturday afternoon and sail their boats, just a little punt and a sail. They used to swim in it too. There was about seven foot of water in the middle. There was one lady found on the bank of that lagoon, drowned. It was all fresh water from Castle Hill, always very clean. No mosquitoes or anything. It was lovely. Then the Council filled it all in and sold the land. Land was very cheap in North Ward then. In those days Stuart Street [as it is] now was known as Honeymoon Row. The whole row was built the same. And Leu the solicitor and Chapmans's that had the sawmill, they came and built here.

We shifted from here to Stanton Hill, next to the Japanese Consul. We lived in a big home called Champions, a lovely big home. We had a water-tank and we had to pump our water to get a shower. There were not many houses on Stanton Hill and we had about half an acre. There was a big rock that we used to sit on. There was no Cutting. They hadn't built it then.[9] It was just all bare rock. There was no Christian Brothers School there then. I remember that getting built. We would cut down the hill to the Central School. There was a private hospital because private doctors would have their own. The General Hospital wasn't big in those days.

All our entertainment was in our own homes. You'd have music and games; you'd have puzzles or something around the walls and you had to guess what they were, then *The Grand Old Duke of York* up and down the verandah. And then you'd sit round in a ring and play games. Then it was more music; singing at the piano.

I could play the piano by ear and mother thought I ought to have lessons. And I made an appointment with Sister Mary Bega down at the Convent for the Saturday afternoon. She was a lovely nun and I heard she was a good music teacher. And she told me to buy *A Hundred and One Exercises* and *Wickhams*. And I'd made all the arrangements, and Saturday afternoon come, and I got to that front gate of the convent, and I couldn't go in! If I'd a' had somebody with me… but I got to the gate and I couldn't go in. Too nervous! From that day to this I never learnt music!

We were Presbyterians and in our home we did nothing on a Sunday. My father he was very strict in that line. And my mother too. You didn't do anything on a Sunday. You went to your Sunday School or you went to your church. And we had Sunday dinner.

We had a lovely lot of ships coming to Townsville: the *Innaminka*; the *Bingera* went every Monday night at nine o'clock; and the *Yongala;* the *Wyrema.* The loveliest sight was the *Mourilyan* of a Sunday night. It was a two-decker boat and came across Magnetic Island, the passage there, and of a moonlight night coming across it was a beautiful sight. The *Kuranda* was only a one-decker. That left every Monday night at six o'clock and got back in Friday night. They only went to Cairns. They called in at the Palms sometimes. You got off and landed in punts. Palms Islands was beautiful. It was a popular spot. Frasers had that, too, like Picnic Bay.

There was a man named Butler had a boat that used to go across to the island. Called the *Scotia*. It was about eighteen pence to go. It could sail over but it was a motor launch, too. We used to land in punts. You had to wait your turn to get in the punt to land. There were no buses, or no cars; you had to walk everywhere from bay to bay, through the bush, just narrow tracks over the hill. It's a lovely island. This would be between 1901 and 1910. I had one brother was drowned at Picnic Bay. They were getting a ride out to catch the boat. He was the only one born in Townsville.

I left school when I was fourteen and went to work at fifteen for half a crown a week, at McKimmins. My sister was a milliner for McKimmins and she worked twelve months for nothing, because, see, they were apprentices, getting taught. But I started on half a crown and got a shilling rise at the end of the year. We worked every Friday night till nine o'clock and then Easter and Christmas Eve – I think we used to go till ten or eleven. I don't remember ever getting any overtime. We got an hour for lunch and I went home every day; climbed Stanton Hill. You could get a lunch, at a place called the Geisha, and straight across the road was a lolly shop, Frasers. There used to be Armatis the chemist and Hastings, and Willmetts used to be further down.

In haberdashery we had soaps and wools and embroideries. And buttons; samples of buttons in big books. And all the colours that you do fancy work

John Oxley Library

Children at Picnic Bay, Magnetic Island, about 1906. From left: May Duffield, Dorothy Cathcart, Edie Hinspeter, Frank Duffield rowing and Rick Hinspeter at extreme right. Barbara Aitcheson's little brother, 'the only one born at Townsville', was drowned at Picnic Bay while 'getting a ride out to catch the boat'.

with, you had to learn all them numbers so that you'd know the colour straight off. I didn't like the wools. Everything was in boxes and we had to climb little ladders to get a box down from the top; different things in, embroideries and laces. Nothing under the counter. At the back of you were big shelves; big green boxes, wooden ones. And you had to climb these little ladders and pull them down and put then on the counter.

And there were what they used to call spiffs – like a sample done up in little lengths – of embroidery and laces and things like that and they used to have little tickets on and some would be marked threepence and some would be marked a penny, and if you sold that, well then, you took that spiff off

HOW DO YOU

JUDGE A FLANNELETTE?

By the appearance, the feel—and the price? Very good. But, unfortunately, few women are sufficiently acquainted with the technical details of cotton manufacture to rely on their own judgment alone. This emphasises the necessity of buying according to standards THAT ARE KNOWN TO BE ACCURATE, backed by a trade mark that guarantees quality and insures the best that can be woven. This unfailing guide is the stamp of OSMAN, which appears on the selvedge of the best Flannelette.

and you kept that and it went to your wages. And there were marks for what they cost; 'g' was for a penny 'l' for twopence, 'd' for threepence, 'h' for fourpence, and so on.

We were in uniforms of course, skirts and white blouses – your white blouses for work were starched and ironed – and long stockings. The best pair of stockings those days was eighteen pence. That would be called a lisle. And then you got the rib stocking. You could buy cheap stockings for sixpence. You wore your hair down low with a big black bow at the back of it. And when you turn twenty-one, everybody in those days, down went your skirt to the ankle and your hair went up. Everybody knew when you were twenty-one. And another thing, you didn't put on creme or rouge on your face. If I'd worn it to work, or doing your eyebrows, or anything like that, well, they would think you were no good.

McKimmins was a big shop. There was a boot department, and a millinery, and a dressmaker. And they had catalogues and did big orders for all the country people. When we served a customer, we couldn't let you go out the shop; we had to call the head girl to see if you were satisfied. If I couldn't help you, or if I didn't please you, I couldn't let you go. I had to call the head. And she'd ask you were you really satisfied.

We used to keep a lot of things in reserve upstairs. Well, you had to know what was up there too, as well as downstairs. Press-studs; well it was during the war, the 1914–18 war, or just before the war, I hadn't gone upstairs and looked in the reserve and I ordered I don't know how many press-studs, oh, I ordered a lot and I got into a little bit of trouble. But, that was all right! Because when the war broke out McKimmin's was the only one that had press-studs!

I worked five years in McKimmin's in the haberdashery department and in the end I had four girls and a boy under me, and the day I left I was getting twenty-seven and six a week!

1 Central School had been established in 1869, in Oxley Street, North Ward, as the National School. By 1873 a separate Girls School had been added and in 1879 an Infants School. The school was still on this site in the 1940s and is described in the author's, *The Morning Side of the Hill,* including mention of the 'little shop on the corner' where lollies could still be bought.

2 Another Narrator in the James Cook University Oral History Archive, Alice Chapman, who lived in Mitchell Street at that time, recalls; 'The Orphanage kids used to march to school in fours. They'd a gray uniform with a white pinny and a straw boater with a band around.'

3 The Townsville Orphanage had been built in 1885. Carramar Children's Centre was later built on the site.

4 See Appendix C for full account, especially, 'Plucky Scholars'; 'The sheets of iron were chasing the refugees and every stump or tree was used as momentary shelter until they reached the gully near the Orphanage.'

5 Alice Chapman remembered Leonta: '... our house was flattened. And we went next door and it was flattened. We run up towards the Sacred Heart. As we were running up the hill Mother said to us kids, "Now, all catch hands and run".'And the wind was lifting us up and we grabbed hold of the billy goat weeds to keep us down. They carried my mother in; she was blown up and her arms were all cut. The roof of the Sacred Heart had gone but we got in because it was safe.'
6 Reckitt's Blue was dissolved in the final rinsing water on wash-days to enhance the whiteness of clothes. Each knob of blue came wrapped in a small square of muslin and was swished backwards and forwards until the right intensity of of blueness was attained. Too little and it was ineffectual, too much and sheets and pillowcases got a bluish tinge. The housewife would establish degree of blueness by scooping up a handful of water and, with a discerning eye, letting it run across the palm of her hand. 'Making the blue-water' was a pleasurable task for children on wash-days.
7 As late as the 1940s there were humpies, or rough dwellings, in the sandhills between Kissing Point and Rowes Bay. Possibly Annie Baggs lived in that area.
8 The short-cut would have been through the previously well-forested valley now cleared for the extension of Stanley Street into Belgian Gardens.
9 The Cutting seems to have been built about 1913 as Joe Clark, a Narrator in the James Cook University Oral History Archive, recalls; 'they were building that Cutting road at the time, 1913, and Dan Galvin, the stone-fixer, was laying the stone…'

9

Charters Towers, 1895–1910 **Harry Pope**

The Wheelwright's Story

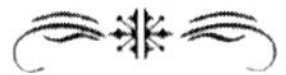

Introduction

This story, though brief, is remarkable for its account of a tonsillectomy carried out 'on the front verandah at home'. There can't be too many of us who do not find ourselves wincing at the thought of, 'He took one off, and I got up to walk away, but he said, "Wait on! There's another one", and he took that one too.' The mere thought makes tears of 'Ouch!' come to the eyes. It also flashes through the mind to consider the alarming possibilities of cross-infection, especially tetanus, and to wonder how thoroughly the doctor had washed his hands – if at all – after handling those sulky reins.

We first meet the Narrator who, as a rather sickly little boy in Charters Towers was nevertheless, like boys of his generation, was brought up to hard work. He and his younger brother got up at four o'clock in the morning to take their billy goat cart out bush for logs, which they then split for the kitchen stove and the 'boiler out the back'. But hard work, and the knowledge that it was a valued undertaking, bred an attitude that stood them in good stead through life. The boys grew up to be among North Queensland's most highly respected businessmen, Pope Brothers Body Builders, Townsville.

The buses which the firm built, with hard, horsehair seats and open sides, were once a feature of Townsville streets. For passengers the world went by *al fresco* with a 'Poop! Poop!' that would have delighted the heart of any Toad of Toad Hall. These wonderful old vehicles were in service, on the Belgian Gardens and North Ward route until the end of the 1939–45 war and were much loved by American servicemen stationed in Townsville. They were later taken to Magnetic Island, their Edwardian livery changed for something less sedate, and were put into service in the tourist trade. What better method of transport could holidaymakers have to view the delights of the island.

The following material from later in Mr Pope's interview is included for the interesting details of technical work methods, possibly long forgotten, in the coach and motor-body building industry.

First we only built horse-vehicles. Lovely work! I used to love it! All in timber. Grey ironbark for the spokes, and blue-gum rims for all the dray wheels and cart wheels. The sulky wheels were made of hickory, American hickory. It would bend; it was springy, a very flexible wood. You could also use Sydney spotted-gum. We used to use a lot of it, but it didn't make such a good job as American hickory. The panels would be maple or silky oak. We had little brass plates with our names on that we used to put on our sulkies. Year after year people used to come to us, especially at show time, to get their sulkies done up. Before the Depression I had nineteen employees.

Or people would just come and say they wanted something; say a baker's cart. Well, you had to build it. Each suburb had a different baker. About four different ones we used to build for. Those bakers' carts were sprung the same as a sulky. Three springs, one each side and one across. A baker's cart was practically airtight. They'd put the hot bread in there and you'd get nice fresh bread. And the driver sat up the front. And he'd get off and open the door at the back.

And pie carts. I'd build them on an ordinary bent-shaft sulky chassis; hexagon shape. He'd put his fire underneath and have his pies on top and he'd open the door at the back. He'd have another space underneath to carry his wood.

People just used to tell me what they wanted and I would design it for them. Greengrocers. Ice carts. They were lined with tin inside. They'd go round delivering the ice, threepence a block.

I made a fruit barrow for a chap they used to call Kangaroo Billy. They say he fell once – walking round the top of a vat of something with molten stuff in it, fat or something, and he slipped, and he hung on to the top but his feet got into it and got burnt. He was crippled in the feet. He had a fruit barrow at the Bank of New South Wales corner there.

The first sort of car we done was a hearse. It was an old second-hand Buick and we took the glass out of the horse hearse for it.

The old cars had wooden rims, wooden spokes. And I was the first in Townsville to put new spokes in those. I had to find a way of doing it with a hollow auger. To get them in nice and tight you had to build then from the inside. You couldn't shrink them on like a horse tyre.

I made a motor lorry with seats on for a bus for Frasers up in Ingham and drove it up in about 1927 or 1928. There wasn't a bridge over any creek. There was seventy-two mile and seventy-two creeks and gullies! Not a bridge! When the creeks would be flooded you'd drive over the railway bridge. Straddle the railway line, bump, bump over the sleepers. Which was illegal! Ha!

When I first come to Townsville in 1915 they had four great heavy Denis motor buses. And then I built four buses for the different motor-bus firms here; built them on the Ford ton truck chassis. They wanted them to carry twenty-eight passengers. I said, 'No. It's too many. It would overhang.' But they would have it! So they'd fill 'em up with passengers. And if the front passengers got out first it would lift the engine up! They'd have to ask the passengers to come forward, else it was like a see-saw! Those buses, they're still running at the island.

The Narrator's words of praise for his brother and partner were, 'He was a good sort of chap. He could do the work of two men!' Doubtless, each brother could have said the same of the other.

⁂

The Wheelwright's Story

I contracted measles when I was about two-and-a-half year old and the mumps about twelve months after. I went to school when I was five, in the January, and I got asthma then, and I had to stay home from school about six months, and one day I was coughing a lot and an old Chinaman came along, and he says to Mother, 'Boyee velly sick.' So he gave my mother a small bottle of liquid to dissolve in water, and I reckon that helped to cure me. I never had asthma again after that.

Then when I was about nine, I got tonsillitis. The doctor came down in his horse and sulky. If your family was in the Lodge, you had the Lodge doctor; Dr Clapwood it was. And he came down, and he said, 'Oh! If he's no better when I come tomorrow, I'll take them out.' So sure enough, they were no better. So he sat me in the chair, in the doorway in the front of the house, on the front verandah, and he put an instrument down m' throat like a scissors. And he snipped one off, and I got up to walk away, and he said, 'Wait on! There's another one!' and I sat down and he took the other one. There was no anaesthetic. And all he told me was to gargle with salt water.

Then when I was ten, I got typhoid. M' brother Frank, he had typhoid, and he was in the hospital. And then I got it and they wheeled me up in a two-man litter. They wheeled me two and a half miles to the hospital and I was in there four and a half weeks. And they used to put you in ice packs. They'd roll me in a sheet that'd been wrung out in ice water, then they'd pack ice all over me and put blankets on me. They'd do that about five times a day. No needles. Just quinine for medicine. I was there four and a half weeks with that. And I come through all right.

We had a little house on low blocks and there was vogavilla [sic.] all over the front verandah, very prickly. And m' father bought m' brother and me some wheels and we made a billy goat cart. It was like a Chinaman's spring cart; they always wanted them built like that. We had a lovely goat for it. I got him out in the bush; swapped a lamb away for him. We took the lamb out and this fellow had about a hundred goats, and I stayed there a fortnight and I picked that goat out of the mob. But those goats, you'd see them going round the ridge with the lamb behind 'em! They were frightened of the lamb and the lamb's trying to mix with 'em! Like a dog chasing them!

The younger brother, Wally; he's four-and-a-half-years younger than me – we used to take this cart out to get our wood in. We'd have two goats in for getting the wood. We used to go out about four o'clock in the morning and we'd be home half-past eight with a big load of wood, long logs. And then we'd have to cut it up; for the stove and the boiler outside for washing. The washing was all done in kerosene tins, no proper boiler. The kerosene came in tins in wooden cases, two in a case. About eight bob a case for four gallons and those tins, you put a length of fencing wire in for a handle and you've got a fair sort of a bucket.

The groceries was all delivered. The orderman would come round on horseback one day and take all the orders in the notebook and the next day the groceries would come round in a cart. Butter was one and ten a pound. Rib roast was twopence a pound. Sausages twopence a pound. Liver they'd give it to you for nothing.

And we started the billy goat racing off in Charters Towers. We used to race at Show days and race days. If there was any races on, the kids would take their goats to the racecourse. And they wouldn't put us on till the last item to keep the crowd there! Everybody would want to see the billy goat race.Then we'd have to take our goats home in the dark, two mile.

When I left school I put in for the railway. There was twelve of us required and I got the highest marks for the

A BRAVE BOY.

(By Telegraph.)

BRISBANE, August 22.

Master Joseph Neilson, of Gladstone Road, Charters Towers, attended at Government House to-day, when the Governor handed him a certificate from the Royal Humane Society, for saving W. Stevens from drowning in the Syndicate Crushing Mill's dam in October last. The Premier and Mr A. Dawson, M.L.A., were also present.

The Governor, with a few appropriate remarks, handed the certificate to the lad, stating that he hoped the same noble impulse would guide him through life.

Mr Dawson said the chief feature of the boy's action was his forethought in telling some other boys to run to the mill while he plunged in and held the man up until assistance arrived.

The Governor said that showed that he had acted on more than impulse, and he certainly deserved the greatest praise. Lady Lamington then shook hands with young Neilson, and complimented him on his bravery. It is thought probable that a medal will be given him on account of his exceptional bravery.

JOSEPH NEILSON

This boy was a slightly older contemporary of Harry Pope and the photograph is of interest for the style of clothes worn. It is easy to suppose that the formal black suit and Eton collar were bought by Joseph Neilson's family especially for him to 'attend' at Government House, Brisbane, to be presented with his certificate by the Governor.

Lady Lamington, the Governor's wife, who 'complimented him on his bravery', was herself later to receive the compliment of having a delicious new kind of afternoon-tea cake named in her honour; Australia's favourite, the lamington.

Above: Boys riding goats, about 1913. On race days at Charters Towers, officials would stage a billy goat race as the last event to 'keep the crowd'.

Below: A beautifully made goat-drawn wagon, about 1895. The harness, too, is a scaled-down replica of that used for horses. Harry Pope tells us that as boys in Charters Towers, he and his brother made a billy goat cart 'with springs', possibly initiating their lifelong love of coachbuilding. Most goat carts of the day were usually a box to which wheels and shafts had been added.

Photos John Oxley Library

examination but they had a lot of bigger boys than me. I was too short so they wouldn't take me. And I was going round on the baker's cart, and this Mrs Parnell asked me what I was going to do. She said, 'My husband wants a boy at the works.' So I said, 'Oh! All right! I'll come to work with him.' So I got this job with the Parnell cyanide works; it was what they called The Fair Rosamund Mill first, then Raines' Mill and Gordon's Mill and it finished up Parnell's Mill. And within about four to five months I could have practically run it for him.

They had what they call vats. Some of them held about twelve tons, some of them about fifteen. And all the sands, or sludge we used to call it, that used to run out from the mills, they would cart that to the cyanide works and spread it all over the flat to dry. Then they had to break the sludge up – it was all lumpy – and screen it; screen the sand.

They had twenty-one vats, some were twenty-two ton, some were fifteen ton. Well, the men had to be directed which ones to fill each day and which ones to empty. Because you had to run the cyanide solution on them for so many hours and you had to know when it was ready. Some sludge was what they call sour. Well, you might have to leave that four days. Some only three days.

Then that solution run down into little sumps, underground pipes down to a big sump. That had to be pumped up, right up high, then run that through gold-boxes with zinc shavings in them. The water used to run in, and there was a little compartment with low ridges, one above the other. The solution would spill over, and come up through the zinc shavings, and then over the next one. Then that would all crumble in time, full of gold.

That had to be taken out and smelted. Then it was ground to get the quicksilver which was attached to the gold out of it, and you'd have to put that through a retort, which was worked by heat. The fumes would come up through a pipe, and say it was an inch pipe, there'd be a two-inch pipe outside of it, with a hose running into that with water, cooling that, and condensing the vapour. And you'd see the quicksilver running down the bottom and the gold would be left in the retort.

I left the cyanide works and got a job with Guthrie and Collins. They was wheelwrights. There was no apprenticeship in those days, but they used to put you through for five years and then they would give you full money. Well, I was only there three and a half years and I was getting full money.

My father had a job in the mill. He was what they call a feeder, shoveling the quartz into the stamper heads. And then he finished up collecting the gold at the end of it. Some of the mills were grinding mills and some of them were crushing mills. This was a crushing mill that he was at. He stayed there till they closed up and they gave him a job cleaning up, and he got a lot of gold out of the old drains.

When our family come to Townsville we come on ahead and Dad stayed behind to clean up the place. Then he brought the horse and sulky down. It took him two, three days to do the trip. It used to take three days to walk up.

And I was going to go out west to look for a job, but on the Sunday, Dave Edwards the wheelwrights, one of his apprentices got drowned out in Aplin's Weir. And on the Monday, blow me, if I didn't go down and ask Dave Edwards if he was going to put anyone on in his place. And he said, 'Can you make wheels?' And I said, 'Yes.I've done three and a half years at that.' And he says, 'All right. You can start tomorrow.' Well, he had a foreman but he could never depend on him – he might get on the booze and not turn up – so I was only there four months and he made me foreman over the other wheelwrights. And I stayed there seven years.

10

Aitkenvale, 1900–1910 **Henry Brown**

It Was All Chinee Apple And Lagoons

Introduction

The hub of the civic life of Townsville has moved in the direction of Aitkenvale, where shopping complexes, commercial premises, medical centres, library and government buildings are now located. The early settlers of Aitkenvale would have been astonished had they been able to foresee this sea change. Once, 'town' was a long, hot, horse-bus ride away, 'fourpence for adults, twopence for the kids'.

Henry Brown recalls what it was like to be one of a large family growing up in Aitkenvale at the turn of the century, a time when children walked barefoot to the Black School, now called the Weir School, and when, out of school hours, they did the chores that kept the family life viable, filling the barrels at the back door with water from a spear two blocks away, weeding the garden, chopping the wood. 'We had no time to ourselves,' he remembers matter-of-factly, but then recalls the pleasurable thrill of drifting down Ross River in flood time; clinging to logs, or hanging in the swift brown current on paperbark branches.

This hard-working family exemplifies much of the spirit of an age when there was no social security safety net of pensions and child endowment. Although Dad seems by modern standards to be a tough old character, taking his belt to boy or dog for disobedience, he is still willing to lend a hand to a neighbour, 'to see what they could do for them', at the height of Cyclone Leonta, going to the aid of one whose house had collapsed. While he is thus engaged the Brown's own house begins to disintegrate and the family struggles along the fenceline towards a neighbour's. Unfortunately, at this point, the Interviewer interrupted with the question, 'What was the house made of?' and we never do get to hear the end of this gripping incident. It is an example of the necessity of never interrupting the Narrator's train of thought, and also of the need for the Interviewer to possess a reasonable understanding of conditions of the period, in this instance that most houses in the Aitkenvale area were built of bush timber and corrugated iron. Interrupted, Henry Brown went off at a tangent on the cost of building then compared with the present, and the story of the family's survival in Cyclone Leonta was never resumed.

Like most of the other Narrators in the series Henry Brown had warmly appreciative memories of the Chinese gardeners around the township, who seem to have been ever generous towards children; 'They would always cut a watermelon for you'. At Christmas there were always gifts from them of 'a couple of pineapples, a watermelon and Chinese ginger, done up'. The 'done up' meant in a blue jar bound with cord. Almost every Narrator who recalls the Chinese of this period mentions this detail, the yearly gift of ginger in a blue pottery jar. To families struggling in poverty it must have seemed an exotic luxury.

Henry Brown gives a graphic account of the life and work of a teamster's 'spare boy' on the Georgetown Road, then the main road leading to the northern goldfields and cattle stations upon which Townsville's prosperity depended. We are left in no doubt about the amount of work involved, but can secretly rejoice with Henry that at the ripe old age of twelve, he acquires his first pair of boots – the mark of manhood in a world of working men. There is a warming little glimpse of Dad, of whom Henry no doubt lived in healthy dread, as he sits by the campfire at night, waiting for the damper and corned beef to cook, thereby ensuring that boy and father will eat on the morrow. The old man sits staring into the embers, the light flickering on the trunks of nearby trees, the bells of the hobbled horses clanking in the distance. Perhaps he is wondering if there isn't an easier way to earn a living than the loneliness and rough living of a teamster's life for 'a shilling a ton'.

⁂

It Was All Chinee Apple And Lagoons

There were thirteen in my family and they reared nine; the others died at a young age. I was born in 1895, down the bottom end of the Weir Road. We were there in [Tropical Cyclone] Sigma', although I was only young then.

And we moved from there to this side of the Upper Bohle Bridge; about a quarter of a mile down. We lived in tents. There was tents to sleep in and a big tarpaulin that was the dining-room, and my mother and father had a tent at the end of it, and the kids had a tent at the back. There was a fly over the tents, a wagon tarpaulin. I was only young when we shifted out there. Dad had a dray; he was carting firewood. We must have been out there the best part of five years. I started school from out there. We used to walk to the Black School every morning. From there we moved back into where Nathan Street is now and we were there in [Tropical Cyclone] Leonta.

I was about seven year old in Leonta. My Dad was away on the road. He had a team, a horse team. He was on the Georgetown road, on his way up to

Ewan, and he was camped at The Bend o' the Bohle. That's between the Alice and the Upper Bohle Bridge. And he arrived in home that morning, right through the cyclone, on horseback. Left the team there. Left the brother out there with the team.

During the day, when the cyclone was on, there was two houses, a high-blocked place and a low-block place, right up the other side of the Chinamen's gardens. And those houses went flat. And Dad and a fellow named Peter Nichols, that lived up the road – they went up to see what they could do for them. While they were away the roof went off our place at the back! So we moved then, hanging on to the fence, the whole family of us, up to Nichol's place.[1]

We built a place up in Charlotte Street. None of these streets were named then, but it would have been nearly halfway down from Ross River Road to the river. Two acres of ground. M' father built it with the timber straight out of the ground, ironbark. We had the brick floor in the front and ant-bed in the back (laughs). We were there a number of years. I suppose there wouldn't have been more than about thirty to thirty-five houses in the whole of Aitkenvale. Aitkenvale run from about Rogers Street right out to the weir. Took in the lot.

Frederick Charles Hall Collection

A tent home. Henry Brown's father worked a horse team on the Georgetown road. For several years the family lived at the Bend o' the Bohle 'with tents to sleep in and a big wagon tarpaulin that was the dining-room'.

Of course, there were no streets in those days. Where Pimlico High School is, Charlie Armstrong had it leased to a Chinaman there, and they were growing potatoes. He had his dairy cattle in there before. And Garbutt's slaughteryard was where Warina is, and somewhere in between Vincent and Heatley, was Billy Pierce's slaughteryard. It used to run right out to where the college is now, Pimlico High. From Hermit Park there was nothing here. It was just a bush track and lantana. All there was lagoons, Chinee apple and lantana.

And I tell you there were a lot of Chinamen's gardens; big gardens. All sorts of things they grew. You could buy a kerosene tin full of ripe tomatoes off the tree for sixpence. And cabbages that today you'd pay three or four bob for, you'd get 'em for sixpence. And you could eat all the watermelons you'd like, but don't take 'em away. They knew most people. If you had to go there and you wanted a watermelon, don't pinch 'em! You could eat as much watermelon as you like; they'd always cut you a watermelon, but don't take any away. They had everything; cabbages, lettuces, shallots – all your vegetables – pumpkin... They used to sell them in town. But there was certain ones that come with the baskets and the stick on the shoulder, they used to walk all the way out there, and then there was others come with carts. There was one Chinaman used to come from way over in Bell Street, a fellow named Tin Wah, and he used to travel one day a week out there. He'd sell lollies and all these vegetables, pineapples. And every year they come round, all these Chinese; the ones with the baskets, and they used to give a Christmas box – a couple of pineapples and a watermelon. Chinese ginger, too, done up. They'd always give you a Christmas box.

Long Kew Yews, they used to import people, the men, like – he had all Chinamen working for him. He had a big garden, and in the morning, at four o'clock, five o'clock in the morning, you'd hear them up and down the road, following one behind the other, carts going in with potatoes, pumpkin and different things, into town, because in town they had the Chinee markets. The Chinaman near our place, down towards where the Seventh Day Adventist School is, he had horses and he used to pump from the river. And some sort of manure. They'd dip the tins in and carry them along.

We had a well. Dad put down a spear and a couple of wells, but the water was no good. After you went down a certain distance, it was clay. No good at all. We used to have to cart our water from next door, two allotments away. They had good water down the front there. You had to hand pump it. And we had hogsheads, the old hogshead of beer... well, we had two of them with the tops knocked out standing on bricks, and us kids we had to fill them every morning with water. And we had to get up in the morning – no boots, and in the wintertime you'd hear the grass cracking under y' feet with frost. Aitkenvale used to be a very cold place. I didn't know what it was to have a pair of boots till I was twelve year old.

I had five brothers. Willy, Jim, m' self, Jack – George was his proper name, but he always went by Jack – and, that's right, Dick. One brother died early in the piece. The one next to me. I couldn't tell you what he had. He was two or three years old. There was twins in the family, but they both died, too. They died at a very young age; only twelve months. If I remember right they had rheumatic fever.

Dad was strict. He might tell you to pick out a certain patch of weeds and if you didn't have 'em out by the time he come home, well look out! I'd've been somewhere about eleven or twelve. You had very little time for yourself. We never used to go anywhere. Might go down the river for a swim. We used to go down where the Nathan Street bridge is now and swim down in the floods. Or we'd walk right 'a way up and wait till a log come down and swim down on it. Or we'd swim out and grab a paper-bark branch and have a spell. But the logs were best, coming down on them!

For colds, kerosene and sugar, they used to give you. That's a good kerosene; White Rose kerosene. So many drops of kerosene on a teaspoon of sugar. That's the only thing they used to give you for colds. It didn't harm you.

Mum worked hard, all right. And of course, as the girls got up they worked too. We had a Beacon Light stove, a wood stove. The boys would chop the wood. Kerosene lights. It came in tins; four-gallon tins. There used to be two in the case. We always had plenty of vegetables, cabbages, beans, potatoes. We had a good bit of meat too. Salt beef most of it. We used to have fresh meat every weekend, from Kierie and Sons. If you wanted twopenceworth of liver they used to throw half a liver at you. If you wanted dripping or suet, you'd get that for nothing, too. A shin of beef for sixpence. Well that went a long way for making stews and soup. There was one butcher there, Ginger Billy we used to call him... he had a hoppy leg… when you went in there he'd cut us kids a slice of sausage.

We went in once a week to get our meat. Saturday mornings, Mum'd maybe go into town. The horse buses, there was two double-decker buses – they brought them up from Sydney – and the driver would flick round with the whip to catch the kids hanging on behind. Fourpence into town, twopence for children. Out to Rising Sun was sixpence, and Aitkenvale was sixpence, right from Tattersall's Hotel; that was the terminal. No stops. Pick 'em up anywhere. Wherever they see people waiting, they pick 'em up, and they could pull the bell and get out anywhere. The bell had like a lever in it and you pull the string and the bell would go. The horse stables, big stables they were, they were where the Rising Sun Hotel is now.

There was a baker's that called out at Aitkenvale, Donald Shaw and Alec Shaw. Grocers too, Rhys Thomas's. They used to have a shop just across the line from the Bellevue. An order man, a fellow named Brown, used to come and take the order and the stores would come out the following day. Pay monthly. You'd go in and pay them.

The Dad used to buy mostly in bulk, from Allen's, and when he was travelling on the roads he'd get a dozen of this and a dozen of that, and he'd get a case of mixed jams, and leave so much at home, and black treacle, and syrup – a dozen tins of each – a sack of Gillespie's flour, a sack of Chinese rice… (laughs) Ha! The good old days! My mother used to make good dampers. She used to make yeast bread, all in the camp-oven. And Dad used to buy a hundredweight of salt beef from Keirie's for when you were going up the road away, and you'd leave so much at home and take the balance with you. And they used to carry that in a sack bag on the shafts of the wagon. And when they get a day's camp they used to hang it out to dry.

I done that trip up to Carpentaria m'self. Spare boy! A spare boy is… you had a certain amount of spare horses. What they used to do when they go away is they used to get horses to break in. Dad used to get a half a dozen from Lawrence up here above the dam, and he'd break them in on the trip. He'd have a certain amount of horses spare. Generally he'd have about eighteen, all depends on what the loading you got. And the spare boy's job was to stand around the horses and hook 'em together and to get the saddle horses – you always had about three saddle horses – and then you ride along behind the team with the spare horses and the spare saddle horses. And when it came to dinner time, y'd go on ahead; he'd tell you where to go, and boil the billy. And get the dinner. I got ten bob a week. I was about twelve year old, so that would have been 1907. There were two of us for two teams, a spare boy for each team.

The only road to Hervey's Range in those days was up cross the Upper Bohle Bridge, and you take that road right through. And when you got to the foot of the range, one team couldn't get up on its own. You had to put two teams of horses on to one team, and they used to have steady riders on both sides and flog them all the way up. Take them all day to get up the range. It was a rough bush road; jump-ups and rocks. When they got on top they used to go about a mile – there used to be a hotel up there, the Eureka Hotel. That was the first stop after they got up the range. And coming down the range, to bring the next team up the next day, they used to cut a big tree down, and hook the horses on to that to steady them; two teams of horses on the one. They nearly all travelled with two.

There'd be no more than two teams. Sometimes with loads for the same station. They used to take their team into town, somewhere down the back of the Post Office, down BP's.[2] there, and the carts used to cart the stuff there from the different stores, and load it on to the wagons; take them all day to load. Then Dad, he'd come home and stop in the yard till he was ready to move off. Sometimes he had some other team going but they'd meet on the road at the first camp, the Bend o' the Bohle. And there used to be a hotel at the Alice, the Alice River. It was on the left-hand side of the old Georgetown road before you go into the creek. No bridges there at all.

Now, the only trouble we had was, at different places, there was no water. You had to take the horses to water. We didn't take them; the men took them. us boys, we had to go and get firewood and boil the billy. Dark time, well we had to cook the corned beef. We had to get up early in the morning and go and get the saddle horses. Then we'd go and get the other horses. Before you got to Hillgrove station... up that road after you get to Hervey's Range on top, there was Running River, Big Star and Little Star, and then there was Big Jim and Little Jim, and then there was Keelbottom, and then there was Greenvale and then Christmas Creek. Then there was the Burdekin, then there was The Lynd. There was a Post Office telephone out there that used to go across to Georgetown. We used to camp on all those rivers.

We had bush-made bunks; we used to fix them up – sticks leaning up, a forked stick, and two long sticks, and two sack bags, corn sacks. M' father used to sleep on the back of the wagon, and I used to sleep in between the two wheels. A lot of them used to just lay on the ground, but we had bunks. And then all we had to do was just fold them up and just chuck 'em up on the back of the wagon. And our tucker box used to be kept at the back of the wagon so's it'd be easy to get at.

Those wagons they used up here were what they call box wagons. They had sides on and they'd be anything up to about sixteen or eighteen feet long. Two shafters, and two abreast, the horses; it all depends on what the load is; sometimes you'd have fourteen, sometimes there'd be sixteen or eighteen. But it was all heavy ground; all boggy country. All across the Bend o' the Bohle, there, it was tea-tree swamp. Bog a duck! But you used to go through; you'd hook the other horses on. Or you'd get horses from the other team.You come to a bad place, you'd take the side horses off one team, put them on the other team. Get out that way. But when it got really too wet, Dad used to camp till the weather took up a bit.

Sometimes there was old swaggies. They used to foot it all the way up. There used to be mobs of them going, backwards and forwards, mostly on their own. Just camp anywhere. Tin scratchers, they used to call them. They used to get a living, too; a bit of tin. It would be sold to the smelters up there. They used to go sometimes with a team, but if they done any work for you, they could claim wages! Ha! We never seen no Aborigines at all, only what worked on the stations. If we got short of food we used to get fresh meat from the stations.

There were two teams with loadings for Carpentaria Downs station. One time there was a murder there two days before we got there. The governess was murdered. They had the station manager up, but I have an idea he got out of it. But they were all away in Georgetown when we got to the Einasleigh – that would be roughly about two or three mile away from the station – we got word that they were all away from the station and we had to camp on the Einasleigh a fortnight. Nine weeks it took us on that trip.

Dad used to make good dampers; cook them in the camp oven. And we'd probably have jam, mostly blackcurrant. At midday, a lump of corned beef. And at night. No vegetables. Never had time. Maybe have a few spuds, sometimes. Mostly corned beef and damper; all the time. Boil the billy for a cup o' tea three times a day. It wasn't a bad life.You got plenty to eat. Sit around the fire at night time. Dad used to make his dampers at night time. He'd have to wait up till they was cooked, and the corned beef. You got good corned beef; not like you get today. All cured with salt and brine.

Dad used to cart for a shilling a ton.[3] Sometimes he worked at Kangaroo Hills on the smelters, carting the ore from the mines to the smelters. He'd be away about three months or more. Ewan was the same. When the line come through from Cairns, it done away with all the carriers on the Georgetown road. So then he went across from Carpentaria Downs to Hughenden; out there he started on the wool. Out there he had to get another team; another wagon, a big tabletop wagon. Did away with the box-wagon, sold it. For years

"SWAGMAN"

WATER BAGS

Hold Water and keep it Cool.

In getting "SWAGMAN" you get the BEST.

VERANDAH BLINDS.—Striped and Green Canvas. These Blinds are becoming very popular because of their neat appearance and durability.

Any size made to your order.

WATER-PROOF CAMP SHEETS AND SWAG COVERS.—A Reliable Waterproof cover for your swag and sure protection against damp ground.

Don't Suffer from Rheumatism, Buy a "SWAGMAN" CAMP SHEET.

CAMP STRETCHERS.—For the Verandah or Camp, giving the maximum of comfort in the minimum of space.

We make all National Flags

TENTS, FLYS, TARPAULINS, MOTOR HOODS, MOSQUITO NETS, SHEEP BRAKE, all Kinds. WOOL SHEETS, MOTOR CAB DUST AND CUSHION COVERS.

"SWAGMAN" GOODS ARE STOCKED BY ALL STOREKEEPERS.

SWAGMAN

William McKenzie, Flinders Street,

TOWNSVILLE

Henry Brown remembers that there were numbers of swagmen along the Georgetown road when he was spare boy on his father's horse team. A waterbag was essential for survival in the bush and as a boy at Koorboora, E. Cummings was told by his father never to go bush without a waterbag.

he used to cart the wool from Stamford, Catoungra, Whitehood and Corfield. When the motor lorries started to come in, that settled the horse teams, so he got rid of his.

When I was somewhere round about fourteen I was up the Hull River with a fellow named Bunting; carting timber. He had two teams, a bullock team and a horse team. The bullocks were for dragging the heavy stuff out of the timber. Horses are too quick, too mad. Bullocks are very handy. You could turn 'em anywhere in the scrub. And it was nothing for them to get their legs out of the chain, not like horses. Horses, you come to a bit of a downhill and they want to go quick. We'd make our own roads, all up the mountainside. Sometimes we used to have to sledge it out to load it.

Sometimes to take the teams in you'd have to make your own bits of bridges across with the big cabbage palm trees, over bits of creeks. And the logs, we'd pull 'em on with the horses. The double wire from the side of the wagon used to go down under the log, and they had skids, and as they come up – it used to have a link in the centre and a wire used to go out sideways from the link, and as they come up we kept the log level and load it on the jinker. The timber jinker, you could shorten it or lengthen it. Then we had to pull them out with horses. You had to have steady horses for it. We used to pull about two logs a day, or three if they was small.

With the bullocks I used to have to get up at four o'clock in the morning. And by the time I'd've found the saddle horses I could've found the bullocks,

Frederick Charles Hall Collection

A horse team on the Georgetown road. Henry Brown had his first pair of boots when as a twelve-year-old he started work for his teamster father as 'spare boy'.

and half the time you couldn't catch 'em so I used to walk – walk through bladey grass up to y' waist. And if you didn't get the bullocks before sunrise – some of them was very cunning! Once it got sunrise they used to dodge in the undergrowth and stop there. There wouldn't be a move all day till sundown. Then they'd sneak out. You'd have to do without those bullocks for the day. But as long as you could get 'em before sunrise it was all right.

Dad always had a dog with the team, a cattle dog, a blue dog. He never let anyone feed it, only himself. If the dog didn't do what he wanted him to do, he'd get it too! Ha! He'd get the butt of the whip! We had a pretty hard life.

1 In the *North Queensland Register* of 16 March, 1903, there is a graphic description of a nearby family's plight in the same area: 'Mr Glover, who owned a very nice property about four or five miles out of town, known as Glenavon, Mount Louisa, started to walk from town to home on the terrible Monday afternoon. He was accompanied by his son, a little fellow of eleven years of age and the short journey occupied two hours and a half. They had to meet dangers ahead of both wind and water, and the telegraph posts on the road came in handy, not only as guides but as friendly supports over and over again. Master Glover received a bad laceration of the hand from a nail sticking out from one of the telegraph posts. The little fellow, however, bore up manfully although suffering considerable pain and Glenavon was eventually reached. Mr Glover found the house nothing but a wreck and his improvements in other directions things of the past. He shortly afterwards discovered that his wife and the rest of the family had secured shelter with a neighbour residing half a mile away and such was the force of the wind that it took Mrs Glover over three hours to accomplish the distance. Mr Glover declares that the ravages of the cyclone at Mount Louisa baffles all description. Big trees were torn up by the roots or snapped off close to the ground and sheets of galvanised-iron had been carried through the air actually twisting round trees and becoming fixed when they came in the way.' See also Appendix C.

2 Burns, Philp and Co. Ltd. James Burns opened a business in Townsville in 1873 as a storekeeper and shipping agent. His partner was Robert Philp. Their joint ventures in timber-getting, pastoral work and shipping helped pioneer large areas of the North.

3 Allingham, Anne, *Taming the Wilderness*, p. 80. 'Cartage was expensive; Hanns paid £15 a ton for loading from Bowen in 1863, but at the same time Scotts were facing £23 a ton for carriage across the Seaview Range. Perhaps 'a shilling a ton' was a phrase used by Henry Brown's father to signify dissatisfaction with the going rate at the time.

11

Bulliwallah station, 1912 **Fred King**

Born To Floods And Drought

Introduction

Fred King had a scholarly voice, unlike that of a typical cattleman. But it was the voice of a man accustomed to giving orders and to being obeyed. He makes it clear that he became a cattleman by force of circumstance rather than vocation, and his story is told in a somewhat academic fashion, with well-formed sentences, grammar and vocabulary. At times one would almost think it was being read from a script, but for the sudden flashes of genuine emotion; of anger – at the memory of police off-handedness following the killing of an Aboriginal stockman; of disgust at the remembered state of the meat house; of delight at the memory of his own resourcefulness in ridding the homestead of white ants; and of humour. It will be a very solemn reader who does not chuckle about the cattle dogs and the beds. Anyone who knows anything about blue heelers will hear, across eighty years, the grumbly snarls of their discontent at being dispossessed of accustomed creature comfort.

We have to admire the sense of teamwork of 'the girls and Mother', as they set about 'cleaning out the building', discovered upon the family's arrival, to be uninhabitable. Mother, was accustomed to the comforts of the homestead at Womblebank, the girls to Melbourne boarding-schools, but they set about turning the fifty-year-old, slab-built woolshed into a home, with a spirit that a later generation can only admire. Before long the woolshed at Bully Creek had become the homestead of Bulliwallah, where evenings were made pleasant by the sound of knives being sharpened to carve the roast, 'two puddings' were served and, after dinner, there were songs around the piano.

Bulliwallah's original owner, Murray Prior, is mentioned by Rachel Henning in her letter of 15 October 1863. Rachel does herself little credit in her description of him as a 'goose' who

> talked incessantly and all his conversation consisted of pointless stories of which he himself was the hero. The witty sayings that he had said and the clever things that he had done. However, we treated him very respectfully

> and Biddulph gave up his room to him and I think he left us under the idea that a mail to Exmoor was necessary for the good of the country.[1]

Murray Prior was no doubt just a lonely bushman, disconcertedly trying to be sociable for the benefit of two strait-laced English ladies. He cannot have been too much of a 'goose' to have coped with the isolation of Bulliwallah, breeding his own stock, and horses for the Indian army.

Some readers will find the terms 'blackboy' and 'gin' off-putting, but these were not used by Fred King in an offensive manner. In the period of which he speaks the term 'gin' was still an acceptable one, having been derived from an Aboriginal word for 'woman'. His voice, when remembering the two 'house gins', Kitty and Judy, conveyed nothing but the warmth of genuine affection. He had the greatest of respect for the indomitable 'Old Judy', obviously a personality of Bulliwallah life. He describes her as 'queen of the tribe' but this should be understood to mean an 'outstanding person'. It is a mistake to think that Aboriginal people had other than tribal elders in leadership roles.

The King family's concern for the Aboriginal people at Bulliwallah was based not only on respect and liking for them as individuals, but also upon the recognition of the vital part they played in maintaining the economic viability of the property.The oft-repeated accolade: 'he was a fine stockman' or 'a fine horseman', used of Aboriginal stockmen, compares more than favourably with those used for the white employees. Fred King had spent so much of his life in the company of his Aboriginal stockmen that he unconsciously adopted some of their thought patterns. Remembering Captain Yagi, on the trip north, as 'a grey-hair fella' he uses an Aboriginal term denoting respect for an older person.

The medicinal powers of tea-tree oil are now well established, but it is interesting to learn that the King family used sheets of paperbark and tea-tree bark to prolong the shelf life of the sacks of flour in the station store.

Although not in the period of his childhood and youth, Fred King recounted during his audio-taped interview an account of an air evacuation from Bulliwallah prior to the establishment of the Queensland Aerial Ambulance Service. It is so graphic that it seems only fitting to include it, possibly one of the earliest aerial evacuations in Queensland, as part of Fred King's story. His wife had fractured her spine in a riding accident:

> We took her into the station on a truck with mattresses. And then I realised it was a case for the hospital, so I broke the record into Clermont, a hundred and twenty miles. And I got on the telephone there to a man who had a weekly plane service to Mount Coolon. He'd take the pay out and bring the gold back. And he had an old de Havilland, with a huge Sidney Plumann engine in it. And he said 'How big is your landing ground?' And I said, 'It's just a natural piece of ground about four hundred yards square.' And he picked me up in Clermont, and we followed the Overland

1 Adams, David, *The Letters of Rachel Henning*, Penguin Books, Sydney, 1984, p. 144.

> Telegraph line to Twin Hills, and then we picked up a line to a big mountain. And we kept that in our sights, and we came straight over the piece of ground. And he says, 'God help us!' He was an old war pilot and he made a perfect landing in the middle of it. And he says 'Well, we're here, Boy! But whether we'll ever get out of it I don't know!'

The story continues with the patient being placed on board the aircraft after four seats had been removed. The plane is prepared for a rather unusual take-off.

> And then he says 'Have you got a rope?' And they dragged the plane about fifty yards back into an opening in the timber. And they tied the tail of it to a tree. And he started this old Sidney Plumann engine. And he got it up to full pace, which in those days was about two thousand revs. And he waved his hand. And my brother got the axe and he cut the rope! And away we went and just cleared the timber about four hundred yards away!'

The flight to Rockhampton was not without further difficulties.

> About half-way down we ran into a storm, Oh! A terrific storm! He butted away into it. I had my wife strapped to the stretcher and I was holding her down but sometimes she and the stretcher and I would hit the roof of the plane. What worried me was that I could see out of the corner of my eye his petrol gauge and that kept going down, going down. I was thinking 'Gee! We'll never make it! It's still fifty, sixty miles to Rockhampton yet, and this old thing eats petrol.' But we finally flattened out of the storm and got in and got my wife settled into the Mater Hospital there. And later he and I were having lunch, and he was a Scotsman, a man of very few words, but halfway though his lunch he said to me, 'You know what, Fred?' And I said, 'No, what, Harry?' And he said, 'A man must have been a bloody fool to try that one on!'

This account of early days at Bulliwallah is of historic interest for the material on red-water fever, brumby mobs, land resumptions, early mail services, and relations with Aborigines. Fred King retired from Bulliwallah in 1962 by which time the station was fully developed, with modern amenities, electric light, reticulated water, motor vehicles, two-way radio, comfortable quarters and a modern homestead. We can but feel privileged to share his memories of the long-ago, sun-drenched days of the early 1900s when the King family first took up Bulliwallah.

⁂

Born To Floods And Drought

My father was a cattleman, of Irish descent. Dad's parents were among a group who were sent out on account of an attempt on the life of a leading politician. Father was born in Penrith. He began stock work on stations then he gathered together three droving plants and droved cattle to the Kiandra gold diggings. Then he got a contract to drove five thousand ewes up to northern New South Wales. He got a chance to manage a property called Womblebank in the Maranoa[1] in Queensland and disbanded his droving teams. Womblebank was a beautiful property with lovely cattle. I was born at Roma on the 21st January 1896.

I only ever had one toy in my life. It was given me on my sixth Christmas Day, by an immigrant couple Mother had as cook and housemaid. It was a crystal ball and embedded in the centre of it was a gilt pug dog. And you rolled that ball along a table, a cloth-covered table so that it wouldn't run too fast, and that little pug dog did somersaults and handsprings. I prized that no end. But somebody stole it. I used to keep it standing in an old serviette ring so that it wouldn't roll off the shelf. And when I went to get it was gone. My mother, she was very charitable, she didn't like you to condemn anyone. She said, 'You must have lost it.' But I didn't lose it. It was stolen.

I began my cattle work at the age of six. I had had an accident to my hands when I was very young and they were like claws. My father was looking at me one day when I was five. And he said, 'With hands like that, you're not going to be much use to me, Fred,' he said, 'but I think you can hold reins. We'll start teaching you tomorrow.' By the age of six I was helping him with the stock work. I became a very good rider. I had no fear in the bush. I never hit a tree hard enough to hurt. I never had any trouble to keep up with the cattle in the scrub.

Father was an expert at making his own hams and bacon and he'd call me in to help him. There was a pickling bench and you rubbed the salt and spice and sugar into the pork. The bench was built for a man but he used to stand me up on the box so that I could rub it in. Cold frosty mornings! Because of the accident to my hands I couldn't straighten my fingers out and I used to scratch the spice into the pork with my fingers.

I was also in charge of the smoking, and we really smoked it in those days, not just putting a chemical in to make it taste like smoke. Dad built a smoke house, he and the men. They dug out a big pit, about eight feet deep, ten feet wide and twelve feet long. And over that they put a framework of netting and over that three or four thicknesses of corn sacks and potato sacks and over the lot they put galvanised iron like a tent. There was a doorway into it, and a big plank running the length of it. And a rail which all the meat was hung on.

And as a smoking agent, we used the sawdust from cypress trees. And no better! It would burn slowly, and smoke gently and impart a good flavour to the meat. It was my job to look after the smoke fires. I won't say that I loved doing it, but I loved the pork!

And my hands remained claw-like and I got into great trouble with our governesses because I couldn't use a pen or pencil. But at the age of twelve I was sent away to boarding-school and I had a very stormy passage there the first year for the same trouble. This was at Wesley College, Melbourne. I was a fellow boarder of Robert Gordon Menzies for three years. I played against him in Form football matches.

At that time there was only one other station boy there. He came from the north-west of Western Australia, from a place called Quandong. He and I were the only two. Came the midwinter holidays we had to stay at school. When I first went there all the other boys gave me a very hard time because I came from Queensland, and there was the great Kanaka trouble at that time.[2] I think they were very surprised to find that I was white.

But the second year I was there I came under the auspices of the prince of teachers. He took me for special tuition and he arranged for therapy for my hands and he taught me to write. I was thirteen and couldn't write. He used to take me Saturday mornings and patiently teach me to write. And by the end of the year, when I was nearly fourteen I could write fluently. And I could write figures well, and do book-keeping. And solely due to this man's care and dedication.

My two sisters were at Melbourne Ladies College. We used to come home once a year. We'd come up by train to Toowoomba then get on to a western train and go on another two hundred miles to Mitchell. My father would meet us in a buggy and take us the seventy miles out to the station.

Then a man for whom he had droved five thousand ewes backed him to buy a property in Queensland. And he looked all over Queensland and he bought a beautiful property halfway between Clermont and Charters Towers, called Bulliwallah.

I hated cattle work, but through force of circumstances I had to take it on. I had intended to go on to university and be a civil engineer. I was always very interested in every thing, and whatever I did I tried to be a perfectionist, although I got more kicks than ha'pence for it. I was only going to be with Dad for a couple of years after he bought Bulliwallah and then go back to school, but the drought broke that up.

Bulliwallah, that's not an Aboriginal name though everybody thinks it is. It used to be called Bully Creek. A huge creek ran forty miles through it from north-west to south-east and that's how it got its name. And when we came there a lot of the old hands refused to call it Bulliwallah. It was still Bully Creek. We were only the second owners of it. The first owner was a man called Murray Prior, who at the time was Queensland's… there was no Federation then… Queensland's Postmaster-General.[3]

We came up through Townsville and Charters Towers to get to Bulliwallah because the Belyando River was in high flood, and there was no chance of it going down. There had been very heavy floods around Clermont. I think thirty thousand sheep were drowned. I can remember the heaps of sheep stacked up along the stock route to be burnt. So my father got us on to a Japanese boat and took us up to Townsville.

SHIPPING.

NIPPON YUSEN KAIRRA LINE
Brisbane, Sydney, Melbourne
NIKKO MARU .... FEBRUARY
Thursday Is., Hong Kong, China and Japan
TANGO MARU .. FEBRUARY 6
BURNS PHILP & CO., Agents

There were five us altogether. Three girls and two boys. I had a sister, five years older than I, and another sister three years older, and then a sister and a brother younger. The boat was the *Nikai Maru* [sic.] and according to old Captain Yagi… he told me one day... '*Nikai Maru* she means 'Sunshine'. I had the run of the ship, down to the engine-room and everywhere. And I used to talk to the sailors with sign language. I was in good with the captain, Captain Yagi. He was a grey-hair fellow. Once I said, 'Captain, what does your name mean?' And he said, Captain Yagi means 'Eight Trees'.

There was no wharf in Townsville in those days. There was no harbour. We pulled up outside Cape Cleveland, and came in by lighters. The train for Charters Towers didn't leave till about five o'clock. Father took us all to the Queen's Hotel and we got in just in time for lunch. There were three or four little Tamil boys, with breechclouts on, and strings from the punkas in the ceiling, and they had their toes through loops of the string, pulling the punkas with their toes to keep the dining-room cool.

We had a very good meal. And then we took off in the train for Charters Towers. Oh, what a train! They were burning wood, you know! There was no coal up here in those days. Well, we got up to the range, and in those days they used to keep what they call a pusher, to push the train over the range. But the pusher burnt wood, too! And it would start pushing us up a long slope with a huge head of steam and the wheels would spin and it would have to stop halfway up.

We got up to Charters Towers about half-past eight and the people from the station my father had bought were not there to meet us. They just didn't bother! We stayed at the Crown Hotel, run by a very fine woman, Mrs Clarke. She could have been queen! She was very kind and a great organiser and knew how to handle servants. We were there a week – at great expense – but she halved it; she knew the situation we were in.

My sisters were taken down the Brilliant Deeps mine, which was over four thousand feet deep. It was very unusual for women to be taken down the mine. You had to know somebody who knew somebody. But I wouldn't go down. I went down the Lord Nelson in Victoria and I suffered so much from claustrophobia that I wouldn't go underground again.

Then my Dad got two wagonettes from a livery stable to take us out a hundred and fifty miles to Bulliwallah. The first day we went thirty miles to Liontown, which in those days was just a plain gold diggings. We stayed at a hotel there, a very plain hotel, and the next day we went on to Pajingo station. Pajingo was half owned by the manager, Mr Adam Black, one of the finest men I have ever known in my life! Pajingo was almost in a direct line thirty-two miles south of Liontown.[4] We stayed there a night.

The next day we went to Natal Downs, a very big property with which I became very conversant. It was owned by two brothers called Salmon, and managed by a Mr Patrick Salmon, and the head stockman was his brother, Thomas.

From Natal Downs we went to Mirtna, fifteen more miles. And from there the livery stables thought they had fulfilled their contract and they went

Frederick Charles Hall Collection

For the 150-mile journey south from Charters Towers to take up Bulliwallah, the King family hired a wagonette like this one. As was the custom of the day, they stayed overnight at stations along the way.

back. Dumped the whole family of us on the Clarke family! They had Tom, Bill, Zara, Harry, Bob, May and Archie in the household and Mr and Mrs Clarke! And there were five of us kids and Mother and Dad! We became very fast friends for years after.

My father thought surely the people from Bulliwallah would be sending a couple of buggies over to take us. They would have been notified. But, no! We were at Mirtna a week. And Dad thought that was enough, so he borrowed a horse, and rode over forty-five miles to Bulliwallah and then yarded up a big buggy and some spare buggy horses and a couple of blackboys and came over to Mirtna and picked us all up.

We landed at Bulliwallah at about seven o'clock at night, a white frost on the ground, a really perishing night; and we were frozen. There was nothing there! No bedding. No beds. Oh, well, there were some beds, but the cattle dogs had charge of them! And nothing to eat! But there was a big log fire of gidgee logs. That was our welcome.

The people that were there, they packed up and left next morning. Well, when we looked round there was no bathroom. Well, we didn't mind that. We could go to the creek and bathe. But there were no privies, either! Nothing to eat. No stores. But we scrounged up a bit of food. We killed a beast and had beef. And there were some milking cows so we had some milk.

It was about a week before we got any stores, and our furniture with them. All our furniture had been sent up by boat to Bowen and put on a wagon there. But the teams were held up at Saint Anns. The water on the causeway was too deep so instead of the teams waiting for us when we got to Bulliwallah, they didn't get there until the week after.[5]

Now, there was a race club that had its headquarters there at Bulliwallah, the Belyando Amateur Hack Race Club. They had a galvanised-iron store-room with all their gear – tents, tables, cutlery – all stored in this shed. And for that week that we were waiting for stores and blankets, Dad opened the door of this room and got out a whole lot of tents and tarpaulins and quite a few blankets, too. We were taking a chance on the blankets, but anything to keep warm!

My first job was to dig a cesspit for a privy. Well, Dad was a bit of a bush worker in timber. So we arranged that Dad and one of the blackboys would get the timber and adze it, and, oh, what an adze was there! Dad had some good tools but, of course, his were still coming on the wagon. Anyway, Dad went on with getting the timber for the privy and another old blackboy and I went on with sinking the pit.

Well, we went down three feet six and struck solid limestone. I knew nothing about explosives, and neither did Dad. So this old blackboy and I we got that limestone out to a depth of about nine feet, with what they call a gad and a sledgehammer. And that was real work! And in due course Dad had the privy built from some of the timber. He ratted a lot of galvanised iron from some of the sheds to close it in.

And then we had to boot all the dogs out of the building so Mother and the girls could clean it. Those dogs didn't take too kindly to that! Then Mother and the girls made soap, caustic-soda soap. The scrubbing brushes didn't have much in the way of bristles on them, but they had to do.

My next job was to clean the meat house. In your wildest imaginings you can't imagine what that meat house was like! It smelt so bad you couldn't bear to go within fifty yards of it. But anyhow, Dad told this old blackboy and I to clean it. It was built the same as the homestead, slabs dropped in slots. The first thing we tackled was the chopping block. Instead of one big block to chop the meat on, it was four, twelve-inch bloodwood blocks twitched together with wire. And the cracks in between them, I swear they had never been cleaned for forty years! So the first thing we did was to build a fire, and the base of the fire was this block assembly. Dad took the other blackboy out bush to cut some new blocks.

The meat house had an ant-bed floor and the old blackboy and I dug that ant-bed out, carted it away about fifty yards and shovelled it into a gully. And then we built another ant-bed floor. We went and got ant-beds and broke

John Oxley Library

Titled 'A weekend at Bulliwallah station – about 1912', this photograph was almost certainly taken by Fred King himself, as in the audio-taped recording he speaks of his interest in photography. The boy at the front would be his youngest brother. His intrepid mother and sisters turned the original Bully Creek woolshed into a comfortable homestead.

them up and watered them and built a floor six inches deep, a new sweet-smelling floor. But first we took on cleaning the walls. You've seen these long-handled brushes they do tarring with? Well, there were two of those. We got some old arsenic drums, dip drums, and made buckets out of them. We had four of these on a big fire and we went over all the walls with these brushes and caustic-soda soap and cleaned down and after about three days they were smelling pretty clean.

The roof was bark, and it was falling down; we couldn't do anything about that. The only ventilation was two windows. And then my father came and he said, 'Look, you'll have to come and swing on to the end of the crosscut saw with me. First of all the saw's no good. And then the blackboy's never used a crosscut saw in his life.'

So I went out with my father and we cut two beautiful river-gum blocks. We had to roll them to the bank of a creek and draw the dray up under the bank to load the blocks, one at a time, on to it. But we finally got them on and got them in to the meat house. And after that we had a clean meat house. Later on Dad got a travelling carpenter to fix the roof and to put ventilation with gauze right around.

The homestead was built in 1852.[6] It was a slab building, floored with slabs, all bush timber, squared with adze and broad axe. There were two long verandahs, twelve feet wide; and one big room, about fifteen feet square, and two rooms about twelve feet square. There was a skillion dining-room about ten feet wide and about twenty feet long.

The kitchen was a separate building altogether. There was one big room with an ant-bed floor. The stoves had a separate room to themselves, which we called the cook-house and in between was another little ant-bed verandah where the bread was made. There was a little ant-bed verandah where they did the washing-up.

It was originally built for a wool store and then they put in partitions. There was a verandah in the front that ran north and south, and another verandah ran east and west. Originally, when it was a wool store, it was built on the ground near the creek, but in the floods of '93 the water went over that ground, so they decided to jack it up and shift it to a slightly higher position. I think that was done in about '94. They put it up on blocks, three-foot-three.

To move it they put it on sleepers on posts then they hooked two bullock teams on it and dragged it along the sleepers till it was over the blocks where it was going to sit. And so it would not be washed off the blocks, they put in eight bloodwood posts, which went from the ground right up to the roof. And those posts were supposed to anchor it, because the blacks told them that the '93 flood was only little fella, that the big-fella flood would come six feet deep. But it never did.

There was beautiful bloodwood timber on that property. They picked the best of them and they had these eight big posts. They were squared where they went up into the building. And because it was a great place for white ants they charred all that part of them that went into the ground. It was the supposition in those days that white ants wouldn't enter charred wood. It was a grandmother's notion! And they put a certain amount of arsenic in the bottom of the hole.

And later, we realised that the house was slowly being eaten by white ants. Well, we sawed all the bloodwood posts in half and put galvanised iron in between them. That cut the white ants off. Then we jacked all the ground plates up and put galvanised iron on top of all the stumps. But then the problem was how to get the white ants out of the building. It was about three-feet-three down to the ground but every night they'd build tubes down to the ground. We'd break the tubes down, but next morning they'd have made them again. And we could lie in bed and hear them eating our house down!

And I had a bright idea. You know red meat ants? And they not only like meat, they like certain vegetables and fruits. But they love condensed milk! So I got an auger, and every here and there throughout the house I'd drill a hole into the workings of the white ants. Then I'd get a stick and poke in condensed milk. And we got up early one morning after about a week and here's a stream of meat ants coming out of these workings, each with a white ant in his jaws! They used to follow it in until they came to the white ants and then, a big juicy white ant, five-eighths of an inch long! He was right up the meat ants' alley! And in about three weeks they cleaned all the white ants out of that house! For years after that we were pestered with meat ants but on account of that fact we never destroyed them. But eventually Dad had to renew a lot of the building where the white ants'd eaten the timber.

The meat ants had another use. My father planted a citrus orchard, and it was invaded by a disease called smut, which covers the leaves with black, like soot on the leaves, only it was greasy; you couldn't rub it off the leaf. And nothing anybody could advise us would do away with this smut. But suddenly the meat ants took to it and they cleaned every tree of it. And whatever was in it, they took it all. So we let them live.

An article appeared in one of the southern papers by a man who had visited Bulliwallah. He said the blacks in that region must have been very ferocious because both the meat house and the homestead had loopholes for rifles. Well, as far as I know there was never a rifle on Bulliwallah, or certainly none when we came there. And there were certainly no loopholes in the meat house! Or the homestead. And certainly, the Aborigines there were a very fine and peaceful race. I don't think there was ever a firearm raised against them.

First of all there was James Daly, who was one of the finest Aborigines I ever knew. He had visions of being a head stockman but he couldn't read. I essayed to teach him but I couldn't. And he couldn't count. I taught him to count up to eighty-one but try as I might I could never get him past eighty-one. We'd run the cattle past him, and he'd be all right until he got to eighty-one, and then he'd 'Eighty-one! Eighty-one! Eighty-one!' He couldn't go past it. But he was a very fine Aborigine; a big man, about six-feet two, and a very good horseman and cattleman. He had a wife and three children, three lovely little piccaninnies, and a South Sea Islander murdered him. Just killed him out of hand. But Dad couldn't get the police to take the case up. And Dad got on to the police about it but they wouldn't do anything: 'Oh, he was only an old boong, anyhow!' And he couldn't get them moving on it.

See, they had made the local Sergeants of Police the Deputy Protectors of Aborigines and those who employed Aborigines had to pay all their wages into the local Sergeant of Police. Well, it was wide open for racket. In those days we had an opium problem. The local Sergeant of Police might 'stick' to the wages and if the Aborigines came into town he'd pay them in opium and not real opium either, but opium charcoal and chlorodyne.[7]

Mother's favourite was old Kitty. We didn't know how old she was, but we found out she was there in 1859 from a man who bought cattle from us. His parents lived at Bully Creeky Creek in 1859. His uncle, a man called James Macleishin, took up Bulliwallah when it was resumed off a ten thousand square mile property called Mount Cornish. After he took it up he died of malaria, but before he died, he left it to his family on condition that they all lived there. Only one daughter, a Mrs Turnbull, undertook to live there. She came up with three small children, all the way from Moree in New South Wales in a bullock wagon with her husband. And she engaged this Kitty, who was then about twelve, as a nursemaid. And Kitty had lived there ever since.[8]

When these Turnbulls arrived they struck a very wet time. They had only tents, which were badly worn from the long trip up, and there was this big slab building, and they thought 'Oh, well! We'll reside in the building. It's on our country.' But they found it was full of wool, from the head station of Mount Cornish, a hundred and fifty miles west. That later became Bowen Downs.

The Aborigines at Bulliwallah lived in a shanty camp down on the bank of the creek about a hundred and fifty yards from the homestead. As soon as we got settled in ourselves, Dad built them proper quarters. And built them a privy, too. But there was an outcry about that! 'Oh, Boss! Long time we go longa bush! What for we want dis somting!' But, Dad said they had to have it because of the flies. But the snag about the proper quarters was that one old fellow died and after that they wouldn't live there any more. We had to shift the quarters to another position.

When Dad killed beef, a certain amount of it was put outside and my father used to say to them, 'You can have all that now, what you want of it. What you don't use, burn.' They used to like to catch a lot of their wild food, ducks and geese on the creek, and kangaroos and possums. They liked their bush food for a change.

For clothing we were allowed to deduction their wages enough for three shirts and three pairs of trousers a year. And tobacco, too. Blankets, the government used to give them; each one, a pair of blankets, cotton, made in India. They were like a thick flannelette, and some of them would have three or four pairs, left over from the years before. Because as soon as the weather got warm they just slept out in the open, not even on a rug.

The best stockmen were Old Jimmy, Charlie Pinkapie, Albert Twist, Charlie Womi, Prince of Wales, and Old Neddy. Old Neddy; if he was white you could have mistaken him for Lord Roberts! He was of an unknown age but he must have been nearly seventy, and a fine old chap too!

Later we had a couple of white fellows working on the place. A raw Pommy from England. We had to get rid of him. We couldn't stand him. We got some more afterwards. Cheeky! One man had the hide to us not to tell him how to ride because he had been taught in the finest riding school in England! He nearly got himself killed out mustering. One we got was a rather superior sort of boy but nothing upstairs at all! Didn't even know how to put a saddle on a horse. And you couldn't let him out of your sight. And wouldn't do anything, anyway.

There was one boy we had as cowboy[9] and Dad heard him in the head stockman's room in the men's quarters. He'd levered up two short boards in the floor and got in, and was going through the head stockman's possessions. And Dad went for him, and he came at him with the file, so Dad kicked him in the knee and he went down like a bullock. Then Dad jumped on him and threw him outside. And he was fired but before he left Dad made him unroll his swag. Dad said, 'This is not the first time you've been searched! Why don't you give this away and live decently?'

And he says, 'Not me! Only fools work!' And he wouldn't have been much older than me; about sixteen.

But the Aborigines were good types, tall and muscular. The best horseman I ever saw in my life was an ex-police boy. There was a murder done by the blacks down at a place called Murdering Lagoon, on St Anns station, about twenty miles to the north-east. He was one of the perpetrators of that. And the police chased him, but he was such a good horseman that when they got him they made him a police boy. And he used to tell us about his police days. He was a very fine horseman.

Mother used to get the women dresses and underclothes, which they wore, except in the camp when they would just throw them off. Everybody went naked in the camp. They slept naked, too. But the two we had, they were very fine old gins. Judy in her young days was queen of the tribe, a tribe of about five hundred. She was of uncertain age, but she was well fitted to be queen of anywhere. She was Charlie Pinkapie's wife. He was her fourth husband. If we were short of a man in the branding and drafting she was there, at the age of about seventy-five or eighty. When you are dipping cattle sometimes you send the first lot out so they won't be standing in the hot yard. And if we were short of a man to dip the second lot she'd be there as good as a man.

One time her husband Charlie Pinkapie went away with the first mob, and we were branding, my brother and I, and she was handing the brands in from the fire, and Charlie Pinkapie came home with the horses. He came round to the branding pen and he didn't like to see her handling the brands. He reckoned it wasn't a place for a woman. He said, 'You git on! Me hand dispella brands!'

Oh, she told him off! 'You git in there, helpim young fella! Me hand dispella brands!' And that was that.

Another time, they were out having their breakfast in the little smoko shed Dad built for them at the back of the kitchen. And Charlie'd got up with a very sore head and in a bad mood. And Mother always went out and spoke to them of a morning, said 'Good Morning', and asked them how they were. And so Mother said, 'Good morning, Charlie. How are you this morning?' And he just grunted, 'Humph! Humph!' And old Judy wheeled round, 'Wadgjabinbin! Wadgjabinbin! Missus tink you bush blackfella!'

'Wadgjabinbin' meant 'talk properly'. Oh, dear, we got a lot of fun out of that!

The two old gins helped in the kitchen. Old Kitty, the one that was there all those years from 1859, she was a very expert laundress. Washing and ironing. All with the old scrubbing board. Her ironing was perfection. And the other old girl, Judy, she was more in the kitchen, washing-up and sweeping out the kitchen and washing floors. We made our own butter. To keep things cool we had what we called Trafalgar safes, with water dripping over.[10]

When we first went there we pumped water up a hundred and fifty yards from a big lagoon, by hand pump. And it was strange to see how the blackboys used to duck out early in the morning so they wouldn't be put on to the pump. But later Dad got an overhead tank and a windmill and pump and laid the water on to the homestead and the orchard.

The cooks had their own quarters attached to the kitchen at the back of the homestead. Early on we had a good cook who was a tin prospector. And he was a mighty baker. But the rains came and he said, 'I must be up and gone now and get back to my tin fields.' And we never saw him again. He was murdered. He bought stores out of the station store before he left. He couldn't read or write and for payment for the stores he handed Dad a two-pound fruit tin stuffed full of notes of big denomination. Dad said at a rough guess there was five thousand pounds in it. And Dad said to him 'You don't want to carry that about. Put it in the bank!'

'Oh,' he says, 'I don't trust banks! I take it with me.' But he never made Herberton. He was found dead on the road and the money gone.

Now, a typical day: generally breakfast was seven o'clock. The horse boy would have the horses run up and the men would have their horses caught and saddled and tied up in the yard. Then they'd come at seven o'clock to the men's dining-room and get their breakfast and cut their lunch and go.

We'd finish depending on how you'd go with the cattle. Sometimes it was a couple of days, or day and night, because you had to be governed by your cattle. You couldn't just turn them loose. You'd have to get them to a certain paddock, or put them into a yard. Sometimes if you were branding or inoculating, what they call bang-tailing, you had to get them finished and out because cows with young calves must get a drink at least once every twenty-four hours. And they will not stand up to being packed in a yard so you get your cows and calves into the yard last thing in the afternoon, just before dark, and you get at them as soon as it's light in the morning, you draft the calves off and brand them. With any luck you'll get your cattle out to water by early afternoon. But you always tried to be back in the yards by sundown.

At night at the homestead we'd have roast or corned beef, or poultry sometimes, or goat, and vegetables and a pudding. Sometimes two puddings because somebody didn't like one and somebody didn't like the other. Tea or coffee, mostly tea. For breakfast we had porridge and grilled steak or grilled goat chops. We used to grow some of our own vegetables and we always had tomatoes. My father's favourite was raw tomato and raw onion covered with pepper and salt. When night came we used to play cards or the girls would sing songs and play the piano.

We bred very good horses on Bulliwallah. We continued what Mr Murray Prior was doing, breeding horses for the Indian Army, each of the four classes. They had to be 100 per cent quality so you bred from good stock. Dad bred horses for working the property. We never bought horses.

We had a lot trouble with brumbies. There was an old couple had thought they would buy into the Indian Army market and they spent £10,000 in buying horses of the four classes to breed from and turned them loose on their property. There were literally no fences for a hundred miles. Those horses ran wild everywhere; big brumby mobs. Our neighbours used to run them over into our country and we used to run them back. But later we used to systematically shoot them. Those brumbies were a problem to all the places for a hundred miles around.

But our main problems were drought and floods. And diseases. When we bought the property it was stocked. It had been stocked by Mr Murray Prior. But then the big drought was on, 1899 to 1903, and when it broke they got re-stocking from Savannah Downs. Those cattle brought the tick fever down, known as redwater. It decimated all the herds in central

ROBERT RUSSELL
AUCTIONEER
LIVE STOCK Salesman
STOCK & STATION AGENT
Charters Towers
Sale Rooms Mosman St.

Queensland. The total loss on Bulliwallah in four years was somewhere about fifteen thousand head.

There were no boundary fences and no paddock fences. Natal Downs, our neighbour's, was round about fifteen hundred square miles, but as the boundaries had never been surveyed and never been fenced we just guessed at them. And we never had a row over cattle. The Salmons at Natal Downs, Mr Black of'Pajingo the Clarkes of Mirtna. They were all very fine neighbours.

We sold to different meatworks along the coast. I went on three droving trips and hated every one of them, but I had to.

The first droving trip I was on we got a mob of four hundred and fifty ready. We were three weeks mustering them, my father and I and two Aboriginals, old Charlie Pinkapie and another to do the tailing. There were no fences. We mustered those bullocks over about five hundred square miles of country. We watched them by night and these two old blackboys tailed them during the daytime. And we were three weeks getting them together and getting them away.

The second trip was four weeks and only one week of that was dry weather. And not only that, but halfway through the trip there was a bush race meeting. And we had put our five hundred bullocks on dinner camp to rest them. I had two blackboys, the boss drover, who was white, and the half-caste horse boy. I got up from my dinner camp and thought I'd better see the boss about moving the cattle on to the night camp, which was about three miles, and found I was on my own with five hundred bullocks! And I didn't even know where the cook had made the night camp!

However, I took the cattle along a creek and watered them, left them feeding and hunted around and found a good secure paddock belonging to Strathmore station. I put those five hundred bullocks in there for two and a half days, taking them out every day to water. And just at daylight in the third morning, the first of the blackboys came in. He jogged in from the races and he was swaying on his horse and the horse jogged up to the campfire and stopped. And the blackboy went right over his head and fell like a sack of flour; just missed the fire.

That was three days lost, and we went on to the next night's camp. But we never saw the boss drover for another four days. He was hanging up his hat to a young lady along the way. And the men were drunk. So after that – that was my third trip; I would have been about sixteen at the time – I said to my father, 'No more droving under any circumstances!' And my Dad wanted to know why I didn't like droving. He said he liked it when he was young.

In the days of the wagons we got supplies every six months. We kept a store for passing people, and drovers. And people going to Mount Coolon mine, taking machinery and a big traction engine from Charters Towers. They would call in and get supplies. We kept all sorts of non-perishables, and some perishables too. Flour; first of all we built a mouse-proof stand for it, with tin tacked round the legs so that the mice couldn't climb up. Then on the stand we'd put a layer of tea-tree bark, melaleuca, paperbark. We bought the flour in 150-pound sacks, about two tons at a time. And on this stand, we'd stand the sacks up on their bottom end, about two or three inches apart, on the layers of tea-tree bark. And in between them we'd put more tea-tree bark and finally cover the stack with tea-tree bark. And that flour would keep free of weevils for an unlimited time.

Sugar was kept on another stand. Now, ants, particularly the red meat ants, don't look for anything up in the air. They like to be underground on the floor. So we stood the sugar in seventy-pound bags on this high stand and it was nearly always free from ants.

Mr Murray Prior, who owned Bulliwallah before us, had the place for forty years, and he established a post office there. In the historical museum in Charters Towers is one of those stamps they close the mailbags with. It still has 'Bully Creek; 1863' on it. About four horse-mails used to radiate from there. The station manager received the mails and gave them to the horse-mail services and got sealing wax, twine, mailbags and three pounds a year for doing it.

We never thought about the isolation. Its a funny thing, which city people can't understand, you never get bored with station life. Every day there was something different. We were born to it; born to the floods and the droughts.

1 McManus, Mary, *The Early Settlement of the Maranoa District*: 'Mr Warnod, having sometime previously applied for all the country now called Toomloombilla and Womblebank…'

2 Reynolds, Henry, *Race Relations in North Queensland,* James Cook University, Townsville.Chapter 11. 'Between 1863 and 1904 62,000 Pacific Islanders were recruited to work as indentured labourers in Queensland, mainly in the sugar industry. They were known as 'Kanakas', from the Polynesian word for 'man'. *The Pacific Islanders Labourers Act* of 1901ended recruitment and provided for the repatriation of the majority of Islanders by December 1906, although over 2,000 elected to remain, either legally or illegally.' 'Kanakalander', now obsolete, was once a derogatory term for anyone from Queensland.

3 Adams, David, (ed.); *The Letters of Rachel Henning,* Penguin Books. '15 October, 1863. A few days ago we had a visit from Mr Prior, the Postmaster-General who was travelling through this district to decide the places whence a regular mail was needed.'

4 Bolton, Geoffrey, *A Thousand Miles Away*, p 271. 'A new settlement at Liontown came to life for a few years after 1903 when there had been a decline in the rich output of the rich central mines [of Charters Towers]. Some attempt was made to compensate for this by reopening neglected "outside" reefs south and west of the Towers, and Broughton, Reshton and Liontown came to life for a few years.' There were nearby settlements of Leopardtown and Tigertown.
5 As early as 1862 there was a teamster route south-west from Bowen, crossing the Suttor River at St Anns by a stone causeway, the remains of which can still be seen.
6 This date is too early to be correct. *Despatches and Letters of Sir George Ferguson Bowen*, Longmans, Green, London, 1889. In a letter to the Colonial Secretary, E. Bulwer Lytton, 6 March, 1860, the first governor of the new State of Queensland, Sir George Bowen, wrote, 'Fresh bands of pastoral settlers, driving their thousands of cattle, sheep and horses before them, are fast pushing out into the wilderness; and it is confidently expected that in the course of the next five years, there will be a chain of stations from Moreton Bay to the Gulf of Carpentaria.' The original Land Claim for 'Bully/Bullie Creek' is dated 11 July, 1865.
7 *Australian Encyclopaedia*, Groler, 1977, Volume 1, p. 57. 'Employment outside the settlements and missions was under individual contract with a separate Aboriginal wage set by the Director of Native Affairs. Many Aborigines lived on small reserves adjacent to towns under the supervision of police protectors. There was a set wage for men under contract. The arrangement for payment into a bank account held by a police protector was very liable to abuse.'
8 Kitty lived at Bulliwallah until her death in 1926. The dates mentioned, in the 1850s, seem very early and may not be historically accurate. Discrepancies of this nature can occur in personal reminiscences but do not detract from their value as social history.
9 On Queensland cattle stations the 'cowboy' is a rouseabout or odd-job man, not to be confused with 'stockmen' or 'ringers' who do the actual cattle work.
10 Other narrators refer to these as Coolgardie safes. 'Trafalgar' was possibly a brand name.

12

Mount Spec, 1901–1908 **Olive Stallon**

Bars Across The Fire To Put The Billy On

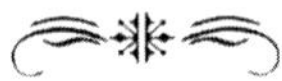

Introduction

Olive Stallon would have been eighty-four when she was interviewed for this remarkable life story, but her voice had the no-nonsense, down-to-earth vigour of a woman who has brought up a family largely on her own. Asked about the Depression she laughed, 'Depression! My life was one long Depression! I had nothing but hard work!' But, as evidenced by the way in which she, a lonely little girl in the mist-shrouded mountains to the north of Townsville, had taught herself to read, 'one letter at a time', Olive Stallon had always been possessed of a tremendous will to make good. At the end of her long life she became something of a celebrity in Mareeba, the town she had come to regard as home, and could say with quiet pride, 'I never learned to sew, but I made m' daughters' wedding dresses. And there was yards in them! And their debut dresses. And at the ball the minister come right down off the stage and he come across the floor and he shook hands with me and congratulated me on my two beautiful debs.'

Even in her later years Olive Stallon showed the same spirit to achieve. 'I had a beautiful garden, and there was this Flower Show. The first year I come second. The second year I come a tie. And the third year I won! I was satisfied then, and I give it away.'

These pleasurable recollections make a satisfying conclusion to the story of a life exemplifying success through hard work. Few remembered childhoods can have been as deprived of basic comforts. The family moved around the lonely valleys at the back of the coastal ranges in search of alluvial tin, never sure that there would be enough to eat, or even water to drink.

'Special Correspondent' in the *North Queensland Register* of 31st May 1900 had described the area:

> Between Running Creek and Running River the road crosses through a mighty gap and a high range of hills. All this country carries tin, but, alas, no water, and deserted bark humpies line the track. All along the road one can see the mullock heaps of little pot-holes with grand, eloquent names

> [sic.]. The two-wheelbarrows-and-a-half over there, that's the 'Silver King' and the broken-down windlass in the middle distance rejoices in the name 'Great Caledonia'. But, to quote Tennyson; 'Dead! Dead! All are dead!'

On one occasion Olive's mother and her children were abandoned in this inhospitable area by a packer, or packhorse carrier, and came very close to 'doing a perisher', or dying of thirst. A kindly prospector, seeing the smoke from their fire 'up in the gorge' came to the rescue just in time.

Graphic reading. Oral historians feel that sometimes the memories of the very old are 'composed' in the sense that, looking back, they review what memories they choose to recall, 'reworking and transforming them',[1] or that much remembering is affected by subsequent experience. Hearing Olive Stallon's story the listener can but believe that she had little need to do much in the way of 'reworking or transforming'. Hers had been a bitterly hard childhood but she had survived. She needs only to state the facts, and she does so, in terse, astringent sentences. She is much more concerned, in the interview, to get on with the story of her adult life, also fraught with hardship but with ultimate success.

For those unfamiliar with the term, 'tin scratching' means panning for alluvial tin, which has the appearance of black, grainy sand, in creeks and riverbeds. At one time quite a reasonable living could be earned in this way in the North. Mount Spec, the 'Cloudy Creek' of the story, is a rainforest area about forty miles north of Townsville. It was well named by the early fossickers, as in the late afternoons, clouds come rolling in from the Coral Sea, obscuring treetops where staghorns, orchids, tropical ferns and wait-a-while vines grow in profusion. One of the three lighters which once ferried passengers and goods ashore from vessels anchored in Cleveland Bay to the new settlement at Townsville was the *Spec*. Perhaps Mount Spec is named after it. Tin scratchers and timber getters were still at work in the area until the 1950s. This beautiful area is now a national park.

Olive Stallon's family – a granddaughter was lovingly present at the interview – are obviously immensely proud of their remarkable forebear, and of the courage and determination with which she overcame the great difficulties of her life. Readers will, I feel sure, share something of their pride and admiration.

1 Dawson and West 'Our Finest Hour' quoted in Alistair Thomson's *Anzac Memories; Living With the Legend*, p. 9

Bars Across The Fire To Put The Billy On

Our father died in Charters Towers and our mother shifted to Townsville. She had five children, four girls and a boy. I was the second youngest. She got a house at Townsville and tried to find work.

One day she dressed me up to take me with her to try to get a job. Then she dressed m' brother and by the time she dressed herself she couldn't find me. I'd wandered away. I was three years old. She got in touch with the police. I'd wandered away across the Causeway bridge and fell fast asleep on the bridge. As luck would have it, it was a policeman as picked me up and took me home and brought me back to her.

Then she married again. She put m' three sisters in the Home because she couldn't look after the lot of us, and she just kept the two little ones, m' brother Archie and me. We got on good together. We was good mates.

This man Johnson she married, he decided to leave Townsville and go tin scratching. My mother must have been mad to go. I was five and a half years old then. They put us on a packhorse, Archie and me in a kerosene case on one side, and m' mother's sewing machine on the other. We went about thirty mile and the next day we were packed up to go up the range.

It wouldn't have been so bad if they had led the horse but they drove us with the team. That track up to Mt Fox, Jacobson's Track, it used to be the old bullock-wagon track. Talk about rough! The horses'd go two strides and slide back one. We got halfway up the range and my mother says, 'For God's sake, Jack, take those kids off the horse before it falls off!' And they just got us off the horse when it went over the edge and my mother's machine went with it! I had to walk the rest of the way, and my brother, well, the packer took him on the front of his saddle. He'd be four and I'd be a bit over five.

That night we got to Hidden Valley. There was a hotel there and a store and we camped there the night. The next day we shifted out to a place called Hoop Creek and moved into a bark hut that was there. We had no bedding or nothing. The only thing we had was flour, tea, sugar and treacle. M' stepfather couldn't seem to get any tin there and we run out of tucker. We was starving. We had to walk into the Valley, Kangaroo Hills, to get a few stores. My sister carried my brother on her back – my mother had got her out of the Home by then. One of them had died of heart, in there. And the other one was married. And there was an old German fellow there. He thought the world of us kids. I got a stone bruise on m' foot and he carried me all the way back, and our groceries, on his horse. My sister carried m' brother because it was too far for him to walk.

My stepfather was going to go to a new field he'd heard about; a place called Hallow. He said that the packer was to take us. This packer fellow, he come once in every three months. And we was on the way to this Hallow with him and he got lost. And he unpacked the horse and just left us there, my mother and my sister and Archie and me, in the bush.

He left us there without any water. It was the 1902 drought. We had no water for three days. The horse fell down in the gully and broke his leg and my mother cut his throat and we drank his blood. We drank our own water. We drank vinegar. We licked the dew off the leaves early in the morning. And what saved us was that this old German where we'd been, he seen our smoke-fire up in the gorge, and he knew something must be wrong and he walked in with a couple of billies of water. By the time he found us he just had enough water to save our lives. Our tongues were swollen. Our lips was cracked. We were in a hell of a mess. And he got another married man to come and help shift us in to Cloudy Creek. They call it Mount Spec, nowadays.

There was only another old miner there called Edward Archer. And there was a bark hut that was already made. There used to be another family there before us but they wasn't getting much tin so they shifted out. And we shifted in. It had a dirt floor, bark beds, bark table. No stove, nothing like that. Camp

Frederick Charles Hall Collection

A bark hut like that in which Olive Stallon's family made their home on the tinfields behind the Seaview Range. Olive remembers: 'We was in a bark hut. It was already made. There was another family there but they wasn't getting much tin so they shifted out.' One family or another would occupy such huts, as hopes of finding alluvial tin or gold rose and fell.

oven, and bars across the fire to boil your billy on. Bladey grass for mattresses. I don't even remember if we had a pillow, but if we'd had a pillow it'd've been a grass one. M' sister and I and m' brother, we used to climb the ladder to get up into the high-hopper, up in the top, up in the ceiling, and sleep up there. Bark huts was good. They didn't leak when it rained if they was all tied down with lawyer vine.

And then the cyclone come, Leonta, and it blew the roof off. Blew m' brother and me halfway across the clearing. Blew all the scrub down and the packer couldn't get in with tucker to us. There was this Jack Lee, he had some horses; there was a big clearing and he used to have horses in the clearing, and him and m' stepfather went down to Townsville to get some supplies. They had to cut a track down.They were gone a week and while they were away all we had to eat was strawberry leaves and potato-tops. That's all we had until they got back.

Mum had a camp oven, a kettle, a teapot and a couple of saucepans. For mugs we had condensed milk tins with handles soldered on, and tin plates. And for the lights an ordinary pickle bottle and you'd have a cork for the top and you'd get the lid of a Nestlé's milk tin and roll it up and put a bit of rag

Frederick Charles Hall Collection

Children were expected to work hard to help keep the family viable. These boys do not look as though they have much time for fun – the old man on the right seems a hard taskmaster. The apparatus is for separating the fine ore from gravel.

through it and that'd be your wick. A slush lamp. That's the sort of lamps we had.

We et wallaby and bandicoot we were so poor. We had nothin' else. Tried snake; carpet snake. It was just like eel; you couldn't tell the difference. But Mum'd only give us one joint. When the packer didn't come we'd run out of tucker. We never got much fresh meat. It was all corned beef. Salt jock[1] we used to call it. Like it? We had to like it, or go without. My brother-in-law would kill a goat, and I had to dress it; skin it 'nd dress it.[2] When I was little I couldn't kill a goat, I couldn't kill anything. I couldn't even cut a fowl's head off. The only thing I could kill was a snake. I'd bash 'em down, or shoot 'em.

An ant-bed oven; to make it they go and gather the ant-bed and wet it, and plaster it all together, and a big hole in the middle and heat it up with wood and when it was real hot you put the bread in and the heat of the oven'd cook your bread. We used to bake in that every second day. We'd make bread in a tub, an ordinary washing tub. We used to put three loaves in each tin, a kerosene tin cut halfways. You cut a kerosene tin in half and knock the ends down and make tins of 'em to bake your bread in.

We used kerosene tins for everything. Water, everything. My stepfather he'd be sitting on a box, and my sister and I we'd have to walk about a hundred and fifty yards down to the creek with two billies each to fill up these two kerosene tins full of water at the door. Whereas he could have carried them up half full and we could have filled them up. But he used to sit just there and watch, and we used to have to do it. That water was for Mum to use at the hut.

To do our washing we'd take it down to the creek; put the dirty clothes in the tub and take it down. We didn't have much in the way of clothes; just one on and one off. We'd make a fire with two crossbars and boil it up in kerosene tins down at the creek. We had a scrubbing board but we couldn't use it much because we just washed in the creek. Mum used to make soap out of caustic soda and fat. She used to make it in a boiler, a kerosene tin. The only fancy soap that was ever bought was a cake of Rexona for my sister's babies. When we finished the washing we'd carry it back up and put it on a bit of rope for a clothesline up home.

I was teaching myself school. I used to take words in syllables. And then there was one miner, he said to my mother, 'Are Archie and Olive getting any schooling?' And she says, 'No.' And he says, 'I'll give them some lessons to do, and when I come back I'll fetch her a present.'

And true enough he brought me a doll. I was about nine then. A china doll, all dressed up. He got this woman off a station to buy it for him. It was the first doll I ever had. It was the *only* doll I ever had! And for m' brother, a pop-gun.

Then mother wrote to my oldest sister in Geraldton[3] and she come down and got me and took me to Geraldton to go to school. I was in Geraldton about two years but I only got about six months schooling. She used to keep me home from school to help her. What I learnt I taught myself. And one day we was doing the washing and it was my job to haul the water out of the well. Forty-two feet deep, it was, that well. And she was washing at the tubs and she looked over and she missed me. I'd gone. I'd fallen down the well. And there was a ladder down it and how I never hit the ladder and killed meself I don't know. And she come running over and singing out to me. And I climbed up the ladder but I was in bed a week with the shock of it.

I never had a pair of boots till I was sixteen. Barefooted everywhere! We used to go shooting wallabies through the bladey grass and everything barefooted. And kangaroo shooting. Oh, I was a good shot![4] And peg out their hides to sell. Once I fired a shotgun at a cocky. They used to come, and they'd eat the pips out of the oranges – and I took this old shotgun and went down and I fired a shot at them. And that old shotgun kicked that hard it knocked me right back over. I had an awful shoulder. Mum had m' arm bandaged up; she reckoned m' collarbone was out. I got an abscess out of it. I had to end up and go to the hospital up in Ingham and they had to lance it. That was the first time I'd ever went to a doctor.

Then a miner, he bought me a pair of boots, first ones I'd ever had. He said, 'Olive, you're too big to be getting around without boots on your feet.' They were brown Bostock kid, buttoned right up here! Oh, they were beautiful! They was a size too small, but I wore 'em! They always hurt me, but I put up with it. I thought I was made! I was that proud of them boots. M' brother and I we went and stood under a bamboo tree and to get m' photo taken. Had m' photo taken in them but they didn't show up for the grass.

1 This is probably a variation of 'salt jerk', meat preserved by being cut into thin strips and dried in the sun; often referred to as 'jerky'.
2 Remove internal organs, head and legs, and prepare for cooking.
3 The original name of Innisfail. There is a story, possibly apocryphal, that a consignment of timber was sent to Geraldton, Western Australia, in error, so the name was changed.
4 The previous 'I couldn't kill anything!' obviously refers to domestic animals with which Olive was familiar, as a younger girl. As an adolescent, hunting became not only a sport but a valued source of income.

13

Charters Towers, 1900–1913 **Marjorie Green**

A Love Of Printers' Ink

Introduction

The voices of many of the stories included in this collection have been those of working people. This account by Marjorie Green (She says, in an aside: 'Actually, we were Hilton-Green') was spoken in the polished accent of one who has had the benefit of an expensive education and has later travelled widely.

The story is of particular interest for the insight it gives into the arduous journey to boarding schools in the south undertaken by many children from well-to-do northern families at quite early ages. Twelve-year-old Marjorie seemingly took it in her stride to 'do it in five days' travelling by train from Melbourne to Gladstone, then 'catching the old *Bingera* north to Townsville', an odyssey at the thought of which many a modern adult would quail. The journey was not without its hazards. Thirteen-year-old Mona Shannon was a schoolgirl passenger among those lost in the sinking of the *Yongala* in 1911.

The Charters Towers remembered by Marjorie Green was, with a population of thirty thousand, the second-largest centre in Queensland, the years of its decline with the failure of the goldfields still a decade in the future. The *North Queensland Register* had taken over the previous *Northern Miner* and under the editorship of Marjorie's father, David Green, had become the most widely read and respected newspaper in the North.

Marjorie Green obviously adored her newspaper-editor father and her brief word-pictures of him, first as a boy, and later as a young man, give us a glimpse of an era in Australian history when schools were a rarity and parents educated their children as best they could. The anecdote of his having shouldered the ailing Scotsman's swag on the Palmer Track is redolent of a time when the 'Mateship of the Bush', much written of by Henry Lawson, was a seminal element in the nascent Australian ethic.

A Love Of Printers' Ink

My father, David Green was the editor of the *Northern Miner.* Then it became the *North Queensland Register* because it was the biggest paper. In those days Charters Towers had about thirty thousand people. Townsville had about nine thousand. But most of the people lived in the bush, so it was the weekly paper that made the money, and the one they worked hard for. It had a tremendous circulation.

They used to call it the 'Bushmen's Bible'[1] and the day that the mail came, station people gave up to read the *Register* and to get their news and to look for anybody that had died, and all that. It was habit. And even years later even when they lived in town they would still give the day to reading the *Register* when it came.

My father's people came from the north of England. He was born near Castlemaine, near Ballarat, in Victoria. When he was young they had an Englishman who taught a district. Then for their secondary education, every Monday morning, he and his brother Jack went into Ballarat to a lawyer and his wife, and lived there for a week, and the wife looked after all the boys… you know, the English way. I think he was a Cambridge man, and Dad talked about him with joy.

So Dad and his brother were better read than most. And when my father was writing a leader or the editorial he could quote Macaulay's essay to so-and-so. He had a photographic mind. There wasn't a Scott or a Dickens he hadn't read. *Don Quixote…* everything.

I understand that two or three papers paid for Father to come north to the Palmer Goldfield. It wasn't going as well as anyone had hoped and expected it to. I think it must have been in its decline. I wouldn't have known anything about this, but my father had a deep scar in the middle of his back and I said to him, once when he was without a shirt, which was very seldom – I never saw him like that – 'How did you get that?'

And he said, 'Oh, I got that when I was young, carrying an old Scotsman's swag on the Palmer. And we couldn't leave anybody behind.' And it appeared that one of the men that they had with them was a miner, and a Scot. And he had made some money and gone back to Scotland and got rather fat and out of condition. And carrying his gear was too much for him. There were about nineteen of them walking. They were going to the steamer at what was known then as Geraldton. It is Innisfail now. And they had to walk most of the way. And they couldn't leave this old man. So Dad had to take his swag as well as his own. Of course, his own was mostly paper and pencil. And I said to him, 'What did you eat?' And he said, 'Well, I had biscuits and bacon.' I said, 'Biscuits?' And he said, 'A sort of dog biscuit. And when it came to the end of the day nothing tasted as good as that biscuit and bacon!'

And then he didn't want to go back to the south; he loved North Queensland so much. He did all sorts of things up North. Some Germans had a smelter in Herberton and he worked there. And he kept writing about the treatment of the men. It distressed him terribly to see the conditions. And the only power he had as a young man was to write, so he wrote madly. And Mr Banfield[2] was on the paper in Townsville here, and saw his work, and asked Father to come as sub-editor.

And then he was asked by some lawyers to run the *Northern Miner* in Charters Towers. The man who had it was rather an old reprobate and didn't care about the truth. And they were proper English lawyers who did care about the truth, and so they bought the paper and so that is how Father went on.

We three sisters were all born in Charters Towers. In those days it was a very gay, bright place. And miners, they are a different type. They were mostly Cornish, and there may have been some Welsh. But my father used to say that sometimes at midnight, in the winter, when they were coming off their shifts, they'd sing, and he would hear them. And he said they were delightful. Those men were very keen on music, and they would be prepared to pay even a guinea, or perhaps two guineas it was, for Melba.[3] And they used to have their own eisteddfods at Easter. They would get together and sing. They had a background of it from where they had come.

I don't remember many of the brass bands, because I went away to school so early, but I do remember once, I must have been ten years old, I was sitting on Dad's shoulders. It was a wonderful band. And they came up and they played in the showgrounds. Lovely music. And then they played some church music, some Elgar, or something like that. And I can remember my father wiping the tears from his eyes, he was so touched. It was such beautiful music! He was entranced with it. He had that love of music and I think most people in Charters Towers did.

At home you would either have something read to you – and we were all in bed very early – we were never up after eight o'clock, and, of course, we loved to be read to. And when we were a bit older we read to ourselves. When my father came home at two o'clock in the morning, if he found you reading he would never scold you. He would just ask you if you had got a good book!

As a family, if we girls wanted money, my father would make us learn some poetry. So we got quite an abundance of poetry. We didn't realise what a joy it was to be in later life. Say we wanted two-and-sixpence for this or that, we'd have to learn, 'Beside the ungathered rice he lay, his sickle in his hand'. You know! 'The Slave's Dream.' Or five shillings we'd get for 'Gray's Elegy'.

And singing round the piano was a great thing in those days. We used to go out for the evening and you'd have to take your music And we had one friend who didn't need to have music. She was Jewish and she only had to hear a song and she could play it. We used to go to one another's places. And we

didn't say we were going to have music, but you would just do it. And when we had parties my father wouldn't let Mother do anything. He used to say, 'Well, you girls can do as you like. But your mother mustn't do the work!'

The house was the merest thing, almost in the office. Because my father always worked until three o'clock in the morning and was down again at eight, we lived there. And the head of the bank who owned the thing would come and he would say, 'David, I thought I ought to come to see the house. It might need some painting or want something.' Well, it wanted a lot of things, but Father would say, 'Oh! It's all right!' And Mr Leuyer said, 'Well, what about letting Mrs Green come out and say something!' So Mother went out and she did get a few things done. But Father didn't care because it was so near for him to go and come.

The only times we ever saw him was when he was in his office. We would rush home from school and peep through the door and if nobody was there, well then, in we'd dart! And we'd have a little time with him. That's how we knew so much about newspapers. And then we would ask, when you were little child, for them to make you a lid with your name on. And there was another

Frederick Charles Hall Collection

The living quarters attached to the office of the NORTH QUEENSLAND REGISTER, of which Marjorie Green's father was editor, were 'the merest thing' because her father liked to live on the job.. This elegant little sitting room has a collection of tropical seashells for the focal point which in cooler climes would be a fireplace.

Monday, January 1st, 1900

Charters Towers
GRAMMAR SCHOOL
CORNER CHURCH AND MARY STREETS.
Principal --- Mr. T. Martin

(Second year Law Student L.L.B. Degree, Melbourne University). Late Classical and Mathematical Master Preparatory Boys' Grammar School, Brisbane; assisted by Mrs. MARTIN, Certificated Teacher.

FIRST QUARTER commences MONDAY, January 22, 1900.

Accommodation for a large number of boarders will shortly be available, owing to extensive additions to the building.

Pupils are prepared for all Public Examinations.

Terms on application.

Evening Classes: Monday, Wednes-

man who did the photography, and we'd always scrounge a bit of sponge.[4]

And they were wonderful men; they were mostly university men from all over Europe. Bismark's nephew was there in Charters Towers. He'd been sent out to New Guinea because he'd been a nuisance, drinking and gambling. That's why we got a lot of people, because they drank too much. Relations hoped that they'd straighten up. But they were splendid men. They could write! I even love the smell of newspapers! When we went down to Melbourne to school, and I'd… (sniffs) and someone would say, 'Smell the printer's ink, Mar?' And I'd say (her voice soft, almost reverent), 'Yes! Printers' ink!'

There was a school in Charters Towers. It was run by a man called Tom Martin. And he was a character. He was an Irishman, and his degree was from Dublin University, in history. And my father was very fond of him and he used to go down and talk. A newspaper being open all night, Father was a man who didn't sleep very well, and he used to go down and they talk about all sorts of things, history and literature and so on. And I think in Tommy Martin's school there were three or four under him to teach; it was for children of ten, eleven or twelve. And Mr Martin had lost his wife and was having a frightful time bringing up his four children. And once, the schoolchildren were sitting in class, and it wasn't an easy class; it was Euclid and nobody was enjoying it. And there was a little garden, a vegetable garden and he was so proud of this. And all of a sudden, one boy put up his hand and said, 'Sir! The goats are in the

State Scholarships & Bursaries.

(By Telegraph.)

BRISBANE, July 13.

The Government has directed that a written competitive examination be held for State scholarships and bursaries, beginning on December 13th next. The conditions are:—

State Scholarships:—Not to exceed 52, of which 40 will be open for boys, and 12 for girls. These entitle to free education at a grammar school, or school approved by the Governor-in-Council, to be tenable for three years, for a period beginning on January 1, 1910.

Fifty district scholarships are to be granted in each currency of three years. Five of these will be allotted to each of the ten State Grammar Schools. The successful candidates must attend the Grammar School nearest their homes. The district scholarships will be additional to the 52 scholarships and 10 bursaries.

State Bursaries are not to exceed ten. Seven will be open to boys, and three for girls. An allowance is attached to these bursaries of £30 per annum, bursaries to be tenable for three years.

Candidates for scholarships and bursaries are to be nominated by head teachers of schools.

garden!' With that Mr Martin threw his hands in the air and the whole school, the whole school, went chasing the goats. And after that, anybody who got into difficulties in their class would suggest there were goats in the garden! But that school was better than nothing and sometimes it as much better than some of the other schools. That was the only other secondary school in Charters Towers.

For boys there was the Grammar School in Townsville. The Townsville Grammar School has been famous! That should never be forgotten. And I don't think we would have got it when we did... long before my day, of course... but the head was a man who was threatened with tuberculosis; and people came out from England for their health. And that was how we got a lot of very able people. But the Townsville Grammar School, it has always had a good name. The old fellows, they were the tops. And they always did tremendously well.[6]

And of course, there was the School of Mines in Charters Towers. I can only quote my father, but at one time he said, 'Do you know, there isn't a mine of any worth, of any value, anywhere in Australia, that isn't being managed by a graduate of the Charters Towers School of Mines!'

In Charters Towers they were just starting scholarships for boys and girls and I think it was 1911 or 1912, the High School for girls, but only a number... I remember when I wanted to do the Scholarship that year Father explained that I mustn't do it, that I was going away to school, and all I would do was stop another little girl from getting one. I don't know, but it can't have been a very big number.[7] And I was weeping at the thought of all the friends who were doing it. So Father said, 'Well, why don't you do it! If you want to sit for the examination.' And he had a talk to the Head. So I did the studying. But I understood it even then, that I would just stop another little girl from getting a Scholarship if I won one, whereas I was going to Melbourne anyway.

And we were all sent away to school. Ethel went first to Armidale, to NEGS and I went to Melbourne because I used to get bronchitis quite often and I had some aunts there and so if anything happened they could contact them. And my youngest sister, she really followed a headmistress that the family thought a tremendous lot of; she had been the head of NEGS and then she went to Abbotsleigh in Sydney, so my sister went to Abbotsleigh.

That was the way it was. It was a great effort to get children away. The expense was so great. Crowds went! They went for the climate, the difference from the tropical climate to go there. Very few of them went to school in Brisbane. Parents thought it was better for them to get a change. And then some went to Sydney. You see, it depends where your parents came from. If your parents had sisters or brothers in a town well then, naturally they would send their children there.

We only got home once a year. We used to come home by ship. That was the only way there was. The train came as far as Gladstone. There was only one time I was able to stay at school for the Speech Night. I wanted to be just in a bit of it; then I had to leave hurriedly. I had to have a cab waiting for me at four o'clock. And then I went to get the train. I got the train to Gladstone. And then I got the old *Bingera* in Gladstone. She was the mail steamer. And so that's how I came home. And in that way you did it in about five or six days, instead of ten. We only had five weeks holiday. You'd get a short one of a fortnight but it would be impossible to get home for that.You couldn't get home and back in the time.

And when you first went you spent holiday time with your relations. And then later you went out with friends. And it was a strange thing, all we who went were Anglicans, and yet we went to this Presbyterian school! The Grooms girls – there were two Grooms in Parliament at the time. And Judge Lucans' daughter. And we all used to come home together. We all used to get the train up as far as Brisbane and then come on together on the *Bingera.*

John Oxley Library

Marjorie travelled five days each way to and from her boarding school in Melbourne, coming home only once each year for holidays. The last leg of her journey was by ship.
In this photograph parents appear to be meeting a girl at the wharf and in the background a boy is dressed in what may be the uniform of The King's School, Sydney. Unease at meeting his parents after the long separation seems to be implied in the way his hands are locked over his head.

Now one good thing about those schools was that everybody was very helpful. I remember we had a plague of… of… smallpox, I believe it was. Or they thought it was. And one day I was hauled out of class. And all the Queenslanders. We were all taken in, and the doctor was there and we were vaccinated. And the telegrams were sent to our parents. Well, the Victorian children didn't get done till a day or two later. I have always recognised how good the teachers were. They did their best to allay the troubles of the parents who were far away. The teachers were a wonderful lot of women. They weren't narrow and they weren't ad lib. But they did their best.

I was a bit different from other children, I hadn't had languages from 'A', and all the other girls had done French or Greek or Latin, or something, and so I was put into what they call a Remove, a class that had to work hard at languages. And I only did Arithmetic three times a week because whenever I came to do Arithmetic I knew it all my own. I didn't even work it out; I put the answer down. And our teacher she hadn't her degrees but she was kept at the school because she got girls through their exams. And she would come round and she would say, 'But, Miss Green, you haven't worked it out!' And I would say, 'But it's so-and-so!' And she would say, 'But I like to see 'equals; equals; equals'. We used to call her 'Old Equals-equals-equals'.

When it rained on a Saturday we all went to the picture gallery. I knew every picture in the Gallery! But being a Presbyterian school they didn't take you to theatres. But my father had written and said that it was part of my education and that he would willingly pay for a mistress to take me. So Irving was there, and Elbar and McCormack. I was a bit too young to appreciate them all but I didn't miss anything. They took us to Clara Butt, but she was in a hall not a theatre. I couldn't see the difference!

When it was raining we wore the navy blue but while I was there they began a new idea. The House Mistress, Miss Vertue, wanted us to have cream coats and skirts. We had white frocks for Sundays, but not one Sunday could we wear our white frocks to church! It was always raining! If it wasn't too cold! And Miss Vertue prevailed upon a whole lot of these old Scots, who didn't appreciate the idea of cream coats and skirts. But we had them, and they were bought at Robertsons and Moffats. And every Sunday when we came home from church we had to go to our bedrooms and take off our 'creams' and the House Mistress would come round and look for any spots. Because they were trying to prove to the men that it was feasible and that the girls looked nice. But sometimes, you see our skirts were fairly long, and mud would splash up. We all had to have a thing of magnesia and rub it on. So we had those and we were known for the first girls who came out of navy blue.

Of an evening we could dress as we liked. That was to give us a chance to express our own style. And two of my friends, one evening, they dressed outrageously. And Miss Vertue didn't turn a hair! She was determined to turn a blind eye!

And we had to entertain each other, to be hostess. First of all you had to write the letter, inviting them, and they had to answer it. And then you had to greet them and see that they were entertained. And I was hostess this night with another friend. And all the time my friends made it so… well, you did it the same to them when it was their turn… they'd look at you with lacklustre eyes, and 'Oh!' (sighs with pretended ennui). It was so difficult to make them be 'entertained'!

And we were told, 'If you are given a present, always undo it. People like to see it!' And I often think when I see people clutch a present they've been given, well, it would have pleased everybody if they had opened it. That's what you want to do, be *pleasing!*

I was seventeen and a bit when I left school. And then later on when Charters Towers was ready to disintegrate (decline), as of course every mining town does, well, Father was ready for that because he had lived near Ballarat. And they bought into this paper down here. I didn't work because Father said the jobs had to be kept for the men.

1 a term usually reserved for the Sydney *Bulletin*.

2 Edmund Banfield was sub-editor of the *Townsville Daily Bulletin* until 1897 after which he lived a reclusive lifestyle on Dunk Island for twenty-five years, where he wrote *Confessions of a Beachcomber*.

3 'Madame Melba's Reception: An immense crowd gathered at the railway station on Tuesday night awaiting the arrival of the evening train, with the hope of seeing the famous "Queen of Song". When the train steamed into the station Madame Melba was met in her special carriage by His Worship the Mayor, Alderman H. S. Thorp, who welcomed her on behalf of the citizens of Charters Towers. Mr John Tilley, President of the local branch of The Australian Natives Association, presented to Madame an Address. A beautiful bouquet of flowers was then presented to Madame on behalf of the Charters Towers Horticultural Society, and little Miss Marjorie Hatton gave her another beautiful bouquet of flowers. Madame Melba responded and said she was deeply touched with the sincere welcome and the presentations which she appreciated very much. She would treasure the Address of Welcome and take great care of it as it would always remind her of her visit to Charters Towers. On stepping from the carriage to the platform at the station Madame Melba was greeted with loud cheers by the assembled crowd. His Worship the Mayor escorted Madame Melba to the Crown Hotel in a motor car kindly lent for the occasion by Mr C. E. Roberts. En route the crowd cheered Madame Melba who responded by bowing and waving her handkerchief.' *North Queensland Register*, Monday 19 July 1909.

4 School slates were cleaned by being wiped with a wet sponge and dried with a cloth. Poorer children had to make do with a scrap of torn rag. Boys were even known to spit on their slates and use their sleeve for drying, a practice much frowned upon. To have a piece of proper sponge would have been considered highly enviable.

5 Charters Towers High School was established in 1906.

6 Townsville Grammar, founded 1896

7 Alice Chapman recalls: 'In those days they picked and chose who would sit for Scholarship. We used to have Higher Class and Lower Class. Higher Second, Lower Second. And if you were in Lower then you worked yourself, and got up into Higher. When it came to Scholarship, well, everybody in the class didn't sit. They picked out two or three.'

14

Stanton Hill, 1901–1911 **Florence Toombs**

Never Much Time To Play

Introduction

Florence Toombs was born in 1896. Her father, a drover, was injured, presumably in a fall from a horse, and the family moved to Townsville to be close to him in hospital. In that era there were no social service benefits of any kind, so hard times were ahead for the little family. Mother took work as a laundress for six shillings a day. She was forced to put the two older girls 'into the Home'. This is a recurring theme when families of that era fell upon difficult times, that of children being 'put into a Home', or orphanage. There was little other recourse for women without a network of family support and no means of income except their own labour.

One of the charms of transcribing oral history is found when Narrators recall actual words spoken long ago. Florrie has a gift of being able to do this, giving her story an engaging immediacy. In the anecdote of Breaker Morant's proposal to her mother she is recalling words of an even earlier period, imprinted on her memory, no doubt, by oft repetition, mother to daughter, of the story. Equally, I am sure that readers will delight in Mother Clare's, of St Patrick's Convent, enchanting Irishism: '...the rest of them sitting down stood out like a sore toe!'

The Rechabites and the Band of Hope which Florrie mentions were Temperance Leagues to which many children belonged as a Saturday afternoon club, but which also provided mutual-aid support for families. The Band of Hope pledge was, 'I promise, God helping me, to abstain from all intoxicating liquors as beverages and to get others to do the same'. A Rechabite profession was, 'Lips that touch liquor shall never touch mine'. These appear quaint now, but at the time children took them seriously, especially as beautifully embossed membership scrolls were presented to those who joined. In the story, we can all rejoice at the kindness of dear Mr Bragge! What better epitaph could anyone ask than to live on in the memory of a grateful child?

Florrie's reference to the loss of the *Yongala* is interesting. The *Yongala* was a well-equipped passenger and cargo steamer, popular with leading Townsvillites travelling to Brisbane, a journey which took about five days. There was no rail link to the south until the 1920s. A famous racehorse of the day, Moonshine, had been loaded in Brisbane for the journey north. The *Yongala* carried no radio and was unaware that a cyclone was imminent between Mackay and Cairns. She went down with all hands on the night of 23 March 1911. Among those lost were sixteen Townsville people, including the matron of the hospital, a thirteen-year-old schoolgirl and three members of the Rooney family, leading timber merchants. The Rooney home in North Ward is now the well-known Yongala Lodge.

Never Much Time To Play

Father was a drover and got hurt and was sent to Townsville hospital. Mother had myself, Hannah, twins, and Baby. She couldn't get a house so she had to put Hannah and me in the orphanage down at North Ward. I'd a' been six or seven. They had wards like a hospital for us to sleep in. When I started to go to school we used to have to walk right down Warburton Street to Central School. It was a long walk for young legs. There was older girls, nurse girls, with us. There was quite a crowd of children; I'd say a couple of hundred.

I got the diphtheria while I was there. They thought it was croup. They had a bit of a hospital at the back on the hill. I was in there when Cyclone Leonta was on. Leonta means 'Raging Lion'. The roof iron was hitting the trees and twisting round. I was there when I got my throat done. Old Dr Humphries done it. I had a tube in my throat for a long time. They wouldn't let me out. Dr Humphries used to get me down in the dining-room, a big long room, the dining-room in the orphanage, and I had to say, 'Miss Ball' – she was the matron – until I cried, to make me talk. He gave me a doll, a lovely doll. But they wouldn't let me take it with me when I left. And years after, when I was about thirteen, I was working for the Nesbits in Stokes Street, and I had to go to the door, and it was Dr Humphrey. 'Oh!' he said, 'It's Florrie!'

'Yes, Doctor,' I says. He says, 'Go to the end of the yard and say, "Miss Ball".'

Mother took a cottage in Hale Street and she got us out of the orphanage. Hale Street wasn't much of a street really, just a bit of a goat track. She was paying six shillings a week rent. The allotment was steep sloping. At the front you could step right off the grass on to the verandah from the hill, but at the back it was high and there was steps down. We had our bathroom underneath. The bath was just a concrete hole in the floor. We'd pull the plug out and where the water run down we had five mango trees, a mulberry tree, a lemon tree and a custard apple. Well, every Christmas the Chinamen used to buy our mangoes. They used to have long sticks, and on the sticks they'd have bags, and when they pulled the mangoes they'd drop into the bag. Oh, we had some lovely mangoes. It made our Christmas!

Mostly we washed under the house; boil up in kerosene tins. We had a tap on the back verandah next the kitchen. The stove in the kitchen, when we wanted to bake, we had to light a fire underneath it. And the oven was in the centre and across the top was bars. Bricks on both sides and the bars. A colonial oven they call it. When you want to bake you used to have to light a fire underneath. Oh, I hated lighting that fire. One day Hannah lit the fire on top and it wouldn't burn so she put kerosene on it and the chimney caught on fire. We had to run next door and Johnnie Matthews brought his hose and put it out.

Aborigines used to come round and sell props for the clothesline. Old King Billy, he was king. He had a thing across his chest with his name on it, a big plate made out of brass. They had a big camp out at Rowes Bay. They used to come to Hale Street and when I seen 'em coming, I'd be scared. There'd be mostly men. Very few women. They'd be 'yabber, yabber, yabber'. I'd close the door if I was on my own. If they seen y' it was, 'Gibbit

James Cook University

Townsville Orphanage about 1900. Florrie and her sister were placed in care when their parents were unable to support them, a not uncommon practice in the days before a welfare system made life a little easier for some of society's less fortunate.

chuga! Gibbit tea! Plour! Anything!' They wouldn't go till you give them something to eat.

Father was in hospital a good while after his accident and after he worked for a man who had the contract to light the gas lamps. He used to have so many men going round of a night, and they had a long stick and they put it up and pulled the gas lamp out. Each man had a certain section to do, walking.[1]

Mother went out washing. She got six shillings a day and she finished about eight o'clock at night. Many a time I went down Wills Street to come home with her. She said, 'Oh, Florrie, don't come down in the dark! I don't like you coming down in the dark. You never know who might be about!'

I says, 'I'm not frightened, Mum.' I used to still go because she would come home that tired. She worked hard, at a boarding house, The Rocks, up on Melton Hill. Two spinsters kep' it. Every Christmas they used to make us a big cake. Took Mum all her time to get it home.

Where the Cutting is now, we used to climb that hill, and we used to go up and catch goats. It wasn't easy. There'd be the four of us and we'd get the kiddies. There were some people called Emlyn that lived on Melton Hill. They used to buy the little kiddie goats off me. They'd pay me five shillings each. It was good money in them days.

Frederick Charles Hall Collection

A bush wedding conducted by the Reverend Charles Frederick Hall. Florrie Toombs recalled her mother's experience at Duckworth station when 'Breaker' Morant burst into the kitchen saying: 'Nellie, the Bush Parson's here! You said you would marry me.'

When it rained there used to be a waterfall come down off Castle Hill, down the gully and down through Wills Street and through Walker Street. It used to go down like a river into Ross Creek. There'd be big waterholes there and we used to go down there and swim in them.

Mother was born in London. She come out as an immigrant girl. And the immigrants had to stop at a place that the government had in Brisbane till they got a job. She was sent to a station called Duckbrook. And who do you think was on the station breaking in the horses! Harry Morant! Yes! And she told me stories about him. Her name was Eleanor, Eleanor Garner. And Harry Morant come into the kitchen one day when she was working, and he always called her Nellie. And he says, 'Nellie, when are you going to marry me?' And she laughed. She thought it was just a joke. And about three or four months later, he comes in and, 'Nellie,' he says, The Bush Parson's here!'

And she says, 'What about it?' And he says, 'You promised to marry me.' She says, 'I did not! I wouldn't marry you! You drink too much!' But he was good with horses. That's why they call him Breaker Morant. She says he was a nice looking fellow, but he drank. And she was a nice, fresh-faced Pommie-girl, you know. Wasn't a bad-looker.

One day at Central School I wasn't well. Miss Caldersmith, she was the head of the school, she says, 'You go into the room then, Florrie, and lay down. There's a blanket in there.' And she shut the door. And I was forgotten. I never came home from school. Mum went to the police. And in the end they thought about the school and they went to Miss Caldersmith's house near the school. 'Oh! she says, I put her in the room!'And they went over to the school and there I was, asleep!

Anyway, when I had to go back to school I sat in the gateway and I wouldn't go in. And they'd try to get me into school and I'd scream. And there was two girls living near us, their name was Williams, Anna and Elsie. They were Catholic. They said to me, 'Florrie, why don't you come to our school?'

I said, 'My mother's Church of England. She mightn't let me.' But I put it to her. Course, we were only just living, and it was sixpence a week. We had to work for everything we got. That's when I started running messages for the neighbours to get m' sixpence a week so I could go to the Catholic school. I used to have a cart, a billy cart, made out of a case with two handles. I used to go down to where Garbutts used to be and get the people's meat. If I got threepence, I'd be rich!

Anyway, I went! And I loved the nuns; Sister Mary Clare, Sister Mary Bega, Mother Clare. My teacher was Sister Mary de Sales. She was one of the Hayles, from Magnetic Island. Oh, she had lovely hair. She was a novice. When she become a full nun she wore a cloth. I said to Hannah one day, I says, 'How does she get all that hair under that cloth?'

'Oh,' she says, 'They cut it off.' Oh, I thought it was that terrible! She had a lovely head of hair. Long!

I was a kak-hander when I went there. They made me write with my right. They'd hit me with the ruler. We had school slates and slate-pencils. We had to buy our own exercise books. One of the Taylor girls – their father kept the Federal Hotel, out towards West End – she was a left-hander too. And she was a Protestant. There was quite a few Protestants used to go there. When they had catechism the Protestants went out. I used to run all their messages for them.

One day the Bishop come; came in suddenly. They all stood up, of course. And I stood up with them. And some of the Protestant girls kep' on sitting down. Mother Clare came to me after. 'Florrie,' she said, 'You're a sensible girl! I was glad to see you standing up. The rest of them sitting down stood out like a sore toe. Drew attention to themselves!'

The school had a verandah right round and steps down the front, and when we come out of school we used to march right round and come down the steps, two by two. Sister Mary Bega, she was a big nun, tall. And when we come out of school, she'd stand at the corner watching for Hannah and me to come round. 'You got to stop behind and sweep the school out,' she'd say. I'd say, 'Sister, I got to get home and cook the tea.' My mother was working and I had to cook the meals. She'd say, 'It won't take you long.' But it would be after five o'clock before we finished.

When Mum was working I'd come home from school and cook the dinner. Sometimes I'd make a stew. One time I made a stew out of some corned beef and it was too salty and Dad hit me. And I got on the steps to get down – our house had steps to the backyard because of the slope – and I got on the steps to get down, and he'd had a few drinks in and he hit me. Oh! Didn't Mum go for him when she got home! Dad was only a little man. Only five foot two. I take after him in that. Small feet; small hands.

And my sister she was a real devil. Many's the time I've protected her and got a hit instead of her. And Mum'd say, 'You leave Florrie alone! There's the one you ought to hit!' If Hannah got a smack she'd roar like a bull as if she was being killed, but me, I used to go away and fret. I was different to her. I favoured Mum more. Mum was quiet. Mum was a lady. She used to write stories; and songs for the Salvation Army. She had a tote[2] full of novels, too. And whenever they said, 'Where's Florrie?,' it was: 'Oh, reading! Reading Mum's books'.

We never had much time to play. I had a lot of responsibility. More responsibility than a child should have. I was older than my years. We never had much in the way of toys. When we got toys it was from the Rechabites.[3] Well, one Christmas Eve it was a Saturday, and we had to have senna tea[4] every Saturday. 'Mum,' I said. 'Its Christmas Eve this afternoon. We don't want our senna tea today.' But she says, 'You got to take it.'

Well, at the Christmas Tree at the Lodge, my little brother Bertie was only about four and he wanted to go to the toilet. There was no toilet and I had'a take him round the back of the shops. And when we went back I'd lost m' ticket for the Christmas Tree. And I was crying. And Mr Bragge, he was the head of the Lodge, he come over and he said, 'What's the matter, Florrie?' And I said, 'I lost m' ticket on the Christmas Tree!' And he said, 'Never mind! The last one on the tree will be yours!' And it was a lovely doll! A beautiful doll. I had it for years. I cherished it, that doll.

I was out working when I was thirteen. Things were bad. I was working for Dr Nesbit where Dad was. Father was a bushman; though he come from London he was good with horses. He was getting thirty shillings a week, starting early in the morning, driving Dr Nesbit around in his buggy. If Dr Nesbit had to go out of a night time, Father would bring the buggy round and take him. Mostly I slep' there.

Mrs Doctor Nesbit used to have Pekinese dogs and Father would have to wash them and he didn't like the job. One day one of them bit him and he

-ARNOTT'S-
MILK
ARROWROOT
BISCUITS.

Look for Arnott's
Name
on each Biscuit.

WILLIAM FRANCIS

ARNOTT'S
Milk Arrowroot
Biscuits,

FOR GROWING CHILDREN AT ALL TIMES WHEN HUNGRY

KEEP A TIN IN THE HOUSE.

They make an excellent breakfast dish in place of porridge, soaked in hot milk, with sugar.

They will be found very delicious and satisfying for lunch or supper with a glass of milk or cocoa.

Arnott's Milk Arrowroot Biscuits---The Childrens Food.

WM. ARNOTT, LTD., NEWCASTLE, N.S.W. MESSRS. R. M. GOW AND CO., MANAGING AGENTS, BRISBANE.

Like Florrie's charges the Nesbit boys, other middle-class boys of the time were dressed similarly to girls in the first years of their lives. Published testimonies of 'satisfied customers' were widely used in the advertising of the era.

gave it a slap. Oh! Didn't she hit the roof! Just about went mad. She had baskets lined with cushions, satin, for the dogs. If they got in the road in the kitchen I daren't touch them. I did mainly kitchen work and washing-up. I used to have to answer the door, and bring in the tea things on a trolley. One of the boys, he was called John. One day I called him Jack. She says, 'His name is John, not Jack.' 'Oh,' I says, 'My brother's name is John and we call him Jack.' She says, 'He's not your brother!'

I'd have loved to have been a nurse but I didn't have the education. I used to get in Dr Nesbit's study when I was cleaning it out, and there was X-ray pictures on the walls and I'd be looking at them One day he come in. And he says, 'You interested in that, Florrie?' And I says,' Yes, Doctor.' And he explained to me about X-rays.

Mrs Dr Nesbit, she used to say to me, 'When Doctor's had his lunch you're not to call him out.' One day a woman came in with a baby that was sick. My mother had lost a baby, a little girl, Clara. There was this girl who lived nearby to us and she asked if she could take Baby for a walk and she didn't bring her back until near night time and when mother went to feed her she took convulsions and died. So, of course, muggins, I told the doctor that there was a woman with a sick baby. He got up and went straight out. Didn't Mrs Dr Nesbit give me the rounds of the kitchen over it! Anyway, he comes to me afterwards and he says, 'If anyone ever comes to me like that,' he says, 'Just knock on the door. Don't come in, but just stand at the door and give me the office.'[5] Oh! I liked him!

I got apprenticed to the shirtmaker at Hollis Hopkins when I was fourteen. That was when I learned to sew. We were all girls in there, about twelve or fourteen of us. The only man in there, he cut out the shirts on a big long table. We got five shillings a week. You got a pound a week for piecework. Piecework was, one girl made collars, one girl made fronts and pockets, one girl made sleeves, and it would go from one girl to the other till the shirt was finished. And we used to have them very fine silk shirts then, and the fronts were devils of things to do and I always used to get them and I used to go crook about it. I stopped home a couple of days thinking somebody else would get them, but they was all waiting for me to come back to. That fine silk! You had to follow the warp of the material or it wouldn't lay straight.

After I was there about twelve months I left. My mother got lawyer's letters, lawyer's letters.[6] It ended up I had to go back. Mrs Hollis Hopkins, she was an English woman. They had the factory at the back of the shop. She was standing waiting on the top of the steps when I come back and she stopped me. 'Good morning, Florrie,' she says. I says, 'Good morning' (guardedly). She says, 'What did you want to leave us for?' I says, 'I was doing piecework and wasn't getting piecework wages! Anyway,' I says, 'you let May Harvey go. Why couldn't you a' let me go?' 'Oh,' she says, 'May couldn't sew like you.' She didn't offer to pay me any more! Eh!

We had steam machines. There was a long table and underneath the machines was a long belt and then when you wanted to sew you just pressed your foot down. You didn't work your feet; just pressed. If you pressed too hard it went! When I first went there I had to make buttonholes and put buttons on but later they got a machine. But when they first tried the button machine it used to smash buttons galore. And the girl that was on it said, 'I wish this thing had gone down on the *Yongala*!' That was the time the *Yongala* sunk. Nineteen hundred and eleven.

Mother had a boarding-house by then, over in Davidson Street, with tea rooms. Mainly for the wharf lumpers. She'd give them their breakfast and tea of a night, rissoles, sausages, nothing fancy. There was a big shed out the back where they slep'. I used to wait on the tables when I come home from work. And this morning I said to one them, 'Didn't you work last night?' He says, 'No, the boat never came in.'

It was the *Yongala*. There was a cyclone that night, and she sunk off the Cape. Some of the Rooneys was on it. Nurse Rooney and one of the brothers. And some nurses that had gone down to do their exams. A terrible lot of Townsville people was on it. They never found any bodies. All they found was a horse's body on Cape Cleveland, on the other side.[7]

In 1912 the grasshoppers come. I was at Hollis Hopkins then and we was watching them from the room. They was just like a cloud. When I went to work that morning everything was lovely and green. And when I come home there was not a blade of grass left. Everything was eaten. And people that had fowls couldn't eat the eggs because the yolks was like blood from the fowls eating the grasshoppers.

1 Another Narrator, Oscar Crowther, recalls that in the first decade of the twentieth century, street gaslighting extended as far as the orphanage in North Ward, and to Stagpole Street, in West End. The first building to be illuminated by gaslight in Townsville had been the Town Hall, in March 1883 when fourteen lamp-posts were erected in Flinders Street.

2 Carpet bag

3 A Temperance Lodge. In pre-Social Security times such Lodges played an important role in the lives of the less well off. Members paid a small weekly subscription which entitled them to benefits such as doctors' fees, funeral benefits, annual outings, etc.

4 A laxative

5 Tip off; advise confidentially

6 If Florrie had been formally apprenticed she was legally bound for five years.

7 See Appendix C for an account of the loss of the *Yongala*.

15

West End, 1904–1914 **Constance Hill**

Mother Always Liked A China Teapot

Introduction

Driving round the North, you sometimes see little old cottages crouched low to the ground, verandahs front and back, a tank-stand and drooping bougainvillaea. Who hasn't wondered about the lives once lived beneath their unpretentious roofs?

Connie Hill's account of growing up in West End gives us an intimate glimpse into the family life of just such a home. There was Alf, the earnest brother, rejected by the Army in the Great War for being a half-inch too short. There was Les, the creative one, who could fashion 'a lady with a baby in her arms' from the clay down in the gully. There was teasing Ray who couldn't resist a tug at Connie's ribbons, knowing he could get away with murder because of his asthma. Last of all there was Connie, busily happy down in the cubby house with her dolls Doris and Phyllis.

Family life is sketched with lovingly remembered detail. The boys rake the leaves in the yard on Saturdays. They help with the washing-up on Mother's big baking day. They look forward with eager anticipation to the event of the year, the Sunday School Anniversary. And always, there is 'the feather duster' hanging on the wall for disciplinary purposes. It can't have been used very often, for Connie informs us 'one word from Father and we knew!' Oh, admirable state of affairs! How has a later generation of parents lost this fingertip control?

Father set such a wonderful personal example that the dreaded feather duster was not often necessary. 'Father was a hard worker'; Father 'loved the ground and could grow anything'; he was thrifty, the mortgage was paid every Saturday without fail; he showed foresight for the family's welfare: the gully was kept cleared so that 'the house was never flooded'. He upheld time-honoured standards: 'The boys went to church with Dad'. He was devoted to his family, and the children knew it. Connie adored him. If Father so much as looked at her with a warning eye it broke her heart. It comes as an enormous surprise to learn that this exemplary man was less than four feet nine inches tall. But later we can rejoice to hear that he lived to eighty-four!

And wonderful Mother! Making calico serviettes 'nicely hemmed' in which to wrap the children's lunches, in an age when newspaper generally sufficed. And taking the children on picnics 'up the Hill' with a tablecloth to spread on that 'big flat stone'. How strange to consider that the rock is still there, warm to the touch in the sun, and all the happy picnickers gone these many years

There are things about which we yearn to know more; of the brother who 'died one month short of his fifteenth birthday', and why poor dear Mother should die when Connie was just eleven. Such grief flooding the once happy little home! But in recording oral history the Interviewer is often hesitant to probe too deeply into long-forgotten sorrows.

Connie Hill's was the first Life History, selected at random from the collection of over a thousand tapes in the North Queensland Oral History Project at James Cook University, which I transcribed. I grew to love her sweet, gentle voice as she related her story – presented here almost word for word – and I found myself identifying with her childhood experiences: the cubby house, the picnics up the hill, the walks to Rowes Bay, the Sunday School Anniversaries, all new white frocks and nervousness. Connie Hill's story inspired me to investigate the life histories of others in the North Queensland Oral History Collection. She was, in a sense, my 'flagship'. I love her, fondly cherishing her memory.

⁂

Mother Always Liked A China Teapot

I was eight when we came to live here in Baxter Street, West End; 1904, the same year as Cyclone Leonta.[1] My mother kept me home from school that day because it was boisterous and the pennants were up at Pilot Hill down near the jetty wharf. They used to put them up when there was warning of a cyclone. My brothers and I were at West End School and all the children were sent home. And one of my brothers and this other boy, they saw a sheet of iron blow off Looby's establishment – Loobys was a plumbing business – and they bobbed down flat; and the sheet of iron flew over their heads.[2]

We used to get a lot of blows, nearly every year. The house we were renting was a little old place, with verandah railings, so my mother said, 'Well, Connie, we'll go over opposite to our friends, Mrs Bradshaw, and we'll see the old home from there. Probably the old home will get blown down.' And mother took clothing for my father and my brothers, dry clothing and lamps for night time. And of course, it blew, and we were looking at the old place, but not a thing happened to it, only a paw-paw tree blew down and a kerosene tin went spinning round the yard (chuckles at the memory).

We were renting that house for five shillings a week; a nice little cottage on low blocks; a front verandah with wooden railings; and a front room, and probably be three bedrooms, and a dining-room and kitchen. There were five children and I was the youngest. I was a babe in arms when we moved there. One of my brothers used to say, 'I can remember nursing you. Mother would say, "Now sit down there against the wall", and she'd put you on my knee and give me the bottle.' That street is called Baxter Street now, but it was called Griffiths Street then.

My father was born in Cornwall. Father was only short but his family were all tall. He contracted rheumatic fever when he was only twelve years old. And he had a bent arm. The doctor said to his mother, 'Now you look after the lad, but you won't rear him', and my father lived till he was eighty-four! But he had to go out to work when he was young, because he lost his father, so it was all hands turn to work. He worked in a flourmill in England, in Cornwall. He used to go down to Lands End; and he remembered where Marconi built his station;[3] Marconi the wireless man.

And when he came out to this country he brought those paperweights from Cornwall. He was seventeen and he worked in a grocery establishment here in Townsville, and he had to sleep on bags of wheat and hay. Then he worked for Jack and Newells, in Cairns. Father was a bulk-store man; in groceries. He didn't drink, and he was in charge of the strongroom.[4] He used to make sauces and colouring for cakes. They had great big tanks and he had like a prop[5] and used to stir the sugar round with it. That was at Hulberts.

My mother was a Victorian. Her father used to work in a bookstore that used to trade between England and Australia. One trip that my mother's father made going over to England, the boat was shipwrecked and all hands were lost. But he had left enough money to educate the children. My mother was a twin and the twins were the oldest and it was decided that they should be sent to England to finish their education. And on their way their boat was shipwrecked too and they were all thrown on to an island. They were there for three days in just what they stood up in. And then they were rescued and taken on to England.

And when their education was finished, my mother's sister wouldn't face the journey again, and she stayed in England and married a cousin. He was from a Scottish family that ran the *Greenock Times*. That's who I was named after, my Auntie Constance, Mother's twin sister, and I was given the two grandmothers' names. 'Constance' runs through the family. My mother was Florence. Mother returned to this country and became a governess, thus meeting father. And how she got to North Queensland was that a sister of hers had married the first Primitive Methodist minister in Cairns. And my aunt was rather delicate. So Mother left the governessing to go and look after her sister. While she was there she met my father, and, well, my uncle married them.

When my father and mother got married, it was the last day of the old year and they came down to Townsville from Cairns on the boat. Their luggage was all packed and put on board and when they arrived in Townsville, which was New Year's Day, the wharf labourers wouldn't work because it was a holiday. And when Father went to get all their belongings the following day, there was one crate missing and this had the silver that my father had bought and had stamped with their initial on, 'H', and the portion of the wedding cake that was left. And that box was never ever found. So Dad had to buy new silver and have the 'H' stamped on. I'm using some of it still.

So, after Leonta my father said, 'You know, there'll be trouble every year'. He meant the cyclones. And everybody was anxious to have their own home, and he was offered this piece of ground, two allotments, a half an acre, and he decided to have the home built. That would be at the end of 1904.

The carpenter's name was Sandy Wyatt. The inspectors in those days didn't leave any stone unturned. It had to be just perfect. There was a back verandah just like the front verandah. The carpenter said to my father that he had made a little mistake and that the dining-room should have been a little bit wider. But he said to my father that if he would let it go at that, then he would lattice in the front verandah. So the front verandah had the lattice work with the railings underneath. The laundry was downstairs with the copper and everything. And the kitchen and dining-room downstairs. We just had our meals and then came upstairs. I was the only girl so I had a room to myself. And of course in those days, lots of people slept on the verandah so the boys were on the verandah.

We never got flooded. The gully came right down out on to the flat towards Garbutt's. And my father and my brothers always kept it cleared and that took the water away. They've put pipes now. Once I was sitting sewing and I thought,'Now that rain's been continuous all Friday, all Friday night, all Saturday.' And I looked out and you could see nothing but water. And we had seventeen inches then. Seventeen inches!

And when we had this home built in 1904 it cost my father two hundred and ten pounds. And Alf, my eldest brother, used to go in every Saturday morning, with five shillings to the bank to pay off the house. Alf, he went to the Central School. He started school there and he liked it and wanted to stay there. He used to walk to Central over the Hill, backwards and forwards, every day. But the rest of us went to the West End because it was nearer.

My father loved the ground. We had everything growing. People used to say, 'What Johnny Hill couldn't grow, nobody could grow.' Paw-paws and mangoes and bananas. And flowers. He loved flowers. And fowls and goats. Everything! The goats used to run on the hill by day, and come home at night. They were just for the milk. Most people had the same.

We used to buy our meat. And bread was sixpence a loaf. If you wanted a stale loaf that was yesterday's bread, it was a penny cheaper. A slice of bread and honey. A slice of bread and dripping. Many people went to school on bread and dripping. The children used to say, 'What have you got on your bread today?' 'Oh, I've got bread and dripping.' If you said, 'Oh, I've got bread and jam', it would be 'Oh, I'll swap you'. Boys would swap. Not so much the girls. I never ever swapped my lunch. George Keyatta, that got into parliament, he never had anything but bread and dripping when he was at school.

In the winter time, it was pretty-well dark when we'd come home from school. We didn't go in till half-past nine. And we'd come out at four o'clock. So in the winter, when we'd walk from West End school, it'd be pretty-well dark when we got home. But my mother always had something ready for us. And when there was a stew, we'd have some gravy out of the stew and a slice of bread. And bread and dripping off the roast. That was lovely with some salt and pepper on it. Oh, yes, plain wholesome food. I don't think the shops closed till six o'clock so my father never came home before half-past six.

Generally for breakfast it was porridge. Rolled oats. And then a boiled egg or a poached egg on toast. Toast made on the wood stove. The menfolk always had a bigger breakfast. Stew that was left over, or steak and onions, or sausages. We had good breakfasts and good big lunches too. Bread and cheese or meat, German sausage; might have chutney, homemade of course. My mother generally made serviettes, calico serviettes to wrap round our lunches, always hemmed and made nice. Oh yes! She'd wrap them in the serviette and then wrapped in newspaper.

Some just had it wrapped up in newspaper. Little lunch, we'd get a sandwich out, or cakes or biscuits. Everybody's mothers baked pretty-well every day. And of course Saturday it was a big day's baking. Oh yes. And of course we lent a helping hand. Wash-up the dishes, and scrape out the dishes that mother had baked in.[6] And, Saturdays, the boys had their work to do. They had to clean the yard. Rake the yard. Everyone had big mango trees and there were plenty of leaves on the ground. We all knew what we had to do.

If there was a holiday we would say to Mother, 'Ma, would you take us up the hill for a picnic?' And there was a great big flat rock and we would take our basket of eats, and perhaps a billy goat cart and leave the billy goat cart at the foot of the hill and climb up where this rock was. And mother would have the table cloth and all the eats. Oh, that was wonderful!

Or she would take us down on the beach. And then we'd walk on down to Rowes Bay. And perhaps friends would take their children too. And there were people called Hobbs, had a brickworks, somewhere just past the railway line. The church people would all go. We'd take our carts, our billy goat carts, and, oh, we'd have a wonderful picnic.

John Oxley Library

Connie Hill's mother often took the children for picnics at Rowes Bay, where doubtless they climbed into the casuarina trees – as many generations of North Queenslanders have done.

The billy goat carts, the boys would wheel it, you know. It was a cart my father had made; might have been the box that the tins the Nestlé's milk had come in, and it had two handles and wheels. Everybody had one.

And we made a cubby house at the corner of the back-yard. And five of us girls used to be in the cubby house and we'd play ladies with some our mothers' old dresses. There were five of us girls. And there was only two names between the five of us; three Connies and two Dorothy's.

I used to say to my mother, 'Ma, do you like Phyllis for a name? Then I'll call this doll Phyllis.' And 'Do you like 'Doris?' Then I'd call this one 'Doris'. Sometimes we'd dress up pegs but mostly we had bought dolls. You might get a doll for one-and-six with, generally, a china face and a straw body. A lot of the girls played marbles. I loved marbles. The boys had their jumping. High jumps and that. Everybody was very friendly. The boys used to climb the trees, but most people used to have a pigeon house in their tree. Everybody had pigeons. They used to kill them and eat them. That was a real treat too.[7] Girls played hopscotch and skipping and at school we had our clubs[8] and dumb-bells. That was part of our exercise. And jacks, too.[9] My word! My word! We loved the jacks. Boys had their cricket and football, way up the back of the school. All after school. Not in school hours. No fear! Too much work to be done in school hours.

And then of course we had our homework to do after tea. I blotted my exercise[10] one time and the teacher said 'that deserves the cane'. And I held out my hand and got the cane. And he said 'I think that deserves another one'. So I held out my hand and got two canes. I nearly broke my heart! Yes. The boys were often sent round to the headmaster. But girls weren't that bad. I don't think we were ever sent round. The boys would say, 'We got the cuts at school today'. That was their slang. But girls said, 'We got the cane'.[11] My mother didn't like us using slang. She would correct us. Very few people swore. And you didn't hear many children swear, either.

When we came to this house there was a lot of clay down in the gully. We made clay dolls, babies, everything. Then my mother would bake them in the oven for us, to make them firm. I tell you what we used to make! Clay pipes! And then we could make soap bubbles! A clay pipe would last up to six months unless you dropped it, then that was it. And once Les made a lady out of the clay and she had a baby in her arms. And Les took this to school, showing all the youngsters in his bag. And the teacher said (a voice of dreaded authority): 'What have you got there, Les Hill?' And, ' Show it to me!' And Teacher looked at it; a lady with a baby in her arms. And he said (imitating, very softly, a wondering tone), 'Could I keep that?' And you know, that was put in a glass case and it was in that glass case until I had finished going to school.

John Oxley Library

Connie Hill spoke very tenderly of her dolls, Phyllis and Doris. The little girls in this photograph, titled 'Christmas Day, 1900', are shown with their new dolls, doll furniture and teaset; enough to make any little girl smile with delight. Their unsmiling solemnity must stem from the photographer's cautionary 'Don't move!' A baby is fast asleep in a stroller typical of the period.

A lot of the men had what you would call a sideline, because wages… well, my father reared us on fifty shillings a week, and paid the house off. Lots of men did a little bit extra. My father had a permit for making baking powder. And in fact he used a *nom-de-plume*. It was 'Mount Etna' powder and he had the labels, and the volcano was always smoking. After the baking powder was made, he used to have a feather duster for dusting the table down. And that feather duster hung up on a nail. And if we didn't do the right thing, father would just get the feather duster.

And at the table, of course we always sat at the table, the whole family. And, (tapping sound) you see that finger, that was enough! One word from my father and we knew. And Ray. He was a terrible torment. I had curls then and I'd nearly always had a bow in my hair. And Ray used to like to get his finger in the bow and pull the bow down. Ooh! that annoyed me! I would yell out! And I'd get the blame then! Father used to look at me and that would nearly break my heart! And Ray would be the cause of it! Oh yes!

Ray was always doing something he shouldn't do. Once Father and the boys were cleaning the gully. We were all hands on deck, Ma and I and all, helping to get the stones and sand out. And Ray would put his finger in my bow and pull it down! So there were big clods of earth, and I picked up a big one and I… I threw it at Ray! Hit him in the stomach. Ray went 'Errh!' (chuckles with remembered satisfaction). And I was called up. And my mother said, 'Well, if it wasn't so near to bedtime, I'd be giving you a hiding!' See, Ray was the cause! But Ray got out of it! That was at night time, a moonlight night. But nothing took about Ray (the hurt of the long-ago injustice palpable in her voice) because we didn't want Ray to cry because it might bring on an asthma attack (said dutifully, as something that had been instilled). So Ray always got out of it. Still, we were all very fond of each other. Ray used to play the mouth organ and the tin whistle.

Mother did everything she could for Ray's asthma, everything. She poulticed him; the poultices were made of mustard. She got him to the doctor. Took him up to the hospital. They said he might outgrow it. Got the Chinese herbalist to him. That herbalist, he did a lot for Ray. Always herbs, a mixture. But the only way he was cured was to go up to Rollingstone.[12]

My father generally used to take the boys to church on Sunday mornings. We all went to Central Methodist, but Alf went with my mother at night. And there were the church concerts. Beautiful concerts. And there was always the Anniversary. We'd practise for weeks and weeks before that. That was a big affair. That would be all day Sunday and Monday night. We always loved our church. We all clung to our religion. Most people went to church then. And they were good people. And no swearing. It was a terrible thing if anybody swore. There was not much bad language. We were brought up in religious refinement.

Mother taught me to sew, do fancy work, and everything. My own mother died when I was eleven. We were three years on our own and then my father married a Scotch woman. And my stepmother, she was more Presbyterian. And there was a little Presbyterian hall just down the road and we were very friendly with the ministers. They would sometimes come for tea here on a Sunday.

After I left school I went dressmaking for a while, in North Ward. I used to ride my bike around the Hill. But then my stepmother was always on the sick list, so I was at home then until my stepmother passed away.

In the First World War Alf volunteered because he thought it was his duty. They got one medical check here and then another one when they went down to Brisbane. But in Brisbane they wouldn't pass him. He was half an inch under regulations. Alf said, 'Look, I know I'm a bit short, but you can put me in the tanks if you like'. And they said, 'No. Physically fit in every way'. Just the height; and they rejected him. So he came back. I was four feet nine and a half, and I was the tallest of the family. My youngest brother who died when he was a month off fifteen, he died when he was five foot six. He was very tall. Mother said he outgrew his strength. I was taller than my father and taller than my brothers. We were all short.

Always, at our home, after breakfast, the stove was let get cool. And then it was put on again at night time to make the meal. But all day the teapot was kept warm on the stove. Some of the older grandmas had a clay teapot on the stove. But we never had a clay teapot. No! Our mother always liked a china teapot.

1 The correct date of Cyclone Leonta is 1903. Connie has confused the dates because she tells us in the following paragraph that the house in which they were living in the cyclone was a 'little old rented place' and that the father built a new house to which they moved in 1904.

2 'At the West End School during the morning there were present 510 children and most fortunately the teachers managed to get the whole of them to their homes, during a slight lull in the storm about 1.30, without a single accident, as far as is known at present. A number of families took refuge in the building during the evening and every effort made to give them all the comfort possible under the circumstances.' The *North Queensland Register*, 16 March, 1903. Flying roofing iron is a frequent cause of death and critical injury during tropical cyclones. See Appendix C, Cyclone Leonta.
3 The site of the first transatlantic wireless transmission.
4 Presumably the spirits store.
5 A prop was a long piece of timber, usually a bush sapling forked at one end, for supporting backyard clotheslines. It was lowered so that the clothes could be pegged out, then pushed high so that the clothes would catch the breeze. Connie's meaning is that her father had a long pole of this kind to stir the vats.
6 'Scraping the dish' was a privilege not a chore. It meant being given the bowl in which the cake had been mixed, to clean of delicious remaining traces.
7 'At the Police Court on Friday before the Police Magistrate a boy named Alexander Marks pleaded guilty to larceny of a pigeon and was convicted and discharged.' *North Queensland Register*, 26 February, 1900.
8 Skittle-shaped items of apparatus which were swung in rhythmic patterns to music supposedly to improve girls' posture and correct round shoulders.
9 Today sets of plastic jacks can be bought, but in Connie's time the jack was the small bone from a shoulder of mutton. They were eagerly collected and much prized. Players sat on the ground holding one jackstone in the hand, trying to catch others as they were tossed in the air in patterned sequences. This ancient game has been depicted on Egyptian tomb paintings. Children in the South Pacific play the same game with pieces of worn coral.
10 The 'Exercise' was done in a special book in copperplate writing with pen and ink. Pieces of poetry, grammar, or arithmetic were copied in the most meticulous fashion, the page being given an elaborate heading in a fancy script such as Blackletter. Girls in particular would spend hours decorating the heading with scrolls and floral designs, creating what were in, effect, miniature works of art.
11 Alice Chapman recalls: 'If you done wrong you got called out in front of all the kids and got the cane, the lawyer cane. I was late one day and when I got into school I got called out and given four cuts. And I was made to stay in and write out a hundred times "I must not be late for school". And I was never late again!'
12 Where Alf had taken a pineapple farm 'just behind the hill opposite the railway-station'. Alf was to farm there for the next forty years. On one occasion, after a heavy flood, generous-hearted Alf slaughtered some of his own goats and waded round to nearby farms with the meat for the stranded families. For years Alf took his produce to the rail siding at Rollingstone on a bicycle, later acquiring a sulky. Sadly, this unsung battler of the North died by being 'knocked down by a bull-terrier'.

16

Belgian Gardens, 1903–1915 **Oscar Crowther**

Just One Big Open Paddock

Introduction

In the background, as the interview proceeds, can be heard the twitterings of budgerigars, happily excited as only budgerigars can be, in a large, well-managed aviary. While telling his life story the elderly man often refers to 'this place', 'around here', and 'down this street'. It is easy to imagine him on the warm afternoon verandah of the house where he has lived since early childhood in Sheehan Street, Belgian Gardens, that most country-townish of all Townsville suburbs. Tucked away from the rest of the sprawling city behind the ironbark-covered shoulders of Castle Hill, flanked on one side by the lagoons and bushland of the Town Common and never far from the sighing of the sea in Rowes Bay, Belgian Gardens has a timeless serenity of its own.

Oscar Crowther's story takes us back to when the suburb was 'all just one big paddock' with a scattering of houses in an area largely given over to small dairy farms and where, once a month, local people congregated at the City Council stockyards down on the Common to dip their household cows. Now that Bundock Street has become a signposted entrance to the city from the busy airport it is charming to consider a time when in the late afternoons the cows, 'hundreds of them', made their leisurely way home to be milked after grazing on the Common, and as Oscar tells us, had such a sense of their own bony-hipped dignity that the motor cars of the day had to give way to them.

Today, few motorists speeding north on the highway from Townsville to Cairns realise that until the late 1940s the bitumen highway ended at Rollingstone, beyond which the road became a dirt track with corrugations and potholes. Experienced drivers knew that the trick was to take the corrugations at speed, or risk having their vehicle shake itself to pieces. Even so there were plenty of places where travellers had to make their own track, winding in low gear in and out of the scrub. A shovel was always carried because of the risk of dry bogging somewhere along the way. In fact, it was the kind of road that would have been not unfamiliar to the teamsters of the nineteenth century. Originally, the route to the north was via Thorton's Gap at Hervey's Range. It was known as the Georgetown road and left the wharf area at Ross Creek via Warburton Street in North Ward, wound around Castle Hill through Belgian Gardens and out across present-day Garbutt to the Upper Bohle.

This road had been crucial to the development of early Townsville, enabling it to outstrip its competitors, Bowen and Cardwell, for pre-eminence as the major port for the north. Townsville had the best road through the range to the hinterland. In the early days the wool industry was the basis of prosperity. Then a succession of gold discoveries, at the Cape River, the Gilbert and Ethridge, ensured Townsville's continuing development in the 1870s. At times there were as many as a hundred teams travelling the Georgetown road. Wayside pubs grew up. John Langton, Oscar Crowther's grandfather, whom he remembers with quiet pride, is said to have been one of the first carriers to take his wagon through Thornton's Gap. He later ran the Range Hotel. An early traveller recalled of the Range Hotel, 'stirring nights when the teamsters assembled to celebrate the ascent of the mountain track and to wish one another good luck for the trip ahead.'[1]

The teamsters of last century would camp during the wet season in Belgian Gardens to spell their horses on the Town Common and have their wagons refitted at Tom Camp's blacksmith shop. Oscar Crowther's recollections give us a charming picture of them as they yarn round their campfires at night or sing to the accompaniment of accordion or mouth-organ, always ready to enthrall the local youngsters with tall tales of their adventures on the Georgetown road.

Just One Big Open Paddock

My mother's people had a property called The Glen, up on the Black River. They bred cattle and horses – principally horses, my father was interested in – for the overseas market; remounts for the Indian Army. But he also bred farm horses that he used to drove up to Ingham. There was a ready sale for them in those times for the canefields. They were a medium type, known as 'compos', halfway between the draught and the saddle type.

I was born, 1st March 1900, in West End, at a private nurse's, a Mrs Flowers, just near St Mary's church. I'm the middle one of three boys. I had a brother; he was two years older than me. And the other one, he was nine years younger.

1 Gibson-Wilde, Dorothy, *A Pattern of Pubs*, James Cook University, 198, p. 154

I was three when we came into town to live, a week or two before Cyclone Leonta. I remember it though I was just a bit of a kid. Dad and a friend had built the house, in 1902, and we come in from the Black in 1903. There was a detached kitchen and what we called the landing, just a walkway between the house and the kitchen. I can remember the walls, they'd move, and the roar of the wind. Us boys, we were quite amused by it. We didn't worry about any danger. Well, the iron off the walkway blew off. Leonta struck twice. First in the morning it came from over the back, and then in the afternoon it come from the sea again. In those times you didn't know what to expect; there was no telephones, no wireless.

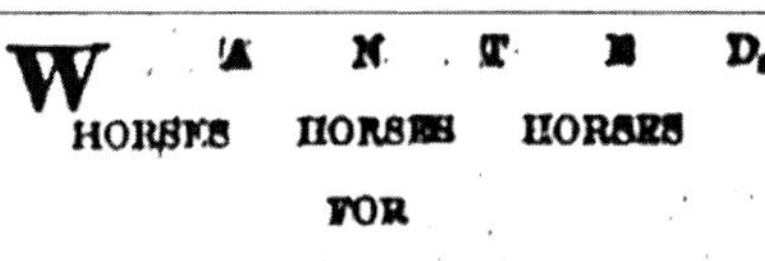

WANTED,

HORSES HORSES HORSES

FOR

WAR IN CHINA.

MESSRS DALGETY & CO., LIMITED, acting as Agents for MR A. J. COTTON, beg to advise that he has a Commission to BUY HORSES for immediate Shipment to China for War Purposes.

The Horses required are Saddle and Light Draughts, broken in, quiet, and in good condition. Ages, 5 to 10 years; height, 14.2 to 15.3. All Saddle Horses to be ridden at inspection. Draughts to be broken to lead or harness. No Greys, Creamies, or Roans will be taken.

MR COTTON will personally attend at the undermentioned places on the date and at the time set against each, and all those having Horses of these ages and class for sale are asked to bring them to one of the places named, as time will not permit buyer to visit the different stations.

TOWNSVILLE.—13th August, from 10 a.m. to 4 p.m. at Show Ground.
REID RIVER.—14th August, from 9 a.m. to 3 p.m.
RAVENSWOOD.—15th August, from 9 a.m. to 4 p.m., at Brown's Hotel.
RAVENSWOOD JUNCTION.—16th August, from 9 a.m. to 4 p.m.
CHARTERS TOWERS.—17th August, from 9 a.m. to 3 p.m., at Show Ground.
PENTLAND.—18th August, from 9 a.m. to 3 p.m., at Taylor's Hotel.
HUGHENDEN.—20th August, from 10 a.m. to 4 p.m.

For further particulars please apply to

DALGETY & CO., LTD.,
Townsville.

There were not many houses here in those days. Ours was the only one, excepting one over at the back where my father's mother lived. The rest was just one big open paddock. There were no houses along the hill. This was known as Dean Street in those days, but there was another Dean Street in Townsville and they were always getting mixed up, so they re-christened this one. After the '14–18 war they altered the names after some of the soldiers. This was named after a chap named Sheehan. There was no street lighting here until 1926.The last gaslight was just near that bridge in Stagpole Street, just this side of the Royal Hotel. And in North Ward, the last gaslight was just near the orphanage.

There was no flood after Leonta like there was after Sigma.[1] My mother had two cousins drowned in that. They were living out on Ross Island, and they were taking them from the houses and the boat capsized and two of her cousins, both girls, were drowned. One body was never found; a family named Rowe. It was their father that Rowes Bay was named after.[2]

I started school at Belgian Gardens when I was five. Our teacher was a chap named Tuffley. He had started the school; *German* Gardens as it was then. There'd be just under a hundred children going there. Round here was all dairies so there were quite big families going to the school; Bentons; they must have had about a dozen kids, then Woods; and a fair number of Pounds; and Nylands, there was about ten of them. Then there was a Chinese family, Ah Moons, had about ten more. The Chinese, they were smart. There was no class distinction. Everybody joined in everything.

The headmaster at Belgian Gardens school wrote a song for the children to sing: 'Shout, boys, Shout! Hurrah! Boys! Hurrah! Won't we have a lovely time driving in our car!' at a time when cars were still a rarity on the roads.

We played cricket and football, but nothing organised, until a chap Lynham, Dart Lynham, he was a school inspector, but before that he was head teacher at Belgian Gardens, and he took a great interest in sport. He was a very keen sportsman himself; good cricketer; good footballer. good footrunner. The result was, then, we had plenty of sport.

We used to take our lunch to school; meat sandwiches or egg sandwiches, in a cloth serviette with ordinary newspaper wrapped around. For tea at night we'd usually have something like a roast, with pudding, sago, or tapioca or vermicelli. If we'd have a leg of mutton over the weekend Mum would make a stew out of what was left. There was always a big kettle on the back of the stove for hot water. Mum would boil up the clothes in the backyard in a couple of kerosene tins, but as soon as they put coppers on the market she had one of those. There was no electricity came out this way until 1926.

Belgian Gardens originally started as the German's Garden. There used to be a hotel, the Belvedere,[3] and attached to that was a garden run by a chap named Bartels, and people used to come out from town, partly attracted to the Sunday hotel and to the German's garden, to come out and buy fruit and vegetables. In the horse-and-buggy days, it was quite a Sunday afternoon's drive out to the German's garden. So then the area became known as the German Gardens.

There was a police station but that was blown down in Leonta and never rebuilt.[4] There was just one police constable; chap named Steve O'Brien. And he was transferred away and never returned. After the hotel closed down,[5] the gardens went to wrack and ruin. And there was a lot of fruit trees, citrus and mango trees, and paw-paw, custard-apple, guava. It was quite an attraction for us kids, wide open and just going to wrack and ruin.

The area was mostly dairies. There must have been a dozen or so. Most of them was about five acres; Kappers, Thorns, Comerfords, Flannagans and Parks, Vines, Rasmussens, Blackmans, Ted Lynham, and two doors down, Alexanders, Cheynes, Woods, Cheam – they was always mixed up with Cheynes – and Morrisons.

The cattle used to go down daily on the Town Common. They would graze for the day; and they'd come back in the afternoons. There'd be a couple of hundred cows coming along this way; been grazing out in that direction. There used to be a cattle trough on the main road and all the cattle would come up for a drink before going home. Oh, there'd be hundreds of cattle coming up. Particular dairies would have about forty cows. They didn't go in for real quality cattle in those times; just a common, ordinary herd. It'd take about two or three cows to provide what one good cow would've. Quiet old cows. Most of them you didn't even have to bail them up to milk them. But,

John Oxley Library

Oscar Crowther 'did the milking before school'. He describes the cows of Belgian Gardens as '...quiet old things. You'd practically have to push them out of your way.' Belgian Gardens house cows grazed on the common by day, coming home in evening processions along Bundock Street.

hundreds of them! It was quite a sight. Even when motor cars became more prevalent, if you were driving you'd have to be careful because those old cows wouldn't get out of your way. You could drive right up to them and nearly have to push them out of your way.

Our family had cows but we didn't make our own butter. Some of the people from the bush used to bring butter in and we'd buy our butter from them. They'd bring it round, door to door. You give them a basin, and you get your pound of butter. The dairies round here found they had sufficient work, looking after the milk side of things without making butter. Lynhams, they had a big family and they used to make butter for themselves. We used to go over and we'd help them, churning, making the butter. They used to have big tin dishes, and they'd stand them on benches under the house, away from the flies. There was a long bench and they'd have about half a dozen of these big tin dishes. They'd put the milk in and in twenty-four hours the cream'd come to the top, and then they'd skim it off. That's what they started off the butter with. They used to have a stick like a broom handle and on the bottom of it there was a disk, slightly smaller than the churn, made of wood. And it had a series of holes in it, and the milk had to circulate through these holes and they'd pummel it, and keep on draining off the buttermilk, until it became solid. Then they had what you call butter coolers. And they used to stand these in water to keep the butter cool. And the buttermilk they used to feed to the pigs or mix it with fowl feed.

Ice was a luxury in those times. There was only one ice works in Townsville. That was Vardy's. This'd be about 1910. It was quite an event, round about Christmas time, or Easter time, Vardys would send the cart out into the suburbs with ice. And the nearest we could get ice was at the little shop in Echlin Street. And we'd go and get our block of ice, and, oh, we were made! A block of ice for Christmas! And you'd put your Christmas ham on the ice, or you might even become rash and make a jelly!

For Christmas we always had our own fowls and ducks. And there was always a big Christmas cake. It had to be iced, with hundreds-and-thousands all over it, and Happy Christmas on it (his voice breaks slightly at the remembrance). Oh, and we'd decorate the house. We didn't have a Christmas tree, but we always had the decorations. Paper decorations, out of crepe paper, or ones you could buy. There was a Japanese shop in town, old Wai Kashima, and he always had things; very cheap, lanterns and things. We'd go and buy these and decorate the place up. Even the blacksmith's shop, they'd go out bush and cut down saplings, and tie them on the verandah posts.[6] Christmas Eve, people all used to assemble in town. The whole of Flinders Street from the railway station up to Denham Street would be closed off, and everybody used to walk down the middle of the street, everybody saying 'Happy Christmas' and singing songs, and plenty of music. My mother's people used to come in from the Black and we'd all have Christmas together.

We always had fowls. Everybody had fowls, and a bit of a garden. And for vegetables there was a big Chinaman's garden. The fence was prickly pears! It went right down the Common. Oh, they must have had ten acres there. And they grew every kind of vegetable there and you could go down and buy, say, a bunch of lettuce for threepence.

The average wage in those times was eight-and sixpence a day.[7] And people worked from about half-past seven in the morning till about half-past four. They'd have half an hour for lunch, so they worked about eight and a half hours a day, six days a week, for eight-and-six a day. And to make ends meet, those chaps nearly always grew a little bit on the side, and if they had any over they'd swap it away; cabbages, radishes, lettuce, tomatoes, pumpkin. That's up till about 1915, and from then on things started to improve slightly.

As for meat, well, when we were in the bush we used to kill our own. Or they'd say, so-and-so's having a kill today. Somebody else'd be having a kill next week. We got plenty of meat always. Popular amongst the bushmen was what they called dried salt meat, dried in very coarse salt. It would keep indefinitely. You'd see it hanging up and it just looked like a piece of leather. But shake the salt out and soak it in fresh water, and then boil it up, and it was quite good. When you had a kill, well, for a couple of days after that you'd have any amount of fresh meat and then after that it would all have to be salted.

Dad was still working out at the Black River property but he'd come in maybe weekends. We always had horses about the place. We had horses there and a couple of cows. I did the milking before school. Holidays, we'd go out to the Black. I'd spend my time running round with a rifle shooting wallabies. Or ducks. Anything!

We always went to the Townsville Show as a family. You hadn't been anywhere if you hadn't been to the Show! That was the big event of the year. You'd meet everybody. 'Course, you had to have the buggy done up and the harness had to be spick and span. The horse had to be well groomed. You had to be dressed up in your Sunday best. You'd drive right in and stand all day in the buggy, watching. Oh, yes!

At Show time all the travelling shows would come. Madame Melba came here at one time. I was only a kid – very small when she came – but we went into town, and the place was booked out. You couldn't get in. But the entrance to the Theatre Royal was down a little lane at the side, and when she was singing, they left the doors open, so that those that couldn't get in could hear her. The place was crowded out. But you could hear her all right. She had a powerful voice. I was too young then to be able to appreciate music, but nevertheless, I have heard Madam Melba sing![8]

But for our ordinary Saturday entertainment, well, there was a cattle dip on the Common owned by the City Council, and a big stockyard. Once a month they used to round up all the cattle and those that wanted branding'd be branded. Everybody that owned a cow and a calf on the Common, they'd be there. There used to be a charge; about a penny to threepence a head. Everybody had their own brand. There was plenty of wood and they'd light a fire to heat the brands. And the cattle'd be dipped and away they'd go.

Or there might be somebody breaking-in horses, and they'd say, 'Aw! Nobody can ride this fellow!' or 'Ten bob if you can ride him!' I wasn't a buck-jump rider but my brother did a bit. There were some quite good riders there! But it didn't pay to fall off! If you wanted a bit of entertainment you'd go down to the blacksmith's shop or to the Common yards. There was always something about to happen. See, we were all interested in the same thing. We all had stock. And in the afternoons and at the weekends, we used to play cricket, just from whoever happened to be there at the time. Everybody'd join in. Adults, too.

And us boys we did a lot of fishing and swimming, and we always had shanghais. We used to put them over our neck, with the fork hanging down.

Frederick Charles Hall Collection

These boys with their guns and kangaroo dogs are the Pilgrim brothers, but Oscar Crowther and his mate Jack Cummings also used to take their rifles duck shooting on the Common or 'out at the Black shooting wallabies'.

You weren't allowed at school with them! Oh, No! You can't bring shanghais to school! We used to cut the fork out of a tree, a green fork; citrus trees was as good as any; nice and pliable and it didn't become brittle. A lot of the bush trees, they get brittle. But, lemon and orange trees, oh, they used to suffer! And we'd buy rubber armbands – all the men used to wear them on their shirts – for the rubber. And for the bit of leather to hold the stone you'd use the tongue of a boot. We'd get old boots and cut the tongue out. Oh, that lasts you for quite a few shanghais. We'd shanghai any anything that flew![9]

We'd go down... boys were allowed to shoot then... on the Town Common, during the duck season, with guns. I used to go down with Jack Cummings... he had a gun. And as soon as I got old enough to hold a gun I had one of m' own. Anybody could own a gun. We had pea rifles as long as I can remember. And we'd go and we'd shoot birds. And we'd take a couple of potatoes and an onion or so, and we'd shoot a couple of birds, sit down in the bush and make stew. And in the duck season we'd go down around the swamps, and you'd often get a duck that somebody had winged the night before and hadn't picked up. We always got ducks.

And we used to go swimming, any waterhole on the Common, fresh water, not salty, in the wet season. There was a chap named Huon, but he was known as Mucker, and he was quite a good swimmer. And, one time, two boys got into trouble in a hole in the swamp. And he was able to pull the two of them out. He was only a bit older than they were. And it caused quite a sensation! And down at the blacksmith's they were saying, 'Wasn't it lucky Mucker was there! Mucker was the only boy that could swim!' And my father came home that night and he said to us, 'You boys will have to learn to swim! You heard what happened down at the swamp today! Mucker Huon pulled 'em out! You'll have to learn!' But, we were just as good as Mucker only our parents didn't know!

There were no waterholes of any account on the Common for fishing. But we used to go out to the Bohle and fish in the Bohle, in the salt water.

And there was a patch of sand down there in Rowes Bay, before you get to the Three Mile; a very flat patch, and Sunday afternoons, before they started Cluden racecourse, there used to be races on the beach. All the hacks, as long as it was a horse. There was one chap used to do a bit of betting on it, small bets, maybe a shilling or two shillings. And then, from that, I think it gave the people the idea of starting off the racecourse at Cleveland.[10] Before that there'd been a racecourse known as Ryebury Park, up at where Yabula is now, where the bush people used to have a few races; just the people round that area, the Saunders, Althaus's, Langtons and the Crowthers. They'd have a few horses there and make a day of it. Everybody would bring bread and meat and cakes, and it was spread out and they'd boil the billy for tea.

My mother was born in 1872. There wasn't much to Townsville then. It only came to life in 1864. My grandfather had a hotel at the foot of the range.[11] His first wife died while they were there and she's buried in a small cemetery at the foot of the range. There'd be about three or four headstones in it and hers is one of them.[12] My mother was only about fifteen to eighteen months old when her mother died. And after that my grandfather kept a hotel at the top of the range. In those days all the carriers used to meet at the foot of the range and they'd double up the horses from two wagons to pull each wagon up. They'd see each other right. There was only one track up the range, a rough bush track. They'd spend a day getting all the wagons to the top, and then when they got to the top of the of the range they might have a day's spell. Then they'd all branch off in various directions. They'd go to all the stations, Dotswood, Karatha Telegraph Station, Wyandot, Christmas Creek. Others'd go on then up through Ewan and up through Georgetown and finish up at Forsyth, Croydon, Normanton, Carpentaria Downs. Some'd even get as far as Butcher's Hill and back down to Cooktown. They were pretty crude roads in those days. Of course they couldn't go in the Wet.

In the wet season, what those old carriers all did, was there was a blacksmith's shop; a chap named Camp owned it, old chap, Tom Camp. Old Tom Camp's son was Hezekiah. He ran it after the old chap died; and then Hezekiah's sons carried it on, and his sons again. Then, of course, as the horse went out of fashion and the motor car took over, there was no need for a blacksmith's shop. But up till then everything was done at the blacksmith's shop, from shoeing horses to repairs to buggies and drays. Oh, it was the meeting place for everyone. Any time of the day you could go down and there'd always be men there. And us boy'd always be down there.

In the wet season all the carriers used to meet there. There was spare ground between the trough and the road and the blacksmith's shop was on the corner.[13] All the carriers, they'd meet there and spend the wet season, and spell their horses out on the Common. And Camp, the blacksmith, would have the job of doing up their wagons. The wheels'd have to be tightened... all the rims had to be what they call cut and shut. With the constant work, the timber'd wear and they'd have to get new spokes and felloes[14] or perhaps new axles. So all the wagons were all done up ready for the close of the wet season. And the teamsters'd arrange a loading for their next trip and then off they'd go, all at once.

We spent no end of time down with them so we got to know them all. They'd camp under their wagons, or they'd put up a tarpaulin, just like when they were on the road. But Ted Lynham, he had about a five-acre paddock and he built a house and his family ran the dairy while he was away. So when he came back he'd put his wagon in for repairs, and he had a house to come to. But the others used to camp with their wagons. Each teamster used to have an offsider, a spare boy, and some'd have a horse boy. We knew them all.

At night they'd have a concertina, or a mouth-organ, and they'd have a little sing-song among themselves just where their wagons were, sitting around the fire. Them that drank used to go round to the Royal. They'd sing *Harrigan* or *The Man that Broke the Bank at Monte Carlo...* or *In the Shade of the Old Apple Tree.* And they'd talk about their trips and make hair-raising tales for us kids about their experiences. About five per cent of it true! They were a good-humoured lot.

Then at the end of the wet season, immediately it was dry enough, about April, they'd all decide among themselves, We've got a loading, and away they'd go. It was all station supplies. The stations in those times used to get one loading for the year; tinned stuff, flour, tea, sugar, jam. And they all had a bit of a store with clothing for the station hands, so there'd be shirts and belts and hats and boots. Five, or six or seven tons of it. Building materials, galvanised iron. Any loading that was offering, they'd take.

They'd get away early but they wouldn't make it to the foot of the range in one day. They used to go to what was called the Bend of the Bohle. There was quite a distinct bend in the river. They'd camp the first night at the Bend and the next leg was to the foot of the range. There were creeks, the Alice and the Canal and the Scrubby... then they'd meet at the foot of the range. That's what the hotel was there for. It was a full day's work getting the wagons up the range. After that they'd branch out in all directions: north, south, west. When they were returning home and the wagons were coming down empty, they used to tie a tree on behind, a tree with all the branches on, to act as a brake, otherwise, the wagon would over-run the horses. The wagons had a brake and they used to wind it on, but they were pretty crude affairs.

There might be from twelve to sixteen horses pulling; heavy horses, not quite the draught. They were a slightly lighter type that they used on the wagons. They wanted them to be a bit active. And they'd have spare horses, and a saddle horse or two for fetching up the others in the morning. The same horses weren't yoked up all the time. They might have, say, twelve in harness but they'd have about twenty horses in the plant; about eight of them spelling from day to day. And the spare boy would drove them along. They'd have the road all mapped out and they'd tell him, 'well, you go on five mile or so', and he'd drove on there and by the time the wagon got there he got the dinner camp ready. And they'd have an hour or so's spell for the horses and themselves, and then head off again in the cooler part of the day, and camp again at night. The horses would graze along the way. They used to go immediately after the Wet when there was plenty of good feed along the road.

When my grandfather, John Langton, had the hotel at the range was way before my time, in the 1870s. After, he sold the hotels, he and his friend Hann took up two properties. It was all empty land and they were branching out looking for properties for stock. My grandfather took up Greenvale station and his friend Hann took up Maryvale. His brand, 2JL, is still the Greenvale brand. In those times you could almost select any brand you wanted. You'd go to the Department of Agriculture and Stock here, and they'd have all the list of vacant brands; 'Which one do you want?' they'd say. You'd say, 'Has 2JL gone?' And that was registered as your brand.

As kids we used to know all the brands. I could've told you thirty or forty of them off-hand. My father's was Z2C… Zachariah Crowther… J12, Mount Sturgeon… (naming twelve to fifteen brands). Just the same as present-day boys know motor cars, we could look at a horse's brand and say, 'He's from Charters Towers or e's from Natal Downs' .In those days everybody had horses. They were as common as motorcars.[15]

I started at the Gardens school in 1905 and I went there until 1913. Then I went to the Christian Brothers for two years. It was up on Melton Hill then. Had I remained at the Brothers I could have sat for Junior that year but I wanted to go to work. I left in the October and sat for the railway exam; which was the same as the Public Service. And I'll skite a bit – I passed First! So I started off in 1915,as a Junior Clerk on £54 a year. That's one pound and ninepence a week! The first thing I did was I bought myself a bike so that I could ride to work.

1 Cyclone Sigma, 1896. 'Sigma, of which it is believed Townsville was the centre, commenced on a Saturday afternoon at the end of January 1896, and the gale, which continually shifted its direction, raged unceasingly all Saturday night Sunday and Sunday night, only abating about 2 p.m. on Monday. On that occasion several lives were lost through some young ladies being foolishly taken away from a safe refuge in a boat manned by inexperienced persons'. *North Queensland Register*, March 16th 1903. See also Appendix C.

2 C.S. Rowe was a partner of John Melton Black who had selected Cleveland Bay as the site for the settlement of Townsville, moving mobs of cattle into the Mt Elliot area in the 1860s.

3 On the site of the present shopping centre in Bundock Street. According to Dorothy Gibson Wilde 'In the 1880s, Henry Bartels, an early Townsville butcher, acquired land on or near the 'gardens' cultivated by Heinrich Frederic Robinson, the original German of German Gardens (now Belgian Gardens) By 1884 he had named the property Belvedere Gardens and erected a large house with a vineyard nearby. It became a popular local resort. The hotel had probably the most beautiful of any setting in Townsville, being surrounded by flower gardens, orchards and vineyard and backing on to the Town Common where tree-shaded lagoons were alive with wild birds.' It is of interest to note that in 1889 tenders were also being called for the erection of a hotel building in the area for James Crowther though there is no record of his ever having been granted a licence. (*A Pattern of Pubs*, pp.125, 126)

4 'German Gardens State School had half of the old school unroofed and the master's residence totally unroofed – both of these places stood Sigma without sustaining the slightest damage. Mr Lynham's outhouses are all gone but the residence is intact. The police barracks are unroofed... Mr J. Cummins' house completely collapsed... Some of the roofing at Bishop's Lodge is gone. Mrs Brabon's house is flat to the ground, and Mr Rintoul's house has vanished and the house opposite entirely gone. Mrs Healy has the frame of the house and the kitchen only standing. Sigma was more disastrous in German Gardens locality than the recent visitation. As the floodwaters in 1896 destroyed stock and property, Monday's storm destroyed considerable property, but little, if any stock is missing.' *North Queensland Register*, 16th March 1903

5 Burnt down in April 1895 (ibid, p126)

6 From a traditional English custom, still practised in country areas, of hanging boughs of oak to celebrate special events.

7 8s. 6d. or eight shillings and sixpence; less than a dollar.

8 'There was a record audience at the Theatre Royal on the occasion of Madame Melba's concert. Curiosity as to the personality of the world's greatest soprano was added to their desire to listen to their countrywoman's vocal perfection... Madame Melba's first number was "The Mad Scene from Hamlet"(Ambroise Thomas) This was in French and the florid character of the music was eminently suited to the prima donna whose runs and trills were a revelation to all present. An enthusiastic encore was gratified by a beautiful rendition of Moore's romantic verse "Believe Me If All Those Endearing Young Charms". The simple but beautiful music was most sympathetically given and the faultless enunciation enabled the audience to enjoy the sentiment as well as the harmony. Madame Melba's next number was Tosst's "Good-bye" which was most exquisitely sung and the dramatic intensity of the last verse is something which will remain a fond memory with her hearers for many years.' *North Queensland Register*, 19th July 1909. This article possibly refers to Melba's Charters Towers concert but it is likely that the programme was similar in other centres, as would also have been the adulation of the crowds.

9 On the audio-tape the remembered wickedness brings a note of glee to the Narrator's gravely serious voice. You can almost see the gleam in the eyes of the ten-year-old hunter-killers of Bundock Street!

10 A bush racecourse at present-day Garbutt.

11 Jack Langton and Robert Williamson are said to be the first carriers to take wagons through Thornton's Gap. For a while they were in partnership as proprietors of the Range Hotel. At first the name Range was that of the hotel at the foot of the ascent, but when this closed down the hotel at the top became known as the Range. Later the name was changed to the Eureka. (*A Pattern of Pubs*, pp. 154, 155)

12 Mary Langton, aged 28, died 1875. Her grave, now heavily overgrown with lantana, is one of several, marked and unmarked, in dense bush slightly south-east of the foot of the old wagon road through Thorton's Gap. The site of the original Range Hotel is marked only by a Burdekin plum tree.

13 The turnoff to the Old Common Road. (ibid, pp. 217, 218)

14 A segment, or the whole rim of a wooden wheel to which the spokes are attached.

15 'At the Police Court on Friday before the Police Magistrate, Wm. Eustace charged with the larceny of a saddle and bridle was remanded till the 5th. inst., bail being refused. The same defendant proceeded against by Tommy Howe for alleged assault. Mr W. F. R. Boyce appeared for the complainant and Mr Cotham for the defendant. On the charge of illegally using a horse the same defendant was discharged, no evidence being offered.' *North Queensland Register*, 26th February, 1900.

Ravenswood and Inkerman, 1904–1916

William Newton

The Eldest Boy In The Family

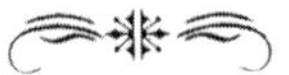

Introduction

The boys of the period were not brought up to be work-shy. In Kelly Newton's story we learn of the way in which boys were inducted into the work practices of the day, by offsiding for their fathers. Kelly (one can only regret that the Interviewer did not ask 'How did you come by your nickname?') stoically accepted that as 'the oldest of the boys' his was the role of helping Dad. At the age of twelve he was loading six-foot lengths of firewood, blowing the forge in the blacksmith's shop, even baling the water from the mine shaft. 'I was only a slip of a kid, but wiry' he says, conveying to us a sense of an earnest little lad doggedly determined to grow into the sort of man his father was. And what an example of hard work the father set. Kelly remembers that his father 'did the work of five men' at the Sunset Extended, 'the last mine that worked at Ravenswood', twelve hours a day, six days a week, singing as he worked.

Gold had been discovered at Ravenswood in 1869 and the tent and bush-shack township which sprang up was soon graced with stores and hotels. It was linked in the early 1870s to Townsville by Cobb & Co. coach, the journey taking almost two days. The easily available alluvial gold was soon worked out and companies were formed to sink deep shafts. By the late 1870s silver–lead was added to gold as a source of wealth. Kelly Newton felt that he had known Ravenswood 'in its heyday', but by the time of his boyhood there, it was already in decline. Today, Ravenswood is a picturesque ghost town, a tiny cluster of once elegant shops and hotels in the midst of abandoned mine workings. A newly established open-cut may breathe fresh life into the historic township.

While growing up in Ravenswood, Kelly seemed to lead something of a charmed life. As a toddler he swallowed cyanide 'set out for the birds' but survived. In the cemetery is the headstone of a little girl who 'died of cyanide poisoning'. Very little cyaniding was done in the mines of Ravenswood after the early 1890s when wilfering tables were introduced but it was possible that individual miners retained some for poisoning dingoes or crows. At thirteen Kelly was struck by lightning and left paralysed. Somehow he survived and we see him, as a fourteen-year-old, working as a horse boy on a cane farm near Ayr. There he catches a glimpse of his first cane loco and knows in that instant that loco driving was the life for him. Anyone who remembers the dramatic fussing, tooting, whistling importance of the steam locomotives that, with fireboxes flaring crimson, once hauled the long lines of cane trucks on narrow-gauge lines to the sugar mills of the north, will understand Kelly's instant fascination.

Amid Kelly Newton's excellent descriptions of the work practices of the day are interspersed laconic accounts of boyhood adventure. Very few would be able to claim, as he can, to have ridden a bicycle overland along the telegraph line from Ayr to Ravenswood, without food or water, drinking from puddles, and lighting a fire at night to ward off encircling packs of dingoes. Again Kelly's qualities of hardiness and quiet determination shine through, qualities that he will soon need as he fights for his life during an almost fatal attack of rheumatic fever, no doubt brought on by the appalling working conditions the loco boys endured. We are told of the practices of not only the local doctor but of the Chinese herbalist – one can only smile at 'the bird's foot sticking up' out of the herbalist's potion. In the end, it is Kelly's will to live that wins the day.

The Eldest Boy In The Family

When I was young I swallowed cyanide set out for the birds. Dad used to put it up on the stump cap under the house. Our house in Ravenswood was on the bank of the creek, and if Mum wanted Dad urgently from the mine she would hang the towel on the front rail. And he seen the towel and of course he made the old bike go fast. And Mum said, 'You damn' fool! Kelly's swallowed the cyanide!'

So Dad, he picked me up in one arm and he took me across the bridge into Pierce's place, where there was a doctor staying. Which was uncommon, a doctor to be staying at a private place. He give me a big glass of milk. I didn't drink milk but he made me drink it, and I stayed there the night and next day Dad come and took me home. But it never come against me, that cyanide.

My father, William Agnew Newton, was a well-known engine driver at the mines. He was the youngest fellow to hold a first-class winding-engine driver's ticket in Queensland. He was also a man of many trades. He could practically do anything. He could build a house. He built our house in Ravenswood. It's at the Burdekin Dam site now. They shifted it out there and it's still there. Not only that, he was a blacksmith, a tool sharpener. He was the best local shot in Ravenswood. He won some beautiful medals – rifle clubs were pretty strong in those days – .303s. There was nothing, really, that he couldn't do, the Old Man.

He worked at the Sunset Extended; that's the last mine going out towards the cemetery, and the last mine that worked in Ravenswood. And they worked twelve hours a day, for six days a week. They had Sunday off. I used to assist Dad. I went home from school and I'd take Dad's tea over on the afternoon shift, and give him a hand to load the cord.[1] If I wasn't there he would have to load two trolleys of cord. And he would have to struggle with his back up against it to push it into the stoke-hole to log the fire. Two big boilers, one on each side. The door opened on hinges, with a roller on it, and he'd put that on and he'd lift the log up, and put it in. This is really hardwood, six-foot logs to just under one foot in diameter. He'd get hold of the end and lift it up and slide it in. He'd have to attend to the boiler, keep the water in; the knock used to go – what you call the knocker-mark – and he'd have to bail water or he'd have to bail quartz.

It even got to the stage when I was coming up a bit, twelve or so, he taught me how to bail water. Not fast, like he did. We'd a seven-foot wheel on the top. You couldn't see the stopes when they're working. Like, you had to do a certain amount on tribute,[2] and he was only getting three pound-ten an ounce when he was doing it. The mining company took half. But he would sing! He used to sing!

When the boilers had settled down and the steam was right, he would go down to the blacksmith's shop and sharpen drills. For the twenty-four hours he was the only sharpener. But he was a kingpin on tool sharpening. I used to have to go and blow the forge for him; help him out with the long drills, hold them up and turn them over for him. Assist him all I could.

On top of that he had the big compressor, which was vital to the men down below, to keep the compressor working. It was a big steam compressor, a double-cylinder job. Today they would have a man on that, one on the engine, one on trimming, one on tool sharpening and one on driving. But he did five men's jobs, that's for twelve hours a day.

There wasn't much of a living in it, but he was healthy. And all those men were because they were working hard. They didn't have time to get sick! Everybody wore Ipswich flannels. They had to. It was hard work sweating around the boilers, and then you get cold. The heat that comes from a fire when you open the doors, when you've got to log it up, it hits you. But the job had to be done.

Only one man on the surface. Two men down below; brace men.[3] You walked to work, a bit over a mile, over School Hill and down to the mine. Dad worked for all the mines. He was winding-engine driver at all that was operating in Ravenswood.

It's wonderful to be in those places in the heyday in the goldmining towns. Everybody is everybody and everybody is happy. There's no such thing as stuck-ups and middle class. Everybody knew one another and they associated with one another. We had no pictures, no ice-cream but there'd be the dance on the Saturday night. We had the library at the School of Arts. There was many Chinese stores. Friday night all the shops are open and you go and pay your bill and they'll give you a bag of lollies.

But then it ended up with a fourteen-months strike.[4] And that practically smashed Ravenswood.

Our family stopped on in Ravenswood through the strike. We had to. There was six children. Maud was the eldest. Then me. I was born in Ravenswood, the 26th January 1901. That was Foundation Day.[5]

Then there was Fred, and Sid, and the two girls, Bobbie and Rita. And if it hadn't been for the Chinaman's shop, Lee Gow's, we wouldn't have been able to manage. Lee Gow had the grocery shop and the baker's shop, and a few clothes. Well, they stuck by the miners through all that period, and they got every penny back. The Lee Gows, they were a wonderful family. They helped everyone.

You had to economise. Everybody in Ravenswood had a little garden and lived on vegetables. And everybody had goats. We had about a hundred and fifty ourselves. You'd have what they call a kiddie every weekend. And the old damper on Saturday afternoon. Mum'd make a Johnny cake on the coals. Just throw the coals around, make up the dough and water, a bit of salt and throw it on. That's bread in the bush. And on the Sunday we always had the plum pudding. That was fifty-two days a year, that plum pudding.

During the strike, Dad went out west to the wool scourers but he didn't like it out there. Eating mutton three times a day, seven days a week. And he just couldn't cop it so he come back again.

Well then, my life was very hard, because I was the eldest of the boys, and Dad had the blacksmith's shop. And of course, it fell to me to be his striker. And I was only a slip of a kid but I was wiry, and I just had to do it. That's all there was to it. Cutting and shutting tyres, big wagon wheels; Dad would re-spoke them and line 'em up. And we'd have to put the tyre in the fire; with the shrinking machine, to shrink it and expand it. We'd have to go and get wood – ironbark – and cut it up into lengths; probably two or three mile out with a billy goat cart. Seven billy goats in the cart, pulling. All harness made by Dad.

The blacksmith shop Dad had was the only one there. When the mines started there was all these big wagons that was carting cordwood in for the mines. Well, of course, they had to go when the mines folded. Most of the wagons went to other districts where they could be employed, because you know there was nothing in Ravenswood when there was no mines working. They didn't need wood.

We used to go out and get this bark, the ironbark, and bring it in and cut it up. Then we'd have to put the red-hot tyres on to the wheel and then everybody available used to grab a bucket and put the cold water on to it. Cool it quickly. Otherwise it would burn into the wood, and the tyres'd be loosened. You had to do it very, very fast. A tin in each hand.

Well, that was very hard work for me, like, and it was very hot work. But I was the eldest boy in the family and I copped it. Well, I done that from when he first started. I'd say I was eleven. Practically, I served me time as a blacksmith and wasn't apprenticed! But I learned a lot. I never lost the formula as a wheelwright to set a wheel.

This shrinking machine, well, it was a big wheel with spokes, and very heavy. It had handles and serrated edges. And you put your foot on the spoke and pulled it down. It used to come together. And then you'd have to belt it to keep it in shape. And you'd lay it on the anvil and you'd have to shape it to the same as the rim itself. Well, then, you had a trammel used to go inside the iron tyre and you mark it. And you go round the outside of the felloes of the wheel, and you'd have to work out your shrinkage on the size of your tyre. If it's a four-inch tyre it would have tremendous heat in it and it takes a lot of cooling. So you have to work out just what shrinkage there would be not to dish the wheel. Because if it comes too tight the wheel is dished. We never had a failure! Never dished a wheel!

Frederick Charles Hall Collection

A goat team probably similar to the one eleven-year-old Kelly used to take out bush to bring back ironbark logs for his father's forge: 'Seven billy goats to the cart, pulling'.

To cool it we had kerosene tins o' water – and big tubs of water – which we used to fill before we started shrinking the tyre or putting it on. And you pretty-well always had two tyres to do on two wheels. Everybody available would pour water on, would have to come and pour water on these big tyres. See, we had no hoses. No overhead tanks; nothing like that. Water all had to be pumped and drawn up out of the well. I think the four-inch tyres were the biggest tyres that ever Dad done. And, after, he would have to do the two forward on this big four-wheel job. The front wheels are smaller than the back wheels and there's this turntable underneath the wagon. Very hard work.

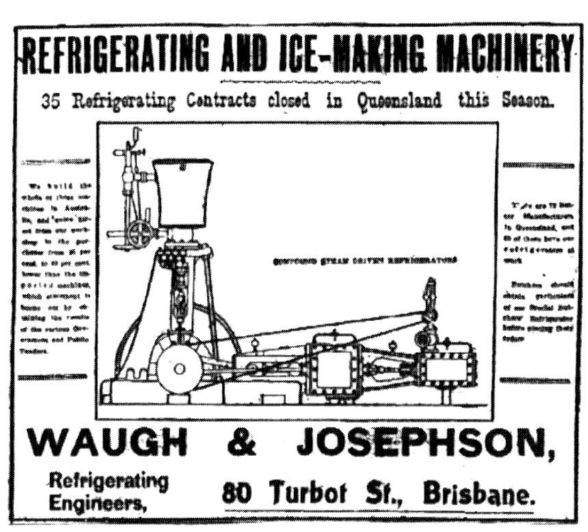

Dad was a very clever man. He could do anything. Make anything. He built a gold-shaker for recovering fine gold. It would be a masterpiece. Made of just ordinary pine-cases; he built it square, about eighteen inches deep; put trays in it; with saddle cloth material in it, which is the best for recovering gold; and a steering gear out of one of them Jumpin' Crows we called them, a Mystery Overland. He got the steering gear off that, and he put it on two blind bearings, which he made himself, and a handle on it. And he put springs on the side of the box, bolted on to the box, that used to hit the side of two pieces of wood that he had nailed to the legs for support. But when you turn the handle it was too sudden. It used to knock the gold over. It wasn't shaking it. It was just jumping the ridges. So he had two ascentrics [eccentrics?—MH] made at the foundry down in Brandon that would give him the right throw, which was about three-quarters of an inch. And he brought them home and put them on and the result was one hundred per cent. But it went missing!

There was this engineer chap, he heard about it and he come over. Wanted to have a look. Dad put it out on the backyard and connected a bit of hose up to it. Then he went inside and he got an Indian Root Pill bottle of fine gold; he'd had that for years. And he put two big shovelfuls of sand, and spread it on all the gold. And I think it was fifty revolutions of the handle a minute, he turned. And he got all the gold back out! He got that bottleful of gold again. It was a marvellous, that machine.

And this engineer chap said to Dad, 'Why not patent it?' And Dad said, 'I got no money to go to all the trouble and patent this!' And the engineer chap said, 'I will do it!' So – he lived in Sydney, this fellow – he went to Sydney, took all the particulars, and the plans. He was going to fix all this up at no cost to Dad. And he had one built down in Sydney that four men wouldn't lift! And Dad had made this one out of pine and a little bit of machinery, built on four legs, so that he could get it to the back of a lorry and slide it on, a one-man job.

But this fellow had it made of steel. No good! Miles too heavy. And we never heard from him. And Dad said, 'Well, That's it! He's gone! And took the plans and everything. We'll never see him again!' And then, a couple of years later, he come back and Dad said, 'I thought you'd gone bush!'

And he said: 'No! No! Bill! Everything's okay. I been up in Darwin.' But, he said, 'I could never build that thing out of wood like you did. So I've come to have a look at it'.

And Dad had left it with people named Spedwell. And when he went back to pick it up, it had gone! Somebody had taken it. Who? Spedwells don't know. Nobody knows where that thing went! But it would be the greatest invention for the little prospector that was ever made.

When I went to school there was the original classroom, and my room in between and they built another room at the back. And the schoolmaster's office was at the back, and then they built a new room in the front. In later years they demolished that, but the original part of the school is still there.

I left school before Scholarship because I was struck with lightning. It was 1914. I had just finished building a billy goat yard, and a big storm come from the south-west. We had a big Chinee apple tree in the back yard with two branches on it. And the clothesline was tied to what we used to call the jujube tree, right through to the back post of the skillion on the back of the house. But the clothes prop was facing the east and it put the wire up against the water-tank.

Well, I was dirty. It had been raining, and I'd just picked up a tin dish and put it on my knee while I turned the tap on, balancing it, you know. And I turned the tap on, and the lightning struck. And it split the tin dish to pieces and it tossed me up against the middle post of the kitchen and from there I went about six feet off the ground and hit the fowl run and fell down. And Mum, and Mrs Wynaman, and Mrs Gregory, the butcher's wife, they was all in the front room. They said, 'Oh, my God! Maud's struck'! Maud's my sister; she was sewing in the skillion. And we had lattice work on the skillion and a blind for when it rains. And they run outside, and Maud was all right. 'Well', they say, 'It's hit something!'

And they looked through the kitchen window and seen me laying down, stupid, on the ground. They run down the high steps, and they picked me up and carried me upstairs, the four of them. I was just like a lump of jelly. Like, I didn't know nothin'.

Well, there's no doctor in town. But the ambulance man, he was as good as any doctor. He rang the Towers and said that I'd been struck by lightning and what procedure? And they didn't know what to do, or how bad I was or anything like that. So they put me to bed, and, oh! I was stupid for a long time. And I lost the use of m' legs and I couldn't get up the school steps. So I finished school when I was somewhere in the vicinity of thirteen or thirteen and a half.

There was no work up there at all. If you wasn't a miner there was no work. Only station work and I just couldn't do it. I wasn't a horsey kid. I hate horses. But I had received word from McDesme, out of Ayr, from cane farmers, McAlisters, to come down and be chop-chop boy. So they put me on the train and away I went down to Ayr, and I went out to McDesme. It was the seventeenth of March, Paddy's Day when I landed on the farm. And I would have to do twelve to fourteen hours of work a day, getting chop-chop, cutting it up, feeding the horses, going out and getting the horses in the dark in the morning. They didn't burn cane in those days and they used the cane tops to make chop-chop for the horses. I'd got to go out and get a drayful in the

Frederick Charles Hall Collection

'Everybody had goats' Kelly Newton tells us. His sister Maude was spared when Kelly was struck by lightning while building a billy goat yard 'out the back'.

morning and get another drayful in the afternoon. There was no tractors, those days. It was all horses. Some of them farmers had forty-five big draught horses, and they had to be fed and stabled and looked after because they were very valuable.

And I'd have to wait till the girls come home from school, from Rangatang. And they wouldn't even unharness the pony. I'd have to feed the pony.

I slep' in a room underneath McAlisters. They had seven or eight people working there. But I didn't stay there much longer! The loco line run past the place and when the Season started, and I seen a cane loco… well! That was mine! I thought to myself, 'I got to get on that engine!' It had me mesmerised, really. I thought, 'I got to get on this thing!'

So I got a job on the loco, at Inkerman Mill, me and two Paterson boys. And I'd just been working two days before the strike, two days, and then the railway strike come on. And Mum had come down from Ravenswood to see the Ayr Show, and got caught when the railway strike come on. Mum didn't know how long the strike was going to last and she had to get back to the other kids that was at Ravenswood. They were going to school and Maud was trying to look after them. So Mum said to me to go home to get the buckboard and two horses to come down to pick her up and take her home.

So the two Paterson boys said they would go with me, and we're going to ride the bikes from Ayr to Ravenswood. We started off Friday afternoon with a loaf of bread and a tin of jam, and a pocket knife to open the jam and one blanket. And Ted Paterson, he'd never rode a bike before and here we're going overland, through rough country. They had hired two bikes. Five shillings a week each. And I had an old Redburn, the heaviest bike you ever seen in your life. Old-type bike, 'cause, I was only young, fourteen, say.

And away we set off. Well, first night, one of them got up during the night and et the bread and finished off the jam. One of those two. So they blamed each other for it and they were going to fight about it but I soon stopped that. I said, 'Well, let's get going!'

And we're going to have a meal at Clare, at the old Clare pub. That's twenty-two miles from Ayr. Maggie Sachell was the owner of the place. So away we kick off. And just after, Hoppy, he broke his chain. So we said he'd have to go back to Ayr and get a new chain and we'd wait for him along the road.

Well, when we got to Clare, no water, hungry. No breakfast. We says, 'Hullo!' And Maggie says, 'Where y'goin?' And we says, 'Ravenswood. Can we get a meal here, Maggie?' And she said, 'If youse belong to Ravenswood,' she says, and she grabs a .303 rifle, 'Get on your way! I hate you Ravenswood lot!' So she put us through the fence, and she says, 'There's the telephone wire! Follow it!' And she says, 'An' if I can see youse in five minutes I'll put one over yer head!' She would've too!

So we went all day! Nothin' to eat! Water in the gullies. We got to the foot of the range at night, the two of us and we lit a big fire. And about five thousand dingoes started. And this other chap started to cry. He reckoned the dingoes would mob us at night and tear us to pieces. So I said, 'Well, we'll just make a big fire and keep it going.' So the next morning we get up the range and we get up to Ravenswood.

It wouldn't be more than about half-past seven. Dad was in bed. 'Somebody at the door! It's Kelly! So Dad jumped out of bed. 'Where the blazes have you come from?' he says. And I tell him, 'I rode the bike from Ayr.' And he says, 'When? When did you leave?' And I says, 'Friday afternoon.' He says, 'This is Sunday! Have you had your breakfast?' And I says, I haven't had Friday night's tea, yet! So Dad makes a good breakfast, and he asks me what I come up for, and I tell him, 'To get Mum back home. We got to take the buckboard down and bring her home.' So Dad said,' Righto! Two days, and we're off!'

When we went back down again for Mum I put the bike on the back of the buck-board and we went overland. And eventually we got Mum back, and, after, when it said in the paper that the strike was over, I went back down to work at Inkerman.

So I was on the locos as loco boy, or what they call points boy. You would have to hand-shunt your trucks, pull them out, and throw the riding points that come from the paddock out. You'd haul the full ones out with a sling, a wire rope attached to the locomotive, then push the empties back, put your trucks in and then flick the line off. It was very hard work for a boy.

Then you had to climb under the trucks – the couplings are under there – and you've got to chop your way under, with sticks of cane in your back, and sticks in your neck. You'd get under and fight your way all the time, no matter how much water or muck that was there. But I don't remember any loco boy getting killed, or only one at Kalamia, and that was just an accident.

I was on the Inkerman Number One loco. That's the one that used to run across the bridge and get the cane from the Ayr side. Our mill was only small then; started in 1914 in a small way. And this loco used to carry a guards van and a guard just the same as the Government line. And we were bringing the cane across: ten, twelve trips a day across the bridge.

I never had a ticket but I did all the driving on the loco. They're small locos, only ten ton; on two-foot-six gauge. My driver just didn't like the job. He'd sit on the water-tank and let me do the driving and the stoking. On two occasions I was sent by the chief engineer with a new driver and I'd be telling him to sit on the water-tank and watch and I'd be tutoring these fellows. I didn't have a ticket.[6] I was just sixteen.

Eight shillings a day we got. Forty-eight hours! Knocked off at midnight Saturday and started again midnight Sunday. Three shifts; twelve to eight,

eight to four; four to twelve. But you had to work overtime because boys wouldn't stick the job. And within three or four weeks, they would leave. They couldn't get boys and you'd have to carry on all the time. I done one stretch thirty-five hours. It wasn't for the money. It was nobody turned up.

At that time there was that bad 'flu, the Spanish 'Flu.[7] A lot of people around Ayr died with it. Oh, yes. Alec Cameron, he was a special friend of mine, he went in twenty-four hours. Lots of people. They died all over Queensland. It wasn't just applicable up here. Anybody could get it though none of the family did. But well-known people around town in really good health, some of them copped it. If you got it in the family somebody else might get it so they had to knock off work, compulsory, and stop home. And you had formalin. You got it at the chemist, and sniff it, and oh, gawd! You could feel it run down to your shoes, it was that strong! That was about the only thing they knew that might help it. But then, like everything else, the 'flu just gradually disappeared.

And they wanted a first-class driver for the platform at the mill. And the chief engineer, Mulholland, I went and asked him about Dad. I said, 'He's a winding-engine driver, and he's a good'n. He's driven for years, and no accidents.'

And Muholland, he said, 'Get on to him now. Straight away! Come with me!' And he took me into the phone and I rang the Post Office in Ravenswood and he went and contacted Dad. And he come down in three or four days and went over to the mill. Later he brought the family down. So Dad stopped on at the Inkerman mill practically the rest of his life!

Most of the men from Ravenswood moved to Kalamia. There was this engineer he went down and he told them, 'I'll get youse all work if youse'll come down.' So they followed him to Kalamia; and most of them retired from there. All Ravenswood men.

And I had rheumatic fever bad. In fact there was three boys from Ravenswood, Wiltshire, Haig and me, all had rheumatic fever, and them two died. Mum fed me with a teaspoon for three months. I was only skin and bone. Well, they all said that I'd die. But the old Chinaman come, the herbalist, Gun Tye. And he seen the doctor's little four-cylinder job, out the front of our place. And he said to Mum, 'What him doctor come oltime for?' And Mum said, Kelly's got rheumatic fever! And Gun Tye says 'Oh! What him doctor savvee this kind fever! Me look!' So he come in and takes a look at me, and he says, Oh! He too far gone! Suppose you tell me longtime before, me bin fixim!' And Mum said, 'Oh! Will you try?' And Gun Tye, he tells her, Yes, he'll come tomorrow.

So, spring cart and horse, he come. Puts his horse in the yard with the nosebag on and gives it a feed. Then he goes in the Mum's kitchen and he makes this big soup-plate of stuff, and comes in and puts it on me chest. I can't move; I got no interest in the world; I got no feeling. But he says, 'You kai-kai 'im!' So I opened me mouth and I'm laying back there taking teaspoon after teaspoon. Anyhow, I happen to look down and I see a bird's foot, sticking up in this soup. That finished me! No more! I wouldn't take no more! Why'n't he take it out, eh? If he only he had the sense to rake it out I would have et the lot!

But as it was, I had about two thirds. But, when that stuff starts to work and shift, it's just like drawing barbed wire through you. There's no pain worse! All I can do is moan and scream. The sweat broke out all over me. They put my hands over the sides of my bed and they say the water ran out from under my fingernails for twenty-four hours. They were all stood around, everyone, and the room was crowded. They thought I was going to die. But I didn't. And the doctor come again and he said, 'How are you?' And I opened my eyes and said, 'Oh, All right.'

And he snapped his fingers and said, 'I wouldn't have given that much for you when I seen you.' Then he said, 'You'll never work again. I'll give you a certificate.' He give it to Mum and Mum put it in the Bible. But I said, 'Nah! I'll be right!' And I was. And later on, I took up boxing and running. And people couldn't believe their eyes when they seen me halfway along the road to Brandon, running.

1 Bush timber used for fuel

2 Often individual miners sub-contracted with mine management for the right to work a mine. 'The Tributors in the London lease struck a new, highly mineralised reef 12 inches thick in their No. 2 level which shows coarse gold freely. We wish them luck in their perseverance. They have about 70 tons of fair stone in their paddock.' *Ravenswood Mining Journal*, quoted *North Queensland Register*, 27 July, 1900.

3 The brace was the platform from the poppet-head.

4 1912

5 Kelly is confusing Foundation Day, 1 January 1901, with Australia Day, an understandable slip as the remembered celebrations of Foundation Day would have been much talked of throughout his childhood. See Appendix A.

6 A locomotive of the type which Kelly Newman drove is on display at Inkerman Mill.

7 The great influenza pandemic of 1918-19, commonly known as the Spanish 'flu, reached Australia in January 1919 and caused more than 10,000 deaths before the end of the year. Young adults were particularly susceptible. Masks were worn, assemblies were banned. Even churches were closed.

18

Irvinebank area, 1910–1914 **Edward Cummings**

Boyhood At Koorboora

Introduction

You drive to these deserted mining towns on a threadbare track through interminable bush. When you get out of your air-conditioned four-wheel-drive the heat hits you. Then the silence. Silence broken only by the harsh protests of crows. Pretty soon comes the 'Zmm, zmm, zmm' of innumerable flies, settling on eyelids and mouth.

For all the dusty miles of travel, the jump-ups negotiated, the dry creekbeds crossed in low gear, there is nothing much to see; a few sheets of rusted corrugated iron where a dwelling once stood; some weed-grown slabs of concrete; quartz edging the ghost of a path to a long-vanished front door; another of green-glass beer bottles embedded upside down; shards of crockery interlaced by lizard tracks in the pale-red sand. There might be the bricks of a long-gone baker's oven through which a wattle has thrust; some defunct machinery strangled by rubber vine; a splash of brilliance where an ancient bougainvillaea has climbed into a stringybark.

Most poignant of all are the long-forgotten cemeteries. Such effort has gone into bringing the marble headstones up from the coast. 'Our Darling Baby'; 'Beloved Wife and Mother'; 'Killed in a fall of rock'; 'Erected by his friends as a token of their esteem'; 'Never forgotten'. The forgetting is complete now. It all happened a century ago, mourned and mourners long gone. But in the dry, pure air the wording is as fresh as though it were but yesterday. Some of the graves once had been fenced against wandering cattle, but white ants have dealt with the timber, its locust-like crust now held together only by number-eight wire. Sorrow broods, despite the cheerful galahs exploding out of paper-barks along the dry creek.

Koorboora was one such township. Named from an Aboriginal word for 'barren place', Koorboora was established in 1889 to serve the nearby tin and wolfram mines. By the late 1890s the population was five hundred; with two hotels, two stores, a Jack and Newell's, Lewis's Cordial Factory and Refreshment Rooms, a butcher, baker and saddler, and Yen Lee the market gardener. There were two crushing mills, capable of treating twenty-six tons of ore a day. Mine strikes of 1911,

1912 and 1913 helped to ruin the little town. After the First World War the battery operated sporadically until it closed in 1927.

You wander round in the heat-seared silence, straining to catch some echo of the life of this forgotten town. Who were the people that came here? How could they not be overwhelmed by the terrible isolation? How did the women cope?

Edward Cummings supplies some of the answers. Through boyish eyes we are given an intimate glimpse of life in Koorboora at the beginning of the century, when the stampers of the battery filled the air with energetic thumpings, the school hummed with the voices of children, and men worked for £2 a week. Women created homes in timber-and-hessian dwellings which had no doors or need of locks. We are given an insight into the demands made not only upon adults but upon children. Boys chopped wood, fetched water up from the creek, and in the dry season, took a cart out to the New King mine and, using a windlass, bailed enough water from the abandoned shaft to fill a twenty-five gallon drum, 'for the house'. The knowledge that these efforts were vital to the family's survival must have had a bracing effect on a boy's emergent sense of self-worth. Few things are more nourishing than to know oneself needed.

Edward Cummings had a lively boyhood at Koorboora. Barefoot, 'soles on our feet like kangaroo pads', he and his friends raced up and down the mullock heaps, went fishing at the Three Mile, rolled boulders down Tennyson Hill and scratched for tin in the school holidays and found it, in appreciable quantities. Not content, in a world of mines and mining, to remain mere prospectors, the boys began an underground operation fraught, to modern eyes, with hair-raising dangers. Fortunately it was an age when boys were 'taught the things they thought you should understand' and no harm ensued.

They were also well taught at the school 'which looked out over the main street'. Jack Cameron 'was the most severe teacher in Queensland, or possibly Australia' and you 'could hear a pin drop' in the classroom. He was, it would seem, also one of the most dedicated, taking the children for botany and geology walks, teaching them to swim in the dam on Friday afternoons and rehearsing them for concerts. Mr Cameron was highly respected in the little town, for when his baby died in one of the recurrent summer epidemics of fly-borne disease, 'everybody walked' to the little bush cemetery for the burial.

Edward Cummings' basic education at Koorboora School served him well. In later life he joined the RAAF and trained as a radio technician. He became a radiographer and made important technical improvements to the equipment then in use. He returned to North Queensland and worked in Cairns and in association with Dr Flecker pioneered underwater photography on the Barrier Reef, designing and using a diving bell for the purpose, filming different aspects of the reef at night in colour on 16 mm film, a first for the period. The hardy, self-reliant boyhood years at Koorboora stood him in good stead. In him the spirit of the bush pioneers of the North, to whom he 'raised his hat', lived on.

Boyhood At Koorboora

I was born in Ravenswood, 22nd of August 1902 and we lived there until I was about five. When Leonta came through[1] Dad was away working at the mine and a big black snake came into the place for shelter and curled up in a cupboard!

From Ravenswood we went to the Hodginson Goldfield, to a place called Kingsborough. Dad was winding driver on a mine called the Monarch. I saw Haley's Comet from Kingsborough in 1910.

In those days the water used to beat the miners, once they got deep. They couldn't keep the waterlevel down. The night shift and the afternoon shift would bail all the time so that the men could work on the day shift. In the end they'd be driven out with the water. They hadn't got the sophisticated pumps which they have today. My father always said before he died at ninety-four, that a great number of the mines – gold, tin, wolfram, the lot – in North Queensland, were all worth opening up again, because now they've got the pumping gear that makes it possible.

Towards the end of 1910 the Monarch closed and they wanted winding drivers at Koorboora, on the Chillagoe line. We moved there in 1911. Before that, Mum and my brother and I were to go down and visit some relatives in Bowen, and Dad said he would let Mum know when to come on. While we were staying with these friends Mum got the letter from him that said we should be able to catch the *Yongala*'s[2] next trip in a few weeks time. My Mum was a very efficient person. She said, 'No! Be blowed to that! We'll get the *Lass o' Gowrie!*' It left in a couple of days. So she packed everything up and we caught the *Lass o' Gowrie* and got to Cairns, and on up to Koorboora. And within a couple of weeks, the news came through that the *Yongala* was lost with all hands! A hundred and twenty-two people! All perished! The only thing saved was a racehorse swam to Palm Island.[3]

Koorboora was booming, then, in tin mining; tin and wolfram. And Dad was winding engineer there.

Dad'd be one of the highest paid. He'd be getting something like three pounds a week. Miners got around two pounds, or two pound ten. I wouldn't say we were well off, but we had good food, and the necessities.

In those days houses were usually bush timber and hessian. But a good galvanised roof. They stood up to cyclones. For the house we had a tank but it wasn't very big and that was kept for cooking and drinking. We were right on the edge of Koorboora Creek and I'd go down and carry water up in a couple of small buckets to use as general-purpose water. The buckets were tins, about the size of what you'd get powdered milk in, and you'd knock a couple of holes in and put a wire handle. They did have galvanised buckets, but they were too big for me to climb up out of this creek. It was fairly steep.

In those days we had Laurel kerosene that came in a beautiful pine box with two four-gallon square tins, side by side, in. Laurel kerosene was for lighting. All kerosene lamps. These tins, they were marvellous. They were used for all manner of things. The womenfolk used to boil the clothes in them, out over an open fire with a couple of bars mounted on a few stones. Plenty of wood, of course. That was the way they did the washing.

And Laurel kerosene boxes were highly prized because you'd get a number of them, and nail them together, then a bit of wire strung across and some sheeting to draw across and there it was, you had a wardrobe, or a linen press![4] There was very little real furniture as we know it today. People had just a few bits and pieces that they'd make themselves.

And other cases which were highly prized were the ones that dynamite came in, by Nobel. They were very well-made cases; dovetailed. Of course,

Frederick Charles Hall Collection

Edward Cumming's home at Koorboora was on the banks of Koorboora Creek 'above the dam', so there was plenty of water for a flower garden – but it all had to be carried up in buckets. In this photograph, an Aboriginal woman seems to be on hand to help with the task that was Edward's. On the verandah is a 'squatter's chair' – sacking stretched between two lengths of timber nailed to the wall. Edward remembered with some pride how furniture in many bush houses was home-made.

there weren't so many of them because one'd hold a good many packets of explosives. In those days the miners, if they're working a small show on their own, they'd just have for a magazine maybe an oil drum set into the mullock heap. And they'd have a bag over it with a few rocks on the top and they'd keep their fuses and dynamite in that.

The stores in town handled the explosives then. There was no special magazine or anything. You could just buy them. Jack and Newell's Store was the main one. It had the basics. Food, and carbide. There'd be only one street at Koorboora, two hotels, and Jack and Newell's. Jack and Newell's Stores was in all these mining towns in the North. They did a marvellous job. The Jack and Newell's[5] made it possible for the pioneers, and the early mining people to survive. They'd give them credit when they'd had a bad time, or were out of luck and couldn't strike payable tin or whatever.

There was one chap, he'd had a very bad time and he owed Jack and Newell's a considerable amount of money. In those days twenty pounds was a big sum, you know. And he explained to the Jack and Newell's manager that he heard there'd been a gold strike somewhere up north and he and his missus were off. And years later this cove came back and he walked into Jack and Newell's, and he said, 'Oh, Hello! I don't suppose you know me.'

And the chap in Jack and Newell's looked up and he said, 'Well, no. I can't place you right away.' And the chap said, 'Well, I'm So-and-So. And you were marvellous to me. I went away owing you about twenty pounds. So I got on my feet, and here it is.'

Yes! Jack and Newell's! They stood by people in those mining towns. Made it possible for them to survive. And another thing about the quality of mining-town people; if anyone had a bit of bad luck, or an injury, everybody was there to help. They were marvellous to come to the rescue. And when you'd go out of your house, you'd never think to lock your door. Well, there were no doors, let alone locks on them. But nothing was ever touched! You might have somebody call out, 'Oh, Mrs Cummings, I borrowed your frypan!' or 'your camp-oven'. And, 'That's all right, Mrs Smith' sort of thing. It was accepted.

There was a very good baker in Koorboora. It was my job to pick the bread up and bring it home after school. And I had the usual chores, chopping the wood, and getting the morning-wood in. And in the dry season, you had to be very careful with water. Once the rainy season stopped you wouldn't get any rain whatsoever and the creeks would stop running. It was my job to cart water in from one of the mines called the New King. It was called after King George V, I think. See, you had to be careful about where you got water. If you got certain minerals it could be not fit to drink. But the New King water was quite wholesome. It hadn't been worked for some time. It was up past where they used to hold the races – it wasn't a proper racetrack but where they held them; there was a bit of a flat. The ridge ran from our place and the New King was at the far end of the ridge. In the dry season, I used to go up to the New King with this little cart and fill this drum up – I had to use a windlass – about twenty-five gallons, and cart it home.

And the butcher boy, he would gallop around on a horse, and you'd call out and tell him what you wanted. And in the morning he would bring it around; the best meat in the shop, lovely roasts, under a shilling a pound.

Butter was about a shilling a pound. The system in the shop, to keep the butter from melting was, they had a big four-gallon drum of water strung up, with a hole in it and it would drip down on to some canvas. And it was over a metal frame, with hessian over. And it'd drip down, and there was a tray under it to catch the drips. But not much water got into the tray because it would evaporate. The air blowing on this wet canvas kept the butter solid enough not to melt. But the trouble was to get it home. Because they'd give you one of these little pine butter-boats. They were made of wood shaved off, very thin, like veneer. A flat bottom and the side came up, all in one piece. Then it had some pins through it up at the end. And they just put this bit of paper on there and smacked the butter on to it with a wooden paddle thing, and that was it. You galloped home as fast as you could before it melted. By the time you got home you were lucky if it wasn't running through your fingers.

At home you kept it in this Coolgardie safe, a frame with the hessian over it and you would have this drum up above it, with just this drip coming through, enough to keep the hessian wet. And this was our system of refrigeration (laughs).

I didn't see ice up to when I was about eleven year old. It was at one of these race meetings where the bands came. It was some big do at Koorboora, not long before the War broke out – the last big get-together. And this chap had this machine for making ice-cream. And he had us boys on turning this handle. We didn't know what it was. But we kept turning away at this thing. And then at the end of it all, when the day had finished, he took his bucket and emptied all this glassy-looking rock out. And I looked and stared and went to pick a piece up and it was cold! Of course, it was ice! So I grabbed a piece, and I got a piece of bark, and ran like mad down the hill to my mother to show her what this marvellous ice was! Galloped all the way home! It was the first time I'd seen ice. Oh, yes! Ice! You know! Of course, my mother was from England, and she'd seen plenty of ice!

The toilet was a hole dug in the ground. It was some distance away. But it wasn't far enough away that the flies couldn't go down it. You'd use sawdust and ashes after, but with that, and the amount of dead beasts about… well, the flies! You had to be very careful of flies. In the summer they were bad and in those days there was very little understood about how they carried diseases. Diarrhoea was one of the worst and in summer it used to get pretty bad. But babies, if they got the diarrhoea they would get dehydrated and die in a couple of days. It was terrible.There was no doctor. So a baby would become ill and the parents wouldn't know if it was a simple cold or something worse. And it was a big thing to go to Chillagoe, and by the time they realise it was getting serious, the baby would die of dehydration. There was no nurses or anything like that. There'd be some housewife who was recognised as knowing a bit more than the others. And the only medicine was Chamberlain's Colic and Diarrhoea Remedy.[6] There wasn't a great deal of knowledge on medical problems then.

The death rate was terrible. And my Mum, if somebody whispered, 'Oh, Tommy Jones was taken to Chillagoe and they think it might be diphtheria'… Oh, the word! The word 'diphtheria' and my Mum's the colour of a sheet. Because you got diphtheria then, (smacks knee) you were finished! By the time they realised that it wasn't just a sore throat, by the time they got you to a hospital where they could do a tracheotomy on you – they put a tube down – you were dead! Diphtheria was a terror.

And for all the other diseases, all we had up there were a few things like Wood's Great Peppermint Cure, and poultices, bread poultices. It somebody had a boil, that's the way you got heat on to it, with a bread poultice. And when it'd burst, they knew to keep it clean. But in those days they didn't understand bacteria and all that.

Well, just trying to sort out whether a person should be taken to a doctor, or it looked as though it mightn't be that serious, you're gambling with time. The doctor never came to Koorboora. In those days the roads were terrible and the train from Chillagoe only ran Monday, Wednesday and Friday from Cairns through to Chillagoe, and Tuesdays, Thursdays and Saturdays down. You'd have to catch one of those. There was no motor vehicles. And until the railway come it was a very difficult trip. Up over The Bump, they called it.

There was a cemetery, a proper cemetery. And there'd be a carpenter or somebody who could prepare a coffin. And there'd be a sulky, or some horse-drawn vehicle. And the people would go along. The cemetery was

> **IN MEMORIAM**
>
> **MILLS**—In fond and loving memory of our darling Norman Keary, youngest son of the late John Mills, who died suddenly on the 19th February, 1899.
>
> You are not forgotten, Norman Dear,
> Nor shalt thou ever be;
> As long as ever life shall last,
> We will remember thee.
>
> (Inserted by his loving mother and brother. Brisbane papers please copy.)
>
> **DOUGLAS**—In loving memory of James Walter Douglas, who departed this life on February 14th, 1899, aged 3 years and seven weeks. R.I.P.
>
> This lovely bud, so young and fair,
> Called hence by early doom,
> Just came to show how sweet a flower
> In Paradise could bloom.
> He is gone but not forgotten,
> Never shall his memory fade;
> Fondest hopes shall ever linger
> Round the place where he is laid.

never terribly far away from the towns. They had to be within a reasonable walking distance. My schoolteacher's baby died and we all went to the funeral. Everybody walked. The women would wear black if they had it. If a brother or sister died a boy would come to school with a black armband for a few weeks. That was the custom, to wear the black armband.

A lot of people had a bit of garden, but, mostly, for vegetables the Chinamen come around. Up at Cooktown, and Maytown and the Palmer River there was very big activity with the Chinese in mining. But at Koorboora all we had were these two who had market gardens, Yen Lee, and Yung Bun. They were terrific market gardeners. Yen Lee, he had a marvellous garden down there by the little creek, by Koorboora railway station. Used to have paw-paws and custard apples, and everything. And he'd come around in a four-wheeled cart – one horse, allowed to go along at his own pace – and he'd pull up and Mum'd say, 'What you got today, Johnnie?'

And he'd say, (adopts Chinese accent): 'Ah, me gottem pum-kin, wata-melon… and sellalee.' Celery, of course. And bananas, two or three of these big hands. And Johnny'd give them to me and the weight'd nearly pull me down! That cost about a shilling!

And everybody had a paw-paw tree, and oranges and mandarins. But lemons! Everybody was giving everybody else lemons.[7]

There were Aborigines around, but they were very well behaved. They'd camp on the creeks and get their own food out of the bush. Except they might come along and say (adopts supplicating voice) 'Oh, Missus. Me chop lil' bit wood, you gibbit lil' bit tea, chuga, 'baccy?' So right-oh, they'd hop in and they'd chop some wood then off they'd go quite happy, down to their camp with their 'baccy. But there was no alcohol, and they weren't disorderly. They were good people.

There were big herds of goats everywhere. Everybody had goats for the milk and to kill for mutton. My brother was something of an invalid and expected to die when he was quite young, but Dr Perkins, and Dr Millet, they both advised goat's milk. And goat's milk saved him. There's something about it.

From the school you looked out over just the one street at Koorboora. Mr Jack Cameron was the head teacher. Don and Jack Mackie and Eva Rumming were teachers. Our teacher, Jack Cameron, he used to put on a concert every year to break up the school. He was a marvellous organiser. On one occasion he got us to go out bush and get grass-tree sticks and paint them all with silver paint. He had us put on what he called the Wand Drill. You'd hold it this way and step; all these different steps, and all in absolute precision. It just about brought the house down.

The thing about Jack Cameron was precision. One act would finish and the next would be ready to move in. When I went later to Mareeba and some of those places, I couldn't believe it! The inefficiency compared to Cameron! 'Oh, where's Topsy Jones? She's supposed to go on next to sing.' And Topsy couldn't be found! And then she'd be found round having an ice-cream! There was none of that! Jack Cameron had it all absolutely precision! One mob'd move off and after the applause the next lot'd come on: 'So-and-so will

John Oxley Library

At the weekends and on holidays, Edward and his friends camped and fished at the Big Hole, near Koorboora. On Fridays they had swimming lessons 'in the dam' under the watchful eye of the redoubtable Jack Cameron. This cannot be one of those occasions as none of the boys is wearing swimming togs.

sing…' All absolutely first class! He did a marvellous job. Anything he did was efficiency.

You could hear a pin drop in that school. You wouldn't be game to even whisper in class. He was the most severe schoolteacher, I'm sure, in the whole of Queensland, and possibly Australia. But we accepted it. That was the norm. I started school at the Monarch, in Kingsborough, but this was the first one that I was old enough to realise what school was, properly. And we accepted it. But while he was severe he was also a marvellous teacher and he was most just and fair and gave us a wonderful founding on the things of importance. He used to take us on prospecting trips, and botany trips. He taught us how to survive in the bush. And great care, if you're boiling the billy, to put the fire out after. In the schoolyard, marbles was the great game. Boys usually played marbles and the girls, they had hopscotch and skippy. No-one had shoes. Bare feet was the thing there. We could race up and down those mullock heaps, sharp quartz and everything. We must have developed soles on our feet like kangaroo pads.

We were all taught to swim up in the dam. Every Friday afternoon was swimming afternoon. That was the only water, and there used to be lovely waterbirds, cranes and others, at the far end of the dam where it backed up into Koorboora Creek. It was quite a big dam, constructed of logs and rocks and soil, with an overflow down through some rocks. The creek had rocky sides and the battery was built at the top end. A good number of people built their homes on the banks of the creek, including us. I just had to climb over a bit of a ridge and I was at school. But our teacher, he was wonderful; Jack Cameron. I owe the progress I made in later life to him. And to my parents who were sensible down-to-earth people.

Parents taught you the things that they thought you should understand. Us boys, we used to go into mines and tunnels and down shafts, and it was all done with a knowledge of how to do it correctly. You got shown the proper way to do the thing. Families taught their children. Now, fire! If you're going out, check the stove before you go. There'd be a flat sheet of galvanised iron nailed on the floor surrounding the stove so that if any charcoal fell out it couldn't set the place on fire,[8] but you had to check the stove to be sure before you went anywhere.

In our spare time, mostly we boys, we went out getting tin; prospecting, and scratching for tin in the creeks and gullies. We were pretty good at it. Our fathers had shown us. Alluvial tin, very good quality, too. Any minerals, tin, wolfram, gold.

I can remember one occasion… (laughs). Of course, all we boys were mad on mines. We all had to have a mine. A couple of other chaps and I had one. We rigged up a windlass on it, and of course, we had to be real miners. We got a hammer and some drills. You'd get drills, they were all over the place.

So we struck some fairly hard rock and we figured it was tin. And there was tin around there too. Later they did find it. Quite a good tin show nearby. Anyway, I decided to bore some holes. So we helped ourselves to a bit of dynamite and a bit of detonator and a fuse.

And, fortunately, we had learnt to… we had a great capacity for learning things properly. And I knew you didn't put this plug in the hole. You take this paper off and you put this plug of dynamite in and then you put the cap onto the fuse, and you don't do any stupid thing like biting the detonator on, you crimp it on with a pair of pliers, and then you ram the hole with dirt, and fine dirt. And you don't use metal on that. You use a piece of wood, wooden rod. And all this I knew.

And we'd fired a hole or two like this, and, this Saturday, we'd bored another hole. And lit it. And we're scampering over the rise a bit, and just as I get on the top of the rise, going down the other side I met my father. On the way over to see what 'the mine' was like! And then it 'Booom!' and there's fine stones and stuff come filtering down.

Well instead of going on at me he said, 'Oh, I see! Well, let's go over and you can show me how you do this, so I'll know you're doing it right.' That was the attitude. They knew we were going to do things, so they'd accept that and show us the right way to do it. Most of the parents were pretty sensible sort of people. They didn't bung on an act about it.

So we went over, and he got me to explain it. And he said, 'Oh, yes.Well… In the future you drill the holes and I'll supervise the charging. So we agreed to that. And he said, 'And I'll provide the explosives.' Once you got mining in your veins there's always an attraction about it.

Christmas holidays, over the six weeks, to do a bit of tin scratching in the gullies, we'd make ourselves a little scraper, a piece of hoop iron, bent L-shaped and then cut off at a point, and then the other end doubled back to make a bit of a handle. There was a gully right opposite our place and it had fairly good dirt in it. And you'd take off the overburden, the sand and stuff, especially after the rain. And if it's raining like mad then you'd put on some old clothes that you could get wet in and you'd go out and you'd break the banks down and let the water run all this dirt away. Similar to hydraulic sluicing.

Then later on, after the rain had finished, and the run off, you'd go down and break the banks down, and down it would come, pouring through, and then you'd go along and you'd scrape the sand back and get down into the crevices. That's where the tin is. Tin or gold or any of the heavies. It gets right down in the little crevices in the rocks.

And we'd scrape along and even use a little brush, made of little grass-sticks that we'd bind together. Because you'd get it exceedingly rich in some of these places. It would be nothing to get a pound of tin to a dish of dirt.

And over this Christmas holiday, I got this tin, and my Dad, he liked to go alluvial mining on his own account, banjoing[9] and hydraulic sluicing. And on one occasion he was taking tin down to Mareeba to sell. It was about £10 a hundredweight bag. And he took mine down as well. And I got £2. That was quite a lot of money in those days, as much as a miner might get in a week.

I'd always wanted a gold half sovereign. Something about a half sovereign was fascinating. So Dad brought me back a half sovereign. And as well, I bought a present for him, and a present for my mother and for my brother. And I still had some left over!

There were some good steep hills around. We'd be climbing the mountains and hills, exploring, out at a place called the Sunset, out past the Iolanthe and the Shakespeare mines. That was a great place for grass-sticks and we'd gather a lot of these and bring them home. Or we'd climb up Tennyson Hill and we'd roll great big boulders down. We'd learned Archimedes Law, 'Give me a lever long enough and an arm strong enough and I'll lift the earth'. So we'd cut a sapling, and that was our lever. And Archimedes was quite right. Because there were these big boulders that weighed tons, and we'd get this big sapling and we'd lever it and lever it and down that boulder would go, right down Tennyson Hill. And if it hit a dead tree and the tree would splatter in all directions, that's what we liked to see!

And we used to go fishing down the Three Mile. We'd go down Saturdays and camp Saturday night. Oh, great fun. I had a couple of mates, George and Ronny Black. We'd go down to what we called the Big Hole, and the Little Hole. There would be garfish sailing up and down. And rifle-fish, with the spot on, and bream and perch. We'd have a line wrapped in a figure-of-eight on to a small stick. You didn't need a sinker or anything. You didn't go any depth. You just swung it around a few times and away it'd go. Smallish hooks. There was nothing that warranted a big hook. And we'd have a piece of meat from home for bait and we'd catch black bream and perch.You never caught rifle-fish on a line. I don't know why. There'd be a shoal of garfish swimming along but you never caught those. If you caught something about six inches long you'd race around, when you got home, and show it to everybody because that would be something really worthwhile. They were all small. But edible.Very fine bones. You wouldn't fillet them; just scale them and gut them, and throw them in the pan, and be very careful about how you went about eating them. George Black, he caught a black bream, it was a bit over a pound weight, and that was deemed a sensation around the place.

And we used to go into these tunnels and down mines, and it was, 'Well, what you've got to watch is that the ladder's safe'. And when we went into the caves we had to be mindful that we didn't get lost in them. The McDonagh boys and us, we'd go into the big caves in Chillagoe and Mungana. And you could get lost in there, no trouble. We'd take an acetylene lamp or a hurricane; maybe some candles. An acetylene lamp gave a good light. More brilliant.

You'd take a waterbag if you were going on a jaunt and only replenish it at a place that you knew was safe. There were certain waterholes, and old mine shafts, that were recognised as drinking holes. You got to know them. Dad always said, if ever water's real clear, don't touch it. Never drink water where it's crystal clear. There's generally some minerals which cause it to be clear. He said it's better to drink water that may have a bit of mud in it. In those days boys acquired knowledge from their fathers on what not to do, and they became very wary.

As for entertainment in the town, well, this is in Koorboora's heyday, at its top before the war, when it was going very well. Koorboora, Irvinebank and Herberton, that area was all John Moffat's Empire. They had a hall there, where you held dances and played cards, one big hall, a community thing. And a man named Gilda used to travel around and put on a picture show. Koorboora had a portable generator engine and this Gilda used to come round from time to time and put on this picture show in the hall. And I can remember the first picture show. It was a Cowboys and Indians thing. Real 'Bang! Bang!' We thought it was great.

Koorboora Notes.

(For the "N.Q. Register.")

KOORBOORA, April 28.

The continual dry weather is making itself keenly felt, most of the residents are already carting water, and at a time when it generally rains most. The outlook is really serious.

Mining matters still continue to be very dull, with no immediate prospect of brightening for some time to come. The Irvinebank Company only have two mines in commission, with a few tributors on the other leases, and the battery running with two shifts has crushed up all the available ore, so things are what we term "just middling."

The school teachers and children are giving an entertainment on Saturday night in aid of the Belgian fund. The tickets for this worthy object are selling like "hot cakes," and as the children are well trained a good night's entertainment is assured.

There was a large attendance at the picnic held at the Two-mile on Sunday last, which proved another one of these enjoyable outings so eagerly looked forward to. Mrs Rumings, with her staff of lady helpers, deserves special thanks, also Messrs Newell, Woodhouse, who worked hard to make everything enjoyable.

Quite a number of famillities departed from here last week, the destination being to the sugar country, which seems more attractive than the tin country.

The Fairplay tributors have just cleaned up a crushing, but returns are not yet available.

The battery is engaged on Coop and Richardson's crushing (Shakespeare's tribute), and is reported to be crushing well.

Messrs Cameron and Lindsay have opened u pa promiscuous tin show in the vicinity of the one-time famous "Lisha." The stone is expected to go twenty per cent.

The Tennyson tributors, Mattley and Treichal, have been operating on good stone, and have a parcel awaiting treatment.

And there would be races, horse races, once a year. Up on the flat. They'd hold this race meeting, and people'd come from Chillagoe and Mungana and Mareeba and all around. Oh, and the Chillagoe and Mareeba Band would come down. The McDonaghs, they were four boys and two girls, and all the boys played something, euphonium and slide trombones and cornets. Oh, Yes! They were extra good. They'd play at the races. For the dances there was just a piano and a violin, or there'd be someone on an accordion.

Another big occasion was the turning of the first sod for the Mulligan Railway. There was big excitement at Dimbulah for that. They decided to build a railway from Dimbulah to Mount Mulligan and they ran excursion trains from Cairns and down from Chillagoe and people came from far and wide. The trains were packed. It was the biggest gathering of the people of the area, a real bumper occasion, with all the bunting, and all the caper. They were giving out toys. And the Governor was there.

And Henry Gunther and myself we're wandering around, there was games and things going on, and our schoolteacher Jack Cameron came along, and he said, 'Oh, Yes! You two boys! Go over to the railway station…' – at Dimbulah the grounds were a little bit away from the station – 'Go over the railway station and he will give you a little box with the gold-plated trowel in, that the Governor will use to turn the sod for the Mulligan railway.'

So right away we raced off and we're given this box and we're coming back and we're dying to have a look at it so we dived behind an ant-bed and opened it up. And it's got an inscription on it in fancy writing but we couldn't even read it. But anyway we got a good look at it. And then when the time came, Jack Cameron said, 'Well, all right, you stand here and when the Governor comes you present him with the trowel.' So I had the great distinction of handing this trowel to the Governor of Queensland. That must have been the last big event before the war, probably the end of 1912 or early 1913.

The day I was fourteen I left school and went to the Biboohra Meatworks just for the season. The cattle used to come from stations up north. They canned the meat; there was no freezers or any of that caper. It was canned and sent down south. When they were filling cans with meat they'd put a little piece of tin inside each one so that when they soldered the cap on, if there's any solder drops through it would go on to this. When I was first there I was putting these into the tin. This was at the start. They used to have presses there, for stamping out the bottom and tops of the tins. And during the smokos I got practising on these presses, and I became pretty efficient at it. And one day, the regular chap who did the job was sick and didn't turn up, and they told the management that I knew how to do it. So they put me on the press and I got five pounds and sixpence a week. Which was fabulous money. And when a boy went on to a man's job, then the management had to keep him on that pay. Couldn't put him back to the other rate. So I stayed on it and was taking home five pounds and sixpence a week! Which was a terrific amount of money, at that time, considering that my father was a winding driver and wasn't getting anything like that. It was a forty-four hour week. An eight-hour day and Saturday till twelve.

I took that envelope home and gave it to my Mum without even opening it. She'd give me back some for pocket money. I didn't want much. Most boys did the same. And we didn't expect much back.

Anything I achieved later on in life I owe it to my parents and my schoolteacher. I raise my hat today to the memory of the pioneers! (spoken in an almost religious tone). They were most terrific *people!* They came from England, from London, from all these places, where everything was worth having. And they gave it up and they came up into these *parts*, right into the wilds, with all the difficulties and terrors that went with it. And they made a go of things! I raise my hat to them!

1 The Narrator is not claiming to remember Leonta, but his mother's recollections of it, especially the snake in the cupboard, a not uncommon experience in the bush. Anecdotes handed down in this way from generation to generation become part of family lore.

2 Using the pronunciation Yon-gla, the pronunciation in use when the ship was on the goldfields run from Adelaide to Western Australia. When the *Yongala* was transferred to the Queensland run, the accent was placed on the second syllable, becoming Yon-gar-la, which is how it is still remembered and pronounced in Townsville.

3 The body of the racehorse Moonshine was found washed up on Cape Cleveland. Newspaper coverage of the day reported initial findings of wreckage on Palm Island. The two are being confused. See Appendix D for the loss of the *Yongala* especially '11 April 1911'.

4 An additional use could be made of kerosene tins by leaving the top, with its metal handle, in position, and cutting out one side lengthwise, turning over the edges for safety. Two tins adapted like this could then be slid in and out of the divided case to serve as drawers.

5 Jack and Newell's stores were a feature of many of the mining towns of the North. They are remembered warmly by many Narrators as being very supportive of struggling families.

6 'Dysentery causes the death of more people than Smallpox or Yellow Fever. In an army it is more dreaded than any battle. It requires prompt and efficient treatment. Chamberlain's Colic, Cholera and Diarrhoea Remedy has been used in nine epidemics of dysentery in the United States with perfect success and has cured the most malignant cases of both children and adults and under the most trying conditions. Every household should have a bottle on hand. It may save a life.' Advertisement, *North Queensland Register*, 1903.

7 Houldsworth, Marion, *The Immigrant Boy: Growing up in Townsville 1912–1918.* Joe Clark makes a cryptic remark about back-yard lemon-trees; 'Of course, the women used lemons as contraceptives…'

8 Older readers will remember the high sheen this sheet of iron acquired with the passage of time and the homely crackling sound it made underfoot.

9 An alluvial mining process named from the banjo-shaped hole dug in the ground into which water was sluiced to wash the pay-dirt.

19

The Bohle, 1912–1920 **Edward Smedley**

Any Fish Is A Good Fish

Introduction

At age seventy-three, Edward Smedley's was one of the youngest life stories to have been included in the North Queensland Oral History Collection, and for that reason I might have passed it over in favour of one from an earlier period. But the eager voice and the zest in the telling quickened my interest. I love an enthusiast! And who else could detail so precisely the way to construct a box fish trap? Or the manner in which the nightsoil pans at the Sanitary Depot at Rowes Bay were tarred so that they shone as though enamelled! We are not to smile! If ever there was an essential service, in pre-seweraged Townsville, that was it! Somebody had to do it, and that being so, how much better that it should have been done with such lively interest.

Edward gives us a wonderful, thumbnail-dipped-in-tar sketch of the Townsville of his boyhood: the tensions of learning to write in ink with dip-pens; the smoodging of fire-crackers off the Johnnie Chinamen; the galloping in fear past the Aborigines' camp at Rowes Bay, ('they could eat you', the boys believed); the finding of spoil from a ship-wreck on the beach at Pallarenda, not to mention a guilty flutter on the fan-tan and pakapoo down in Flinders Lane.

Mouths can only water at talk of plentiful barramundi, and of crabs and oysters by the bagful. And for a profitable sideline for the family there was the shellgrit. As Edward Smedley talks you can almost feel the heat of the sun, smell the salt, sense the luminous vastness of sky arching above the empty coastline at the mouth of the Bohle. And in charge of the whole operation, indomitable Mum, 'head boss', making two trips through the sandhills into town each week, the spring cart laden with the produce of the sea.

A noticeable feature of Edward's narration on the audio-tape is that there are moments when he is not merely telling about the past, but somehow slips through the mesh of years and is back again in his wild, free boyhood, actually living it. The voice, as he remembers the canings at Belgian Gardens School, is filled with unfeigned dread. Then he chokes with laughter at how he and his brothers tormented the boys at the orphanage in Warburton Street, with shouts of 'gi's a suckin' pig!' He has no idea what the taunt meant. It was just something to provoke the orphans into counter-attack, at which he and his brothers would run for their lives. It could have all happened ten breathless minutes ago, so great is the glee of the telling.

Similarly his sorrow in recalling the drowning of one of the orphans in the lagoon at Kissing Point; the audio-tape winds on for long moments of silence before the Narrator startles back into the present with an invisible shake of the head and the comment. 'Sad, eh!' Sad indeed, but only to Edward Smedley, in reverie, all these years later. Everyone else has forgotten. And the saltpan and lagoon have long been filled and built over with streets of houses.

Early in his account Edward expresses regret that his parents had not given him a better education. But the lack of formal schooling has not detracted from his ability to observe keenly, and to recount his experiences with a winning immediacy. The tumbling words and the scrambled syntax have the power to carry us back to the sunlit days of circa 1915, to a time when barefoot boys could range like wild ponies through the sandhills, lagoons and bush of Rowes Bay and the Townsville Common, and when, for the boys of the Smedley family, home was the mouth of the Bohle.

⁂

Any Fish Is A Good Fish

Dad had the fish trap at the mouth of the Bohle. Mum used to help him run it. She was head boss! There was twelve children in the family and I was born out there. Mum and Dad come from England. Father was terrible smart. He could add up five rows of figures at once. He could dance or sing or anything. He could write a poem in five minutes. And he used to do anyone's income tax, quick and lively. But they never give us the education.

When we come to school age we stopped in town. They had a place in North Ward there, and one sister, the biggest one, looked after us. And Mum come in there twice a week and stayed overnight. They'd come and take us out to the Bohle every weekend. We'd come back Monday for school. Sometimes we'd be late and miss a day. We had the spring cart, or the sulky; three horses. It was a bad road out across the Common, all sand.

We all went to Belgian Gardens School. I started school about five. We had a very strict teacher. When you went in school, there was none of this running out. You go into the schoolyard, and you're going home to dinner, well, you're allowed out, but otherwise you weren't till it's going home time. And when school went out, everybody had to be out of the schoolyard in about ten minutes. There was no squealing, no whistling. He used to patrol the schoolyard like a policeman. If you done anything wrong you get the cane. And when the headmaster caned a boy it'd always go down in a book. And he had the control of your comings to school and your goings from school.

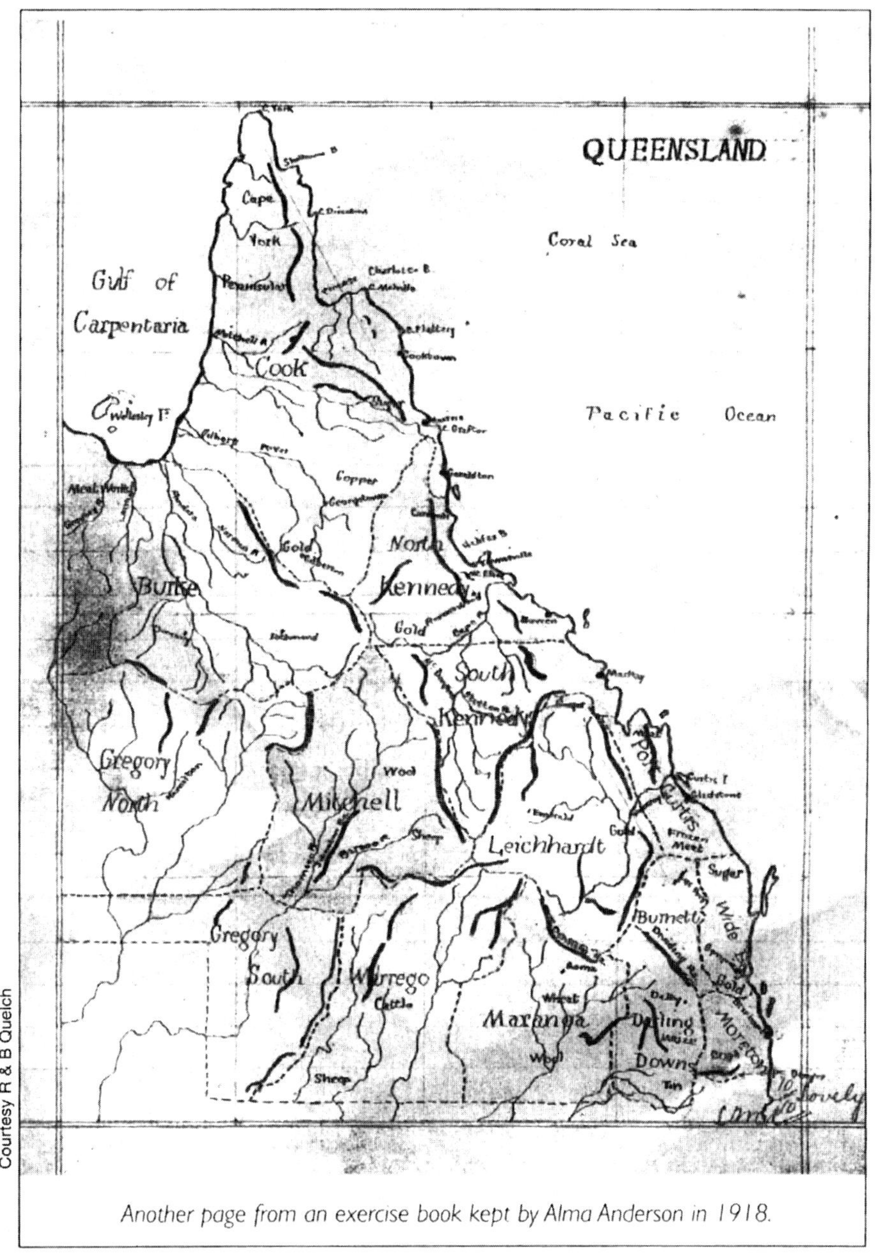

Courtesy R & B Quelch

Another page from an exercise book kept by Alma Anderson in 1918.

And you couldn't talk in school. If you wanted to go to the toilet, well, if you'd only been once for the week he'd let you out, no punishment. But if you went two times or three times in a week you'd have to write a hundred words

John Oxley Library

Edward Smedley grew up in the sandhills near the mouth of the Bohle. The cheerful face of the boy posing for this photograph doesn't quite mask his wariness as two of his charges reach for his 'bit' or 'crib'.

after school. I suppose he thought you were just trying to get out of doing your work.

We wrote on slates with a bit of sponge to clean them up. You put them down the rack in front of you in the wooden desk. And of course, when you got up a bit in the big classes, you use ink. You all had a little hole in the desk with a ink-well in it, and you use nib pens. And sometimes the ink would come down in a big dob. Or you get a bit of fluff on it and it goes all… awrrr! (the memory is still infuriating). You couldn't make a mess. You had to buy your own exercise book. You could only use one side of the page. And if you went and done a drawing or something inside, you'd get the cane for it. You had to be neat. You couldn't fool with it.

There were four teachers, the headmaster and three others. We had Primmer One, Primmer Two and Primmer Three [primary classes, named for the reading text books, Primer I, etc.]. And then it was Fourth Grade, Fifth Grade. They used to ram times-tables and spellings down your throat. And when you get up in the big classes, you had homework. You had to have three passes out of five otherwise you get on the floor and get the cane.[1] He'd check you out for the week, and he'd say, 'You only got two passes. You haven't got three. Get out on the floor.' He used to call the cane 'Peter'. And he would say, 'I don't like bringing Peter out but I've got to.' And he used to bend it and he'd stand on the tip of his toes and hit you across the legs with it. And if you run to get away from it he'd say, 'Come back and get your change, Boy! Come back and get your change!' Oh, God, yeah!

And there were female teachers too. Some of them were quiet, but there was one there, aw! She could use a stick like billy-o! We had another little piece there, Mrs Bowen. She always used a ruler. But, aw! She could hit! I don't know how many rulers she broke on kids' legs! The way she'd snap 'em! Oh, yeah!

And Breaking-up Day, first you'd have a bit of a sing-song and things, and they give out prizes. Then we'd have races. Then you'd go down and you'd get as much soft drink and cake as you could eat. Then you'd line up and you'd all get a bag of lollies to take home. You always got the lollies.

And us kids were always going down the beach. We'd poke along towards Pallarenda down to Three Mile Creek. And, once, the *Bombala* got caught out there on Salamander Reef.[2] It was loaded with pineapples and bananas and mangoes and coconuts, going away down south. One of our schoolteachers was on it, too. And it couldn't get off the reef, so they threw everything overboard. And us kids, we seen a case washed up on the beach, and we looked and it was full of pineapples. Well, boy! we tore into it! We et and et until our tongues was bleeding with the h'acid. And we went along and we got cases and cases of 'em! All washed up. And mangoes! And bananas! But the bananas all went bad. They wouldn't ripen. We got the cases and we dragged them up and hid them in the grass up in the bush. Then we got the coconuts. They was already peeled. Oh, we had a picnic with them! And on the Monday we took all the schoolkids down, and we showed them all these pineapples. And didn't we slip into them!

In them days Rowes Bay had a big camp of Aborigines, just before the bridge, with what they call gunyahs, only sheets of iron; you crawl in, dirt floor. They had a heap of dogs. Oh, we used to run past them. We thought they'd eat yer! We thought the blacks'd... you know... eat yer! We used to keep away from them!

There used to be old blackfellows, they'd come around selling wooden props, with a fork on the end for the clothesline. Everybody used a prop in those times. They'd cut them out on the Common and sell them all round the town; cart 'em round on their back, four or five at a time. He'd come round and ask you to buy one for two bob. And there used to be old King Billy. He had a copper plate, with King Billy of Ross River on it, polished, on a chain. Aw! An old fellow he was. Another old fellow, Old Tim they call him, by gee, he was bandy! But after a while the government sent all those Aboriginals to Palm Island.

There used to be Chinese gardens up on the lagoon, and old Chinamen with baskets. They all had pigtails and a pole over the shoulder. They could carry a load, by gee! Potatoes and pumpkin. And you know, the kids ... if the Johnnie was carrying a load... they used to hit the back basket and spin it round on him. Boys! You know! And, Christmastime, us kids used to go up to the Chinaman's garden and buy threepence worth of mint or something and he used to give you a big packet of crackers for Christmas. We didn't want the mint. We used to just keep going back and buying it to get the packet of crackers.

And the Chinee, they have their New Year different to ours. Flinders Lane – Ogden Street it is now – you'd see them decorating all the poles with crackers for New Year night. They used to do right down the poles. And no, there was no pinching them. In our days there was no pinching. Not even for fun. In those days, like, whatever we done, we never done any pinching.

Only thing was, we used to do a lot of shanghaiing. Beggars for shanghais[3] we was! We used to wear 'em round our hat; think you was great if you got a shanghai over your hat with the fork sticking out in front! We was champions with 'em! We used to go down the Common every weekend. Oh, gee, yes! We could knock a bird from fifty yards, sixty yards! But one thing we never done, we never fired at any telegraph cups, or anything like that. Never damaged anything a-purpose. Just the birds.

You couldn't take shanghais to school! No fear! If you got found out – or if a girl put you in: 'Sir! Sir! He had a shanghai!' you're gone! (tone of dread of retribution to come still palpable in voice). We used to hide them along the road to school and do a bit of shanghaiing going home. But you had to watch where some of these tell-tat girls was, see! If a girl would say, 'He had a shanghai going home', the teacher'd bring you in and question you, and if he found out you had, you'd get the cane! Oh! God, yeah!

To make a shanghai we'd go and buy the rubber rings off an old woman that had a shop in Cook Street. She used to say, 'Now what do you want to makes shanghais for! You're only chasing and killin' little innocent birds!' Those rubbers come off the armbands men used to wear; kep' their sleeves up, see. But what we used to do, we'd stretch 'em and look to see where the join was, otherwise if you didn't cut 'em on the join they'd break. Oh, powerful they were! A lot of people cut theirs out of inner tubes but that's got no stretch compared to the ones out of armbands.

Years ago where Eyre Street is, that was one big lagoon that very seldom went dry. We used to swim there in six feet of water. Right across from Kissing Point that was all salt water. A bloke there had a twenty-foot boat floating where there's houses are now. You couldn't credit what they filled in down there. Same with Rowes Bay, there was big sandhills.

The orphanage was down along Warburton Street; fifty or sixty boys and girls there'd be. And Central School used to be along where the clinic is now.[4] The teachers used to march them up every morning for school and march them back for dinner, then back again. They had a proper uniform; the girls had a blue pinafore sort of a thing and the boys had blue striped pants and a coat and a blue hat. The orphanage had all that property where the Crippled Children's is now.[5] There was a well with a windmill, and their own dairy, big proper Jersey cows, and they grew their own corn. Some of the biggest boys had to do the milking. We used to ask them for a sucking pig. When you sang out 'Gis a sucking pig!' they'd be over the fence and pelt you with stones. And, boy! Did we hadda go!

And, gee, it was sad. The Head that was looking after them, he took them down for a swim one day, down to where that twenty-foot boat was, the lagoon. They had to cross the saltpan, see, and it was up to their middles in water. And this bloke didn't know there was a deep gutter where the tide come in. Two of the kids slipped and went under. They were all diving and looking for them and they got one bloke out. And they couldn't find the other bloke and they thought, 'Oh, he got out! He's all right!' But his brother was crying and he said, 'No m' brother ain't come out!' And they found him when the tide went out, caught on the limb of a tree (extended period of silence). Bad luck, eh! Of course, it's all filled in now. When they was filling in the corner of Rowes Bay they cut the big sandhill down and the big high sandhills that was all along the front and they got enough to fill in all that big lagoon.

We had to help with Dad's fish traps. He had traps on both sides of the Bohle with a punt to get across. Now a fish trap, you've got a square box, six by six foot each way, and what we call a receiver. And you've got two round funnels, a big one and a smaller leading from the receiver into the box, and you connect your wings out on either side. You get nine or ten-foot sticks, mangrove, and you come off to the side with a long wing, ours'd've been about a hundred and twenty yards. And the one on the other side, would have been about thirty yards, you bring it back on to the bank. You got to have galvanised wire, or she'll rust out in no time. We've had three boxes on the one trap. The fish come along and they hit the wing and they follow him all the way along and they go into the receiver and through the funnel into the box. Very seldom do they come back out. You very seldom lose a fish. Once they're in they stop in there.

The weather's everything. If you get good weather you get good fishing. Like the mackerel. And when the salmon come you'd get a hundredweight of 'em. Shark is alright to eat. The shovel-nose has got a beautiful taste, as good as a barramundi. And another fish that is good, and that's a catfish. The catfish, the little brown one, he's a lovely fellow to eat! People get the idea that just because he's a catfish he's no good, but his flesh is snow white! Beautiful! But if you're hungry, any fish is a good fish.

A fish trap works while you're asleep! The only thing is those little doggy-mackerel, you had to be there once the tide's out, to take them out or you'd lose em. They get stuck in the wire and they'd be rotten. And when the salmon come you get hundredweights of 'em mashed [meshed] in your wire. Round about three pound they mash in your wire, see. The big one can't. The big fish go in and you have 'em knee deep in water. We'd dig a big hole for the box and they'd swim round. That's how we kept them. We never had no refrigeration.

Mum used to keep the fish in deep water and when she thought she had enough she'd go into town. It'd take her two hours to go in; that's not forcing the horse. I'd go with her. The Chinamen took all she took. When I was little I used to be frightened of the Chinamen. If you done something wrong they used to say, 'I'll take you to the Chinamen!' They told you that the Chinamen took you home. But he always had money in the earhole, and he used to pull a sixpence out and give it to you. In town there were Chinamen running everywhere with their baskets. Twice a week they'd all go with their carts in to Flinders Lane, that's Ogden Street now, and have a market there. And that was where my Mum sold the fish.

And Flinders Lane had these Chinee gambling dens. Us kids'd sneak in and there'd be old Johnnies laying everywhere, and there'd be a peculiar smell; they reckon it was opium. They burnt a lot of those josh sticks. They had these pakapoo tickets, like Pool tickets. They was numbered, up to a hundred marks, and you mark your numbers on a sixpenny ticket. You had to get eight to do any good. If you got seven marks you might get a shilling, or two bob.

My big brother won a couple of bob once. But I never stopped long because I was scared. The police used to come in. One day a bloke said, 'Look! Big Khaki Boot coming!' And I went out through the window! Oh, they'd arrest you, you know. Fan-tan was illegal.

Women didn't go down Flinders Lane, but a lot of businessmen used to have their lunch down there. There was, like, a big shop, straight in, nothing flash, big tables, and they'd all be sitting down having a meal. Chinese cooks are good. And oh, the way they cooked the pork! Just the smell'd make y' hungry!

Crabs was thick in those days. Us kids'd go out with crab sticks and get three or four dozen in a couple of hours. We have a hook on it, a bit of fencing wire bent round, pull them out of the hole. Then there was always plenty in the traps. They'd eat all the dead fish. But if you get too many in the one trap they'd fight, and maybe lose a nipper and you've got to put two to get the price of one. But there wasn't much sale for crabs. We used to get twelve bob a dozen! And that would be big crabs! And we'd take the punt up them creeks back of the Bohle, get those big gold-lip oysters. We'd bag 'em and sell 'em in town. Every cafe always had a corn sack of oysters just inside the door.

And Dad done the shellgrit, too. See, all fowl feed's got to have lime in it. Well, when Dad started out at the Bohle, no-one couldn't get lime, so they'd

John Oxley Library

A billy goat cart of the less-elaborate sort, an empty packing case with shafts and wheels cut from a log, circa 1908. Simple it may be, but the boys in the photograph are obviously proud of it, along with the team and its harness. Such an outfit would have been the envy of any small boy of the era.

use shells instead. They used to buy the loose shell off of us and crush it. But that was no good. They'd get a corn sack of shell but only get a sugarbag of shellgrit out of it. But then Dad got a good idea. He got a square of wire mesh and us boys'd used to have to shovel the shell on; let the grit fall down of itself. It was cheap and quick to get. You could go along the beach and you'd get about twenty bags in about half and hour. And we had pits; we'd dig down fifteen feet. But other times you got to do a lot of work; sieve the sand out. When them poultry farmers bought two hundredweight of shellgrit off of us, they got two hundredweight, it was that fine. They could pour it straight in their chook feed.

I was fourteen when I left school and I worked for a bloke that had a poultry farm at Shelly Beach, a big place. I was feeding the fowls, must have been a thousand of them, driving the sulky into town and bringing the eggs in. He had a fish trap too. I used to help him with that.

And then Dad took a contract on at the Sanitary Depot, trench digging. Then he hurt hisself. He fell down and got three ribs broken. The contractor asked me if I'd take his job on. And I worked there, trench digging and tarring all the tins. It was hard work. There were no fans in those times and the fumes'd nearly kill you. You had a big vat of boiling tar; it would hold thirty gallons, and you've got a big fire underneath. And then three lavatory pans at a time, you spin 'em round. You've got to watch them; you got to know when

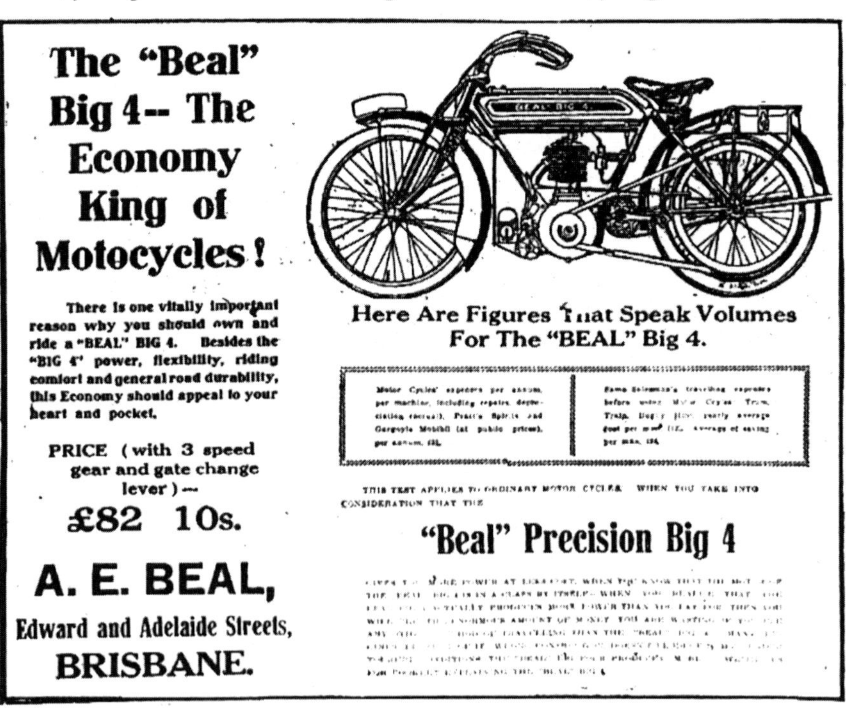

to take 'em off, and then you stand them up and they come out like enamel. You can take 'em away and in five minutes, they're warm and dry. If you boil your tar it dries straight away. But if you've got it boiling too long it goes into bitumen.

And with my pay I bought an old belt-drive motorbike, a Douglas, a little old 'ttt-ttt-ttt' of a thing, with a proper little runnin' board to put your foot on. You could practically pick it up and run away with it. And, one time, I was speedin' round North Ward to get a billy can to go on a picnic, and the bar broke. And, gees! Didn't I come a cropper and a half! Done me h'elbows and me back. I was all split down the head, and blood everywhere. But I got up and dragged the bike off the road. For about six hours after I felt like I was going to pass out. After, geez, I done a silly thing, but! Where the bar was broken I got a bit of broom handle, and I rammed that bar together with it, jammed it in tight to hold it. I rode that Douglas like that for a good while!

We used to go swimming down at the swimming basin. It was cement and had salt water pumped in. Many a time I cut my foot on the oysters and things on the bottom. See, a barnacle will form in a week. If you put a stick in the water, and you come back in a week it's like sandpaper; it's all young barnacles. They grow terrible fast. The swimming basin should have been emptied every second day and scrubbed, but sometimes it never got an empty for months. But it was calm and you could dive off anywhere round the sides so we used to always go there.[6]

And sometimes we'd dub in so much each and hire a truck and go up to Rollingstone to the swimming hole. Be about forty of us'd go, sitting along the side of the truck with your legs out, and sing, *Daisy, Daisy*, and *Pack Up Your Troubles*, and all them, going along. The girls'd bring the food and the boys get the drinks. All soft drinks. I never know none of the boys to have a hard drink! And the whole lot of us'd go swimming. Then the boys'd make up the fire and boil the billy up for tea and the girls'd get the food all laid out, cakes and sausage rolls and sandwiches and that. Oh, yes! We used to have plenty of fun!

1 Go out to the front of the class.

2 9 December, 1919

3 Catapults, also known as gings.

4 The present Townsville Dental Clinic is on the site of the original Central State School, built in 1872. The Moreton Bay figs are a reminder of the times when most Queensland State Schools grounds were planted with these trees for shade.

5 Carrara Children's Centre

6 The semi-circular wall of the Swimming Basin in which generations of Townsvillites swam and 'cut their feet' can still be seen on the seaward side of the Tobruk Baths on the Strand. The actual baths have long been filled and grassed over. It is said that the concrete rubble from the wartime air-raid shelters in Flinders Street was used as fill.

Appendix A

From the *North Queensland Register*, Monday, January 7th 1901

COMMONWEALTH CELEBRATIONS

The Procession At Charters Towers

It would appear that the thrilling events of the past year have aroused a capacity for enthusiasm among Australians, for certainly the procession in honour of the inauguration of Federation exhibited a striking evidence of the thorough abandon with which the British nature, somewhat thawed under our warmer climes, gives itself up to the celebration of an agreeable occasion… It is not surprising that the procession was such a huge success… Early in the morning, and notwithstanding the late hour to which the welcome to the New Year had been extended, large crowds began to assemble in the streets, and small armies of bright, happy-looking well-dressed children were seen proceeding to the rendezvous at the railway station.

One troop of tiny tots, 700 or 800 strong, who had been denied the long hot march with the procession, walked in a body to the park in the deliciously cool morning air.

At the railway station, the numerous bodies were marshaled into order under Mr Benjamin Toll and at the stroke of 10 o'clock, the Cyclists, who led the van, moved off. The order was then as follows: Sub-Inspector McNamara, the Band of the Kennedy Regiment under Bandmaster Emmerson, A, E, and D Companies of the 3rd Kennedy Regiment, under Captain F.W. Toll, Charters Towers Rifle Club, Members of the Charters Towers Municipal Council and Dalrymple Divisional Board, Highlanders in kilts with Pipers G. Cowrie, A. Miller and J. Kennedy, Central State School Scholars under Mr R. Lester, Queenton State School Scholars under Mr J. McLaren, Richmond Hill State School Scholars under Mr J. Hastings, Scholars of the Charters Towers Grammar School under the Principal Mr T. Martin, Protestant Alliance Orange Lodge – Royal Banner of Ulster and Star of Queenton, Combined Methodist Band, The Ancient Order of Foresters, St. Paul's and St.George's Lads Brigade with Bugle Bands, The Australian Natives Association, The Layabouts, Manchester Unity Order of Oddfellows, Star of the North, United Miners and Hope of Millchester Lodges, Order of Rechabites, Members of the Fire Brigade under Superintendent Walker with hose and reel, Charters Towers Branch of the Ambulance, Hibernian Society, United Ancient Order of Druids, Messrs T. Buckland and Co., Butchers.

The procession was at least one-and-a-half miles in length. The cyclists, of whom 68 took part, made a brave display, many of them being in fancy dress, providing much fun. The Defence Force, in review order, scarlet uniforms with blue facings, lent a spice of brilliant colouring to the procession, rendered all the more noticeable by the homely khaki of the Rifle Club who followed them. The real charm of the procession was undoubtedly the large number of gaily and appropriately dressed children, who numbered probably about 4000, and almost everyone of whom waved a flag.

Long before the procession reached Lissner Park, hundreds of children were assembled there feverishly awaiting the advent of the procession. Streams of people could be seen coming from all directions and soon the place had a quite animated appearance. The committee in charge of the children had their time fully occupied in keeping the youngsters in their places... Soon thousands of children with their variously coloured flags were marshalled in a compact square to the west of the flagstaff.

Mr B. Toll, spurring through the crowd on his horse, had a lively few moments getting the various parts of the procession into their places as they arrived, also keeping the crowd back, but his untiring efforts, helped as he was by the different workers and members of the police force, were soon successful, and all was ready at about 11 o'clock for the unfurling of the Union Jack and the Federal Flag.

Miss Clarrie Benjamin, youngest daughter of the Mayor, then stepped forward and prettily performed the ceremony of unfurling the flags. At the same time the Defence Force presented arms, and the band struck up *God Save the Queen.* At this stage of the proceedings the enthusiasm of the great crowd could be repressed no longer and they burst into hearty cheers. The Defence Force then fired a salute in the form of a *feu-de-joie*, after which they gave three cheers for the Queen, the assemblage of people taking it up. At this stage the inevitable goat appeared, having made her way through the crowd with her kid, and marched up to the aldermen and committee and bleated her allegiance to the flags. An effort to make the old lady take her place in the ranks of spectators proved unavailing until a second volley was fired when with a disgusted toss of her head she marched off.

Alderman W. J. Paul, addressing the gathering, said that the motto, 'One People, One Flag, One Destiny' was very appropriate... They now witness the birth of a new nation whose voice would be heard in the councils of the nations of the world...'

A great rush was then made towards the fountain which was to be christened and formally presented to the people by the Water Board...

Three cheers having been given for the gift, the children were invited to go to the bridges and receive the bags of provisions prepared for them. Each bag contained sandwiches, rock cake, lemon buns, and sweets. The members of the Defence Force took up their positions shoulder to shoulder, thus keeping back the crowd and letting the children pass through... The scene was a most interesting one – the different expressions on the faces of the little ones as they eagerly stretched out their hands for their bags, or watched over some little ones in their charge…

AT RAVENSWOOD

RAVENSWOOD, JANUARY 1. A procession, headed by the band and Military under Capt. Twine, started from the railway station at 12 o'clock last night, thence to Mr Dowd's residence, where the band played a patriotic selection, thence to the courthouse, where speeches were delivered and the band played the national anthem and *Rule Britannia.* The official programme then closed but large crowds were in the streets until the early hours of this morning.

The procession today was a good one. The band, military and Friendly Societies and school children formed an imposing sight, the scarlet uniforms of the soldiers showing conspicuously. Mr A. Lawrence Wilson was Marshal of the procession leading it to the Show Grounds where swings were provided for the children and other amusements. The Donnybrook and Sandy Creek children were conveyed by wagons covered with boughs.

Luncheon and afternoon refreshments were provided for the children in the drill-shed. Beautiful weather prevailed and everything went off without a hitch reflecting every credit on the Committee. The Irish Team defeated the Natives in a tug o' war rather easily. The band played choice selections throughout the day. A concert will be held in the School of Arts tonight, followed by a dance.

CELEBRATIONS IN TOWNSVILLE

TOWNSVILLE, JANUARY 1. (By our Special Representative) At an early hour this morning gangs of men were busy in Flinders Street decorating buildings with flags and bunting, and by the time the people began to assemble to take part in demonstrations the main thoroughfare presented a gay appearance. A platform raised about five feet from the ground had been erected at the intersection of Flinders and Denham Streets and a temporary flagstaff erected. Here many of the more prominent citizens assembled along with a numerous choir. Forming a guard round the platform were the Mounted Infantry and detachments of the Naval Brigade and Garrison Battery. Shortly before 10 a.m. His Worship the Mayor addressed a few words to those assembled. He said they had met that morning in Townsville as the integral part of a new nation. Throughout the island continent that day, each city, town and village were doing the same as the residents of Townsville. That morning they would hoist 'our' Federal flag. Hitherto it had only been called 'the ' Federal flag but now it belonged to all. That flag was the symbol of the unity of the nation and it was their duty to stand by it and defend it. He then hoisted the Federal flag to the head of the flagstaff and called upon Bishop Barlow to dedicate it. His Lordship said, 'By virtue of the will of the people of Australia, we declare this flag to be the Federal flag of the Commonwealth of Australia. May it fly over a free and happy people. If it is to lead us into battle may it be in the interests of right rather than might... may we hand it down to those to come unstained and unsullied. I dedicate this flag to the Glory of God and to the service of humanity.'

The Mayoress, Mrs McCreedy, then unfurled the flag, a ceremony which was greeted with applause. The choir immediately sang the National Anthem while a firing-party on the opposite side of the creek fired a salute of twenty-one guns. The procession, which was a lengthy one, then formed and marched to the Show Grounds. The streets were lined with crowds of spectators. At the bottom of Stoke Street a picture of the Governor-General was raised twelve feet high and presented a good appearance. During the day a long programme of sports was gone through. Tomorrow the children will be entertained at the Queen's Park and there will be a display of fireworks.

AT HUGHENDEN

HUGHENDEN, JANUARY 1. The Commonwealth celebrations passed off successfully today. They consisted of unfurling the flag in the school grounds, the presentation of medals and the planting of trees. The athletic sports take place tomorrow. A good deal of dissatisfaction is felt at the additional medals not arriving in time.

AT CROYDON

CROYDON, JANUARY 1. The Federal demonstration was a huge success. There was a large gathering in the Town Hall which was addressed by the Mayor (Ald. Morrison) the Police Magistrate, Mr Millican, and Bishop White. There was a procession of children and Friendly Societies through the streets, and a children's picnic at the racecourse was enjoyable. At Golden Gate the children had a picnic on the Golden Gate racecourse.

AT COOKTOWN

COOKTOWN, JANUARY 1. Six hundred children were entertained at a picnic in the Queen's Park. There were sports and other amusements and a procession of the bands, local bodies, Friendly Societies, etc. The demonstration was an unqualified success. The weather was fine.

SOME IDEA of the importance of membership of Friendly Society Lodges such as the Oddfellows, Foresters, etc., can be gained by the numbers taking part in the processions in various communities. In a period when there were no social security benefits available from government agencies Friendly Societies, organised into District Lodges, offered some peace of mind to members, who for a small weekly subscription were entitled, in the event of illness or accident, to financial assistance. In the case of death, widows and children would receive help with funeral arrangements and a fund would be raised for them. On public occasions such as the Federation Day processions described here, members of the Lodges would parade together as a sign of group solidarity, behind large, splendidly ornate banners.

The celebrations at Charters Towers are given lengthy coverage because in 1901, with a population of nearly 30,000, it was the largest centre in the North. The date of publication, 7th January 1901, is six days after the events described as the paper was published weekly. Accounts of events in other centres were necessarily brief as they were forwarded by telegram.

Appendix B

From the *North Queensland Register*

THE PLAGUE IN NORTH QUEENSLAND

Monday July 10th 1900. Rumours were current this morning, in today's *Townsville Star* that another case of plague had been discovered on Ross Island. Up to one o'clock Dr Row was engaged in setting inquiries but was not then in a position to state definitely whether it was a true case or not. The patient is a boy named Owen Redding in McIllwraith Street and was employed as night messenger. Dr Row was unable to obtain any serum and therefore was unable to say definitely whether this is a case of plague. The symptoms point strongly to it and the lad is in a dangerous state, so much so that it was found advisable not to move him. When the doctor called this morning the boy was unconscious. As a precautionary measure the house has been isolated, and on the arrival of Dr Turner from Mackay tomorrow morning he will be asked to pronounce upon the case.

The swallowing of the prophylactic, is not a new theory, but in diseases in which it been applied, only evanescent immunity has been obtained. Sufficient time has not been allowed by Dr McDonald to prove the efficacy of his experiment.

CAIRNS, JULY 13TH (By Telegraph). A fourth case of plague was reported this afternoon, the victim being the eight-year old son of Mr. John Boland, storekeeper. The attack was discovered in a very early stage and Dr Koch is hopeful of pulling the patient through. The contacts are Mr John Boland, his wife, and daughters aged 11 and 12.

The council's offer of a shilling each for rats is producing little response.

BRISBANE, JULY 13TH. Information has been received that the Netherlands and East India Governments have declared Rockhampton an infected port, and the same measures are to apply as in the case of Brisbane, Townsville and Cairns.

AUGUST 31. A boy named Charlie Kennedy, 12 years of age, residing in Palmer Street, Ross Island, was discovered by Dr Row this afternoon to be suffering from plague of a mild form. He was conveyed to the plague hospital during the evening.

THE PLAGUE HOSPITAL is listed among other buildings badly damaged in North Ward by Cyclone Leonta in 1903. It seems to have been in Gregory Street close to the old gaol, the administration building of which now forms part of Central School. To parents of the time, the talk of the 'prophylactic' that offered 'evanescent immunity' can have been of little comfort. Although it was not widely understood that rats carried the disease, Townsville people seemed to have steered clear of the offer of 'a shilling a rat'. Suburbs like Ross Island, close to the wharves, were at greater risk. Dr Ashburton Thompson, New South Wales Government Chief Medical Officer, had established that the infection was carried from infected rats to man by fleas, and as a result of his work the *Commonwealth Quarantine Act* was introduced in 1908.

Appendix C

Cyclone Leonta. Extracts from the *North Queensland Register*, Monday March 16, 1903

Frightful Gale at Townsville
SEVERAL LIVES LOST
GREAT DAMAGE TO PROPERTY

About midnight on Sunday the sky became overcast and the wind changed with startling suddenness from North to North-West. Sunday had been very hot and dry and the night was very oppressive. At 11 a.m. there was quite a gale and from 11 to 12 a.m. the shrieking storm increased to a hurricane. By this time the public were thoroughly alarmed and fought to make things safe during the hurricane. The tremendous forces of Nature, however, swept aside the puny efforts of man, and stout buildings in many instances were brought low. At a quarter past two in the afternoon the barometer stood at 28.586 which was the lowest recorded in any portion of the town. From noon the hurricane raged with fearful intensity and terrible damage was done in the town and suburbs.

The Church of England Cathedral, the Rectory and the new Catholic Church are all badly damaged. St James' presents a sorry spectacle. The roof is gone. The Methodist Church at the top of Stokes Street has been entirely unroofed. The walls are shattered and the interior badly damaged. Other buildings to suffer very extensively are the School of Arts and the Queens Hotel. The Grammar School is a complete wreck. It is unroofed and the walls are cracking. When these substantial structures suffered severely it can be realised that the more humble structures suffered terribly.

Numerous buildings were unroofed and the scene during the hurricane was of a weird and appalling nature. The iron roofing was flying about like pieces of paper in a whirlwind and all the while the stinging rain accentuated the misery of the situation… The streets are strewn with debris and hundreds of people are homeless. The seven hotels from the Newmarket to the Causeway suffered very severely and two are practically demolished. In the North Ward the greatest damage was done and in Hermit Park it may be said it is hard to find a building uninjured. The streets are strewn with debris and hundreds of people are homeless but are being sheltered as far as is possible in warehouses, offices and hotels.

The most heart-rending disaster occurred at the hospital which is situated on the north slope of Stanton Hill and facing out to sea. The Harvey Ward was a two-storied detached building and the appalling wind had such an effect on it that Dr Bacot decided to remove the typhoid patients from the top story. He had just got them removed from the top story at 2 p.m. when a frightful gust of wind lifted the roof clean off. The gale was then raging at its fiercest and after the roof had gone the 14-inch brick walls collapsed and fell on the unfortunates in the lower storey, killing five persons instantly. Among the injured were Nurse Grant, who sustained a broken leg and compound fracture of the skull. William Harrington, 8 years of age, was extricated from the ruins with one arm hanging by a shred of skin. The scene after the walls of the Harvey Ward toppled over and buried the unfortunates beneath was appalling but many stout-hearted residents of North Ward came to the rescue. The gale was possessed of prodigious force and it took a strong man all his time to keep his feet, while the driving sleet stung like a whip. The rescuers, however, braved all danger and directed by the hospital staff, worked through the debris to those portions of the ward where the injured people were. The dead bodies were removed to the morgue and those persons injured but alive to the main ward.

The Barometer

Mr. C. S. Norris writes: The weather in Townsville during Sunday the 8th March was very hot and unsettled and in the morning of the 9th a moderate breeze was blowing from the south-west which gradually increased to very ugly threatening weather. At 9.15 a.m. the barometer registered 29.556 which was sufficient indication of a probable hurricane. The barometer continued to fall rapidly and the wind to increase with very heavy rain squalls from the south-west, and very thick weather. These squalls in crossing the bay lifted the spray to a considerable height, in many instances forming miniature water-spouts. At 11 a.m. the barometer registered 29.305 and still falling, the wind increasing to hurricane force and still from the south-west. At 1.30 p.m. the barometer had fallen to 28.868 the wind still increasing in violence. About this time it was noticed that the water in the bay was blown out from the shore and the bare sand was seen for a considerable distance very much further than I ever saw it in the lowest spring tides. At 2 p.m. the barometer registered 28.617 which is by far the lowest reading ever recorded by me in Townsville. After 2 p.m. the wind gradually veered to the south-east and moderated considerably, and the barometer commenced to rise. The calm centre of the hurricane was evidently then passing over Townsville. The wind continued to veer until it reached about due north, when it again commenced to blow with hurricane force and very heavy rain squalls, the barometer, however, rising very rapidly and at 8 p.m. it registered 29.641, being a rise of nearly one inch in the 6 hours. At 9 p.m. it registered 29.719 from which it was evident the hurricane was passing away, and after this hour the wind and squalls moderated considerably and at 10.30 p.m. the barometer registered 29.800 and the wind had moderated to a gale with occasional heavy rain squalls. This hurricane is without a doubt the heaviest experienced in Townsville for a considerable number of years and although not of so long duration as 'Sigma' hurricane of the 26th and 27th, January, 1896, it was more fierce, while it lasted, about twelve hours. The lowest reading of the barometer during the hurricane 'Sigma' was 29.262 as compared with 28.617 the lowest reading during this hurricane.

Townsville Grammar School
PLUCKY SCHOLARS

That fine brick building, the Townsville Grammar School is a complete wreck. The cyclone struck the building with greatest force about twenty minutes past one, but in the morning when the wind was blowing from the north-west the building was unroofed. This left the dormitory and masters' rooms uncovered. Still the walls were intact and remained so until after the first gong for dinner had gone. The brick chimney of the kitchen fell with a crash just where the cook had been standing a second or so previous. A crack in the masonry over the big schoolroom drove masters and boys into the fourth-form room in the north-west corner.

Mr J. G. Leadbeater, the second master, took the girls to a place of safety, and the headmaster, Mr J.T. Miller and the other two members of staff remained with the boys. The wind suddenly veered to the south-west and the wind practically demolished the brick building. The north-east corner of the room in which the masters and pupils were taking refuge fell and left a gaping space, but luckily the walls fell outwards. Then in good order, the masters helped the boys through the northern door, and leaping over the mass of spiked timber, galvanised-iron and bricks and mortar, they ran into the open. Under the circumstances the open park was the safest place. If a substantially built brick building would not afford shelter, there was little chance of protection in a wooden structure. Even when away from the falling debris they were not assured safety. The sheets of iron were chasing the refugees and every stump or tree was used as momentary shelter until they reached the gully near the orphanage. Here there seemed to be just a lull in the gale and less danger. With such numerous charges there was grave responsibility at such a time for the masters, but Mr Miller was favourably impressed by the coolness of his staff and the excellent discipline of the boys.

North Ward Losses
HEARTRENDING DISASTER

Passing towards North Ward yesterday by way of Stanley Street it was to see devastation writ big on every hand. In each direction were carpenters – amateur and otherwise – busily engaged in effecting repairs. Strewn in heavy profusion along the hillside were broken timber, crumpled iron and everyday effects of home life. In fact, looking afield from this point one hesitates wherewith to adequately tell of the deplorable damage. Houses throughout the ward have suffered, more or less, while many have been totally destroyed. Houses stand empty, houses lie razed, owing to Monday's typhoon. Residents are to be seen in disconsolate groups talking of the horrors experienced. Paxton Street shows much damage done. One feature hereabouts is the dismantled condition of both park and Botanical Gardens. The first has trees and sheds stripped whilst the latter is shed of all its glory. Going along Gregory Street it was to find further desolation. Mrs Heffernan, a widow woman, has lost her store, and in this, her all. The thoroughfare known as Eyre Street also experienced disaster. Eyre Street from the Queen's Park Hotel to the orphanage was badly treated. The entire top storey of the hotel was carried away at the height of the storm and Mr Short's store on the opposite corner was crumpled up under a mass of flying iron and woodwork from the hospital. The Plague Hospital was severely handled. Indeed, except for the old gaol which proved a safe refuge in the worst of the storm for many of the homeless residents of the neighbourhood, hardly a stick has been left standing. To view the broken and ruined home-treasures strewn about was a sadness. The residents are bearing their losses with fortitude which may be said of all who have experienced loss in the trying ordeal. On the Strand the first sight to strike one is the dismantled condition of the trees and the timber-strewn beach. An almost miraculous escape from death is reported from the residence of Mrs Conn. A huge piece of 4 by 3 timber hurtling through the air crashed through the window of the kitchen where but a moment before Mrs Conn had been standing.

Miss O'Brien of the Sea View Hotel has had heavy loss. Neighbours all aver that Miss O'Brien has been most kind to those in distress, near upon 150 had recourse to her premises. The night of the storm and the day following it was more a public haven of rest than a fashionable hotel. Mrs Quilter, wife of the Sub-inspector, had a very narrow escape while in shelter here, a piece of timber crashing through the roof quite alongside of her. The body of a woman, as yet unidentified, has been found at Stanton Hill, which has evidently been dead since Monday.

General Items

The homeless men, women and children who were sheltered in the Court House on Monday night and fed through the instrumentality of Mr J. A. Boyce, P.M. and Sub-Inspector Quilter were removed to the Immigration Barracks yesterday where the Government will provide for them until they can arrange for new homes.

Our representative heard of the death of Mr Thomson. While occupied repairing the roof of his house a squall flung a piece of iron upon him and striking him on the head it killed him almost immediately. Mr J.J. Fanning, while proceeding home to lunch his right arm was caught by a piece of flying iron and is severely cut. Constable Walsh of Walker Street West was met by his wife and children seeking shelter from the brow of the hill, his house threatening to carry away with every gust of wind. The Great Northern Hotel had parts of its parapet blown through the roof causing flooding below. Frightened horses released from vehicles and stables are galloping madly about the town.

On Monday afternoon the Ambulance received a call to Hubert Wells and between 5 and 6 o'clock in the evening a party was dispatched. On their arrival they found the two-storey brick engine-house had collapsed. The one-story brick engine-room at the Wilmett Well also being completely demolished and several of the residences in the neighbourhood were completely wrecked. At the Hubert Well it was found that Mr George Haylett, Assistant Resident Engineer had sustained very serious injury (George Haylett later died) and Mr W. N. Treen, Resident Engineer, had also sustained a dislocated shoulder and nasty scalp wound.

On the way in the ambulance also attended to a Miss Belton, an elderly lady who keeps a little shop, which it appears was bodily overturned and then again rolled over by the wind, the unfortunate lady being imprisoned all this time.

At Mundingburra they found several houses levelled to the ground, The Anglican Church of St Matthews was demolished and the Rising Sun Hotel had ceased to exist while the verandah and roof of the Royal Oak hotel were gone. Pullen's 'bus stables, next the Rising Sun are unroofed and in a very bad way. Mr T. A. Gulliver's splendid fernery and plants were destroyed and the house so much knocked about that it was rendered uninhabitable. 'Mysterton' Mr. Danner's residence at Aitkenvale had the back verandah carried away, kitchen, storeroom and back premises all unroofed. The brick chimney fell into the kitchen and all the outhouses and stables being completely destroyed. Everywhere there is destruction and ruin and many are the unfortunates who are homeless and one might say with Milton, 'Let these describe the undescribable.'[sic.]

Meagre news has been received from the lower Burdekin and Bowen recording damage relatively as serious as that which has occurred in Townsville. The Bowen news is rather conflicting but when the full effect of the hurricane there is told it is feared that the story will be a sad one. Cairns also reports a severe disturbance.

Mr George Butler made a trip to Magnetic Island in the *Hephzibah* yesterday and was naturally surprised that no damage had been sustained. The tight little island showed no evidence of the gale other than a few trees had been stripped here and there.

Stewarts Creek Gaol

At Stewart's Creek Gaol the old stockade is down. The A and C wings of the main building, the hospital building, kitchen, storeroom, visiting justice's room and the chief warder's residence were all unroofed. There are about 140 prisoners confined in the gaol. B wing still being sound they have as far as is possible been distributed in the weather-tight cells in that portion.

Message to Premier Philp

This morning His Worship the mayor, Alderman W. A. Ackers, dispatched the following telegram to the premier; 'We have just had a cyclone surpassing Sigma in violence. It has caused more devastation than experienced by Townsville before. Many people are absolutely ruined. I have visited various portions of the city and suburbs this morning and the scene is heart-rending. I am afraid we shall have to invoke your aid in affording relief. The hospital, Grammar School, Customs House and other public buildings have suffered seriously. Five patients in the hospital have been killed by the collapse of portion of the building. I hear that other lives have been lost in the streets… Weather now fine.'

Meat and Bread

His Worship the Mayor this morning notified Messrs. Johnson and Castling to supply with meat and bread deserving persons who have suffered from the gale.

No Water Supply

His Worship the Mayor informed us this morning that in consequence of the serious damage done to the pumping machinery at Mundingburra, the municipal water supply would probably be cut off for the next three or four days.

Appendix D

Extracts from the *North Queensland Register*, April, 1911.

The Loss of the *Yongala*

THE YONGALA

WRECKAGE FOUND AT PALM ISLAND

APRIL 9TH, 1911. A resident who has spent the last fortnight at Palm Islands and who returned last night has afforded a representative of the *Northern Miner* the following interesting information as to the wreckage found on Palm Islands and which has been noticed there since Sunday March 26th.

Mr Butler, the lessee of Great Palms, and the guests of his pleasure resort first noticed wreckage coming up on Sunday March 26th when they discovered three tins of kerosene bearing the mark 'Tidewater' Oil on the south side of Great Palm. Next day they made a more systematic search and picked up small pieces of freshly painted and newly broken boards, among which was a fair quantity of some dark dressed timbers, cedar or teak, and which had been varnished. Some of these bore the figures '736' in conjunction with the words 'Officers' Room', 'Pantry' or 'First Saloon – Smoking'.

For the next few days the weather was very rough and wet and nothing could be done. On Thursday March 30th, a further search was made. Esk Island was examined and there were found a half-grating from No. 5 forehold which they gave to the captain of the Kuranda. At this island they also picked up a red plush cushion. It was a cushion which would be expected to be found in a first-saloon cabin and a remarkable feature about it was its most abominable stench. The cushion was opened and found to be stuffed with feathers and there was nothing in the contents to account for the odour. On Sunday notwithstanding rain, another party went over and again examined the north side of Great Palm. They picked up further wreckage with nothing to identify it except occasionally the figures '733'. Another party found apparently what had formed part of a settee in the second-saloon. They also found what looked like a piece of the taffrail and a rather large boat's mast, marked '4', and rigged, on Orpheus Island.

On Thursday last Mr Butler and two well-known amateur beachcombers made a thorough investigation of Eclipse Island and found on the lee side a seaman's chest painted a very dark green, and broken open. Near it was a canvas-covered lid and between the two was scattered a considerable quantity of clothing, notably a dark-blue top-coat of good quality, a white mess-jacket but no papers or any marks of identification except an handkerchief bearing the initials 'R.D.G.'.

The party then visited Brisk Island and discovered further pieces of broken gratings and a number of kerosene and benzene tins which by their marks appeared to have been consigned to Jack and Newell, a half-door, apparently from the chartroom or a deck-cabin, parts of several cabin doors and two of the weather beams of the central coverings of lifeboats. Portions of oak fiddles were also found, a broken sweep and two 56lbs. boxes of 'Silverwood' butter. On Esk Island they picked up the bottom of a cane chair apparently from the music-stool or a saloon or dining-room chair.

On Friday morning the *Teal* put in and the capt. reported they were still engaged in the search and had that morning thoroughly examined the weather sides of Great Palm and Caracca [?] Islands and had seen a considerable quantity of 8 x 8 Oregon pine and other wreckage but nothing to indicate the presence of human beings.

CAIRNS, APRIL 10TH (By Telegraph). Captain Campbell, of the *Muriel* arrived from Townsville. He reports, while at Lucinda Point, more traces had been found of the missing *Yongala*, a good deal of wreckage being found in Hinchinbrook Passage and to the southward of Lucinda. It was too rough to secure the debris which was floating about. Two bags of mail were found five miles south of Lucinda. It will be possible to make out the addresses of fully 90 per cent. The contents of the wreckage found consists of broken cabin doors, broken wooden chocks, boards, pillows, etc. Seven hatches were also brought to Lucinda Point.

INGHAM, APRIL 10TH. A police party returned from Cassidy's Creek early on Monday morning, bringing five bags of mails, one bag being taken on to Halifax. The bags were discovered scattered over a distance of four miles along the beach. Four bags were opened by Kanakas who took the bags to their humpies leaving the letters. The letters included a lot of correspondence for Townsville and Cloncurry; with very few exceptions the address of the letters were legible. The newspapers were mostly pulp. The other wreckage consisted of a box of butter, potatoes, onions, also a piece of board with the word 'Yongala' on it, evidently part of a boat.

TOWNSVILLE, APRIL 11TH. The Inspector of Police has received a report from Constable Portly, of Mundingburra station, with respect to the carcass which was discovered on the beach at the mouth of Gordon's Creek, about three miles down the coast from Ross River. The bones of the horse are there minus the head and hoofs, whilst a small piece of the hide shows that the colour is bay. There is a strong odour coming from the hide which is evidence that the body has not long been there. The remains at high tide are under water. In the position the horse was found it would be impossible for it to have got there from the land as the country is too broken and it must have been washed up by the sea.

An Aboriginal boy named John Murray who resides in the neighbourhood of Gordon's Creek, and who is a very intelligent lad who can read and write, informed the constable that he saw the carcass there on the 2nd of April, when it was very much swollen. It is thought that these remains may be the horse Moonshine from the *Yongala* wreck. The Aboriginal lad stated that on the same day that he first saw the horse he also saw a quantity of swede turnips scattered along the beach.

Inspector Molone on Tuesday evening received the following telegram from Sergeant Horan of Halifax:

'Taylor found at Victoria Creek a portion of a life-boat with the name 'Yongala' on it in raised letters on a plate. Also a lifeboat water-cask. The former has since been stolen from his cutter.'

BRISBANE, APRIL 10TH. In consequence of the continued heavy weather, the proposed visit of the small steamer *Pelican* to Nares Rock for purposes of sending a diver down has been abandoned.

CAIRNS, APRIL 10TH. A special memorial *Yongala* disaster service was held yesterday morning in St John's Church, the Masonic, Friendly Societies and others attending. The building was filled. The Reverend C. W. Tomkins preached an eloquent sermon. The special music included 'The Dead March' in Saul and Chopin's 'Funeral March'.

A memorial service was held last night at the Methodist Church. In the course of the service the Reverend H. M. Wheller said, 'Perhaps we know as much now as we ever shall know of the *Yongala.* The public, though, they have a right to demand an analysis, as far as possible into the circumstances surrounding the event. No stone should be left unturned to get as much light as possible on the subject. Adequate lighting on our coast now that the public conscience was aroused. Those were the questions we trust should not rest until this information be supplied. We have the right to demand, whatever the cost may be. The dangers which surround our coast would have the sting extracted from them by adequate lighting.

Bibliography

Historical Background

Adams, David (ed.), *The Letters of Rachel Henning*, Penguin Books, Australia, Ringwood, 1969

Aitkinson, R.L., *Bush Tales and Memories*, Pineville, Mareeba, 1984.

Allingham, Anne, *Taming the Wilderness*, James Cook University, Townsville, 1978

Blainey, Geoffrey, *A Land Half Won*, Griffin Press, Adelaide, 1980

Bolton, G.C., *A Thousand Miles Away: A History of North Queensland to 1920*, ANU Press, 1972

Cannon, Michael, *Who's Master? Who's Man?: Australia in the Victorian Age*, John Currey O'Neil, Melbourne, 1982.

Clark, Manning, *A History of Australia*, Volume V, MUP, Melbourne, 1981

Crowley, F.K., *Modern Australia in Documents,* Wren, Melbourne, 1973

Darian-Smith, Kate and Paula Hamilton, *Memory and History in Twentieth-Century Australia*, OUP, Melbourne; 1994

Gibson-Wilde, Dorothy, *Gateway to a Golden Land: Townsville to 1884*, JCU, Townsville; 1984

Gibson-Wilde, Dorothy and Bruce, *A Pattern of Pubs: Hotels of Townsville*, JCU, Townsville; 1988

Gibson-Wilde, Dorothy and Brian Dalton, *Townsville 1888,* JCU, Townsville, 1990

Holt, Tonie and Valmai, *Battlefields of the First World War*, Pavilion, London, 1993

Hooper, Colin, *Angor to Zillmanton: Stories of North Queensland's Deserted Towns*, Townsville; 1993

Macdonald, Lyn, *1915 – The Death of Innocence*, Headline, London, 1993

Macintyre, Stuart, *The Oxford History of Australia*, Volume 4, MUP, 1993

Shaw, A.G.L., *The Story of Australia*, Faber, 1960

Wilson, Charles, *Australia, The Creation of a Nation*, Weidenfeld and Nicholson, London, 1987

Unpublished Transcripts of the James Cook University North Queensland History Project: Barbara Aitchison, Henry Brown, Violet Allingham, Alice Chapman, Joe Clark, Oscar Crowther, E. Cummings, Susan Gallagher, Marjorie Green, Mary Grimwade, Constance Hill, Elizabeth Hinspeter, Fred King, Ethel McLeod, Julius Mathieson, William 'Kelly' Newton, Harry Pope, Edward Smedley, Olive Stallon, Florence Toombs, Francis Valenta, John Walker.

Oral History

Caunce, Steven, *Oral History and the Local Historian*, Longman, London, 1994

Frisch, Michael, *A Shared Authority: Essays on the Craft and Meaning of Oral and Public History*, State University of NY Press, New York, 1990

Humphries, Steve, Joanna Mack and Robert Perks, *A Century of Childhood*, Sidgwick and Jackson, London; 1989

Lummis, Trevor, *Listening to History*, Hutchinson, London, 1987

Perks, Robert, *Oral History: Talking About the Past*, Oral History Society, London, 1988

Thomson, Alistair, *Anzac Memories: Living With the Legend*, MUP, Melbourne, 1994

Thompson, Paul, *The Voice of the Past*, OUP, Oxford, 1988

Thompson, Thea, *Edwardian Children*, Routledge and Kegan Paul, London, 1981

Yow, Valerie, *Recording Oral History*, Sage, Thousand Oaks, 1994

Methodology

Abrams, Jeremiah, *Reclaiming the Inner Child*, Thorsons, London, 1991

Dovring, Folke, *History as a Social Science: The Nature and Purpose of Historical Studies*, Nijhoff, The Hague, 1960

Robson, Colin, *Real World Research: A Resource for Social Scientists and Practitioner-Researchers*, Blackwell, Oxford, 1993

Stanford, Michael, *A Companion to the Study of History*, Blackwell, Oxford, 1994

Newspapers

North Queensland Register

Northern Miner

Index